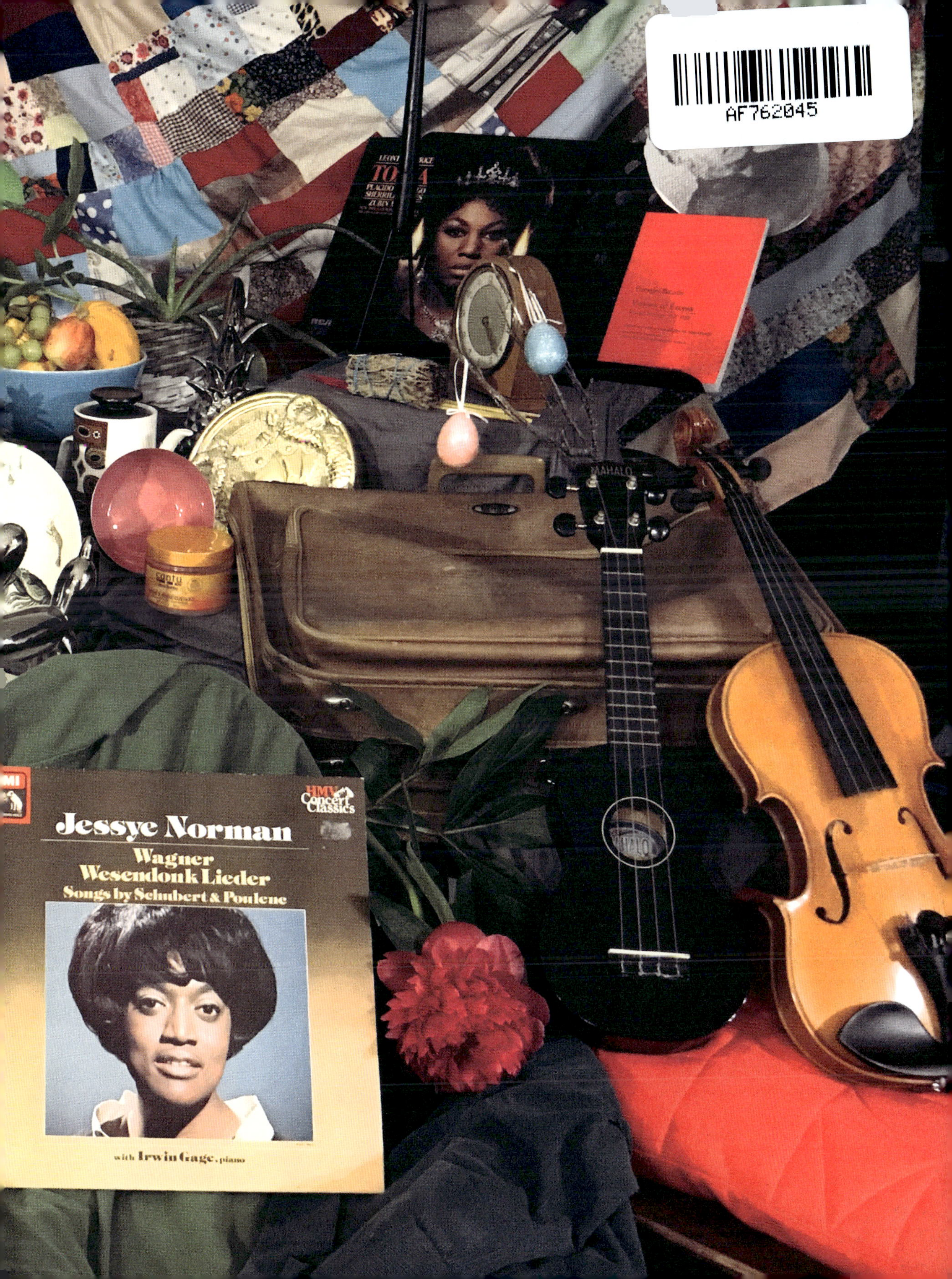
Jessye Norman
Wagner
Wesendonk Lieder
Songs by Schubert & Poulenc
with Irwin Gage, piano
HMV Concert Classics
MAHALO

Rediscovering Black Portraiture

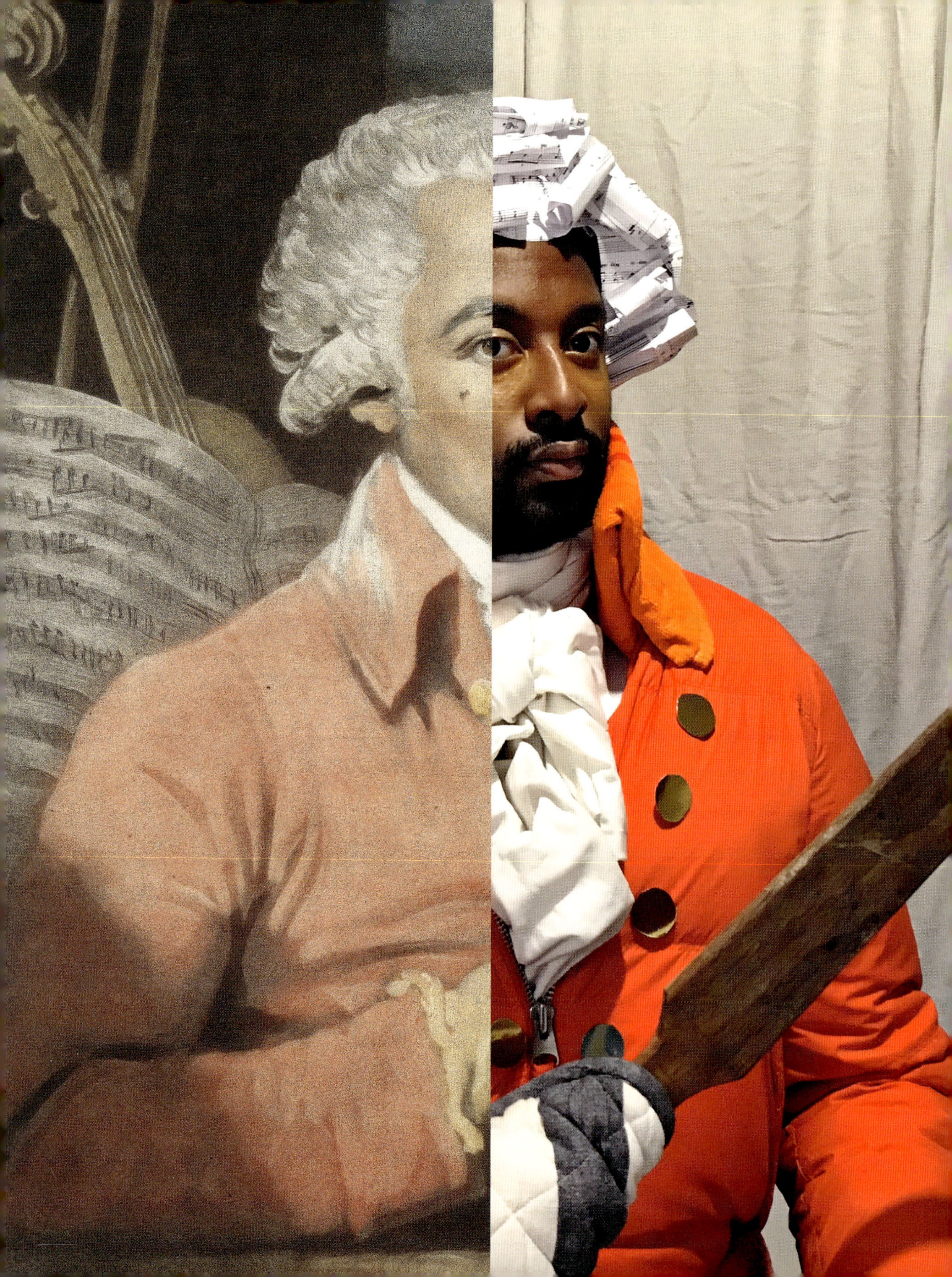

Getty Publications Los Angeles

Peter Brathwaite
Rediscovering Black Portraiture

With contributions by
Cheryl Finley, Temi Odumosu, and Mark Sealy

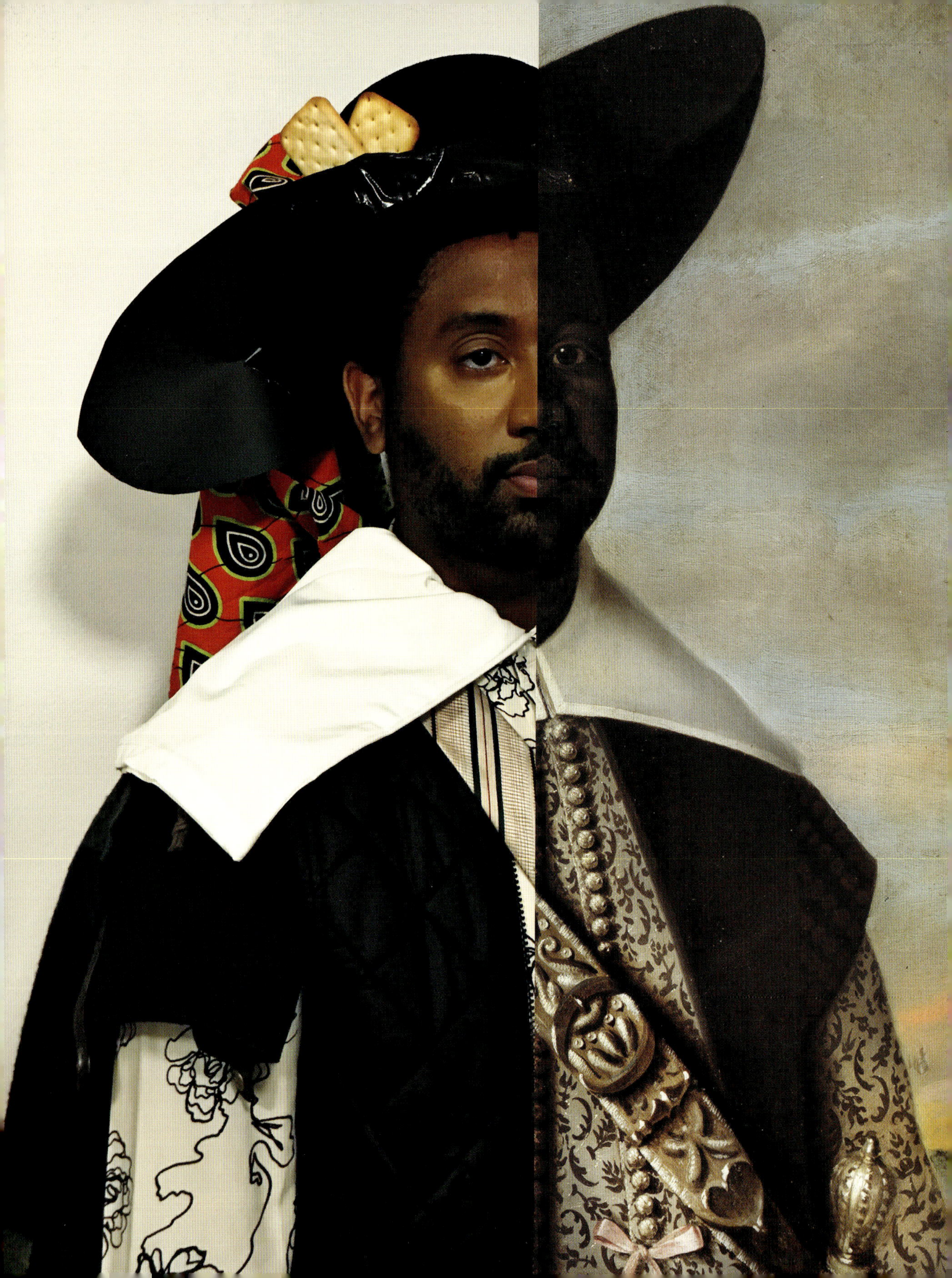

This book is dedicated to my great-great-great-great-grandparents Edward (Addo) Brathwaite (ca. 1742–1831) and Margaret Ann (Peggy) Brathwaite (1780–1860) and to the enslaved ancestors who came before them, whose names and stories have yet to be rediscovered.

Published by Getty Publications, Los Angeles
1200 Getty Center Drive, Suite 500
Los Angeles, California 90049-1682
getty.edu/publications

Karen A. Levine, *Project Editor*
Lindsey Westbrook, *Manuscript Editor*
Dina Murokh, *Editorial Assistant*
Jeffrey Cohen, *Designer*
Victoria Gallina, *Production*
Nancy Rivera, *Image and Rights Acquisition*

Distributed in the United States and Canada by the University of Chicago Press
Distributed outside the United States and Canada by Yale University Press, London

Printed in Italy

Library of Congress Cataloging-in-Publication Data
Names: Brathwaite, Peter, author. | Finley, Cheryl, contributor. | Odumosu, Temi, contributor. | Sealy, Mark, contributor.
Title: Rediscovering Black portraiture / Peter Brathwaite ; with contributions by Cheryl Finley, Temi Odumosu, and Mark Sealy.
Description: Los Angeles : Getty Publications, [2023] | Includes bibliographical references and index. | Summary: "Explores representations of Black subjects in Western art, from medieval Europe through the present day"— Provided by publisher.
Identifiers: LCCN 2022049095 (print) | LCCN 2022049096 (ebook) | ISBN 9781606068168 (hardcover) | ISBN 9781606068441 (adobe pdf)
Subjects: LCSH: Black people in art. | Black people—Portraits. | Black people—Portraits. | Portraits, European.
Classification: LCC N8217.B535 B73 2023 (print) | LCC N8217.B535 (ebook) | DDC 704.9/42—dc23/eng/20221108
LC record available at https://lccn.loc.gov/2022049095
LC ebook record available at https://lccn.loc.gov/2022049096

Cover: *Portrait of an Unknown Man* (ca. 1525–30) by Jan Mostaert, with re-creation by Peter Brathwaite (see pp. 28–29)
Endsheets: re-creation by Peter Brathwaite of *The Paston Treasure* (ca. 1665) by an unknown artist (see pp. 48–49)
p. 2: *Monsieur de Saint-Georges* (1788) by William Ward (after Mather Brown), with re-creation by Peter Brathwaite (see pp. 84–85)
p. 4: *Don Miguel de Castro: Emissary of Kongo* (ca. 1643) by Jasper Becx, with re-creation by Peter Brathwaite (see pp. 40–41)

Illustration Credits
Every effort has been made to contact the owners and photographers of illustrations reproduced here whose names do not appear in the captions or in the illustration credits at the back of this book. Anyone having further information concerning copyright holders is asked to contact Getty Publications so this information can be included in future printings.

A Note on the Type
This book is set in Freight Text and Freight Sans, fonts created in 2005 by the African American type designer Joshua Darden. Inspired by historical typefaces, these bold and innovative fonts may be familiar to visitors to the National Museum of African American History and Culture in Washington, DC, where they have been adopted as the brand typefaces.

8
Prologue
Peter Brathwaite

13
Act 1

50
Feeling in the Dark: Rediscovering Black Portraiture as Speculative Metadata
Temi Odumosu

59
Act 2

100
The Imagined Museum: A Conversation about Erasure, Encounter, and Entanglement
Mark Sealy and Peter Brathwaite

117
Act 3

148
Encore
Cheryl Finley

155
Backstage

160 **Acknowledgments**
161 **Suggested Further Reading**
163 **Illustration Credits**
164 **Index**
168 **About the Authors**

Break a vase, and the love that reassembles the fragments is stronger than that love which took its symmetry for granted when it was whole. The glue that fits the pieces is the sealing of its original shape. It is such a love that reassembles our African and Asiatic fragments, the cracked heirlooms whose restoration shows its white scars. This gathering of broken pieces is the care and pain of the Antilles, and if the pieces are disparate, ill-fitting, they contain more pain than their original sculpture, those icons and sacred vessels taken for granted in their ancestral places.

— Derek Walcott, "The Antilles: Fragments of Epic Memory," Nobel lecture, December 7, 1992

Prologue

Peter Brathwaite

As a Black British opera singer, I am used to being a rare breed—still. Moreover, I am accustomed to having quizzical glances cast in my direction, as if I am something of a novelty or a curious anomaly. A large part of my musical career to date has been based on balancing and reconciling the tricky dichotomy of otherness in relation to myself and the canon of Western classical music that I love and love to perform. And given that they are so few and far between, representations of people who look like me in the classical canon have always been of interest. As a student of opera, I clung to the album covers of the African American soprano Leontyne Price and a black-and-white postcard portrait of the Black British composer Samuel Coleridge Taylor.

These totemic images, my superheroes, became talismanic, protective figures when I found myself on the receiving end of everyday racism from fellow musicians—things like "You're the whitest Black man I know"; or, "Your performance was so good, I thought you were a white singer blacked up"; or, "You would have been a slave when this opera was written." Or the time a singing coach put her finger in my mouth because she just didn't understand how I, "a Negro," could have an alveolar ridge.

In opera, I have been cast as an enslaved African man twice. Both times turned out to be opportunities to humanize Black characters that have all too often existed on the stage as one-dimensional stereotypes. With one of these roles in particular—the enslaved African Kaidamà in Gaetano Donizetti's *Il furioso all'isola di San Domingo*, a nineteenth-century opera set in the Caribbean—there was an urgent need to restore agency to an operatic character who has been portrayed in blackface well into the twenty-first century. This is a "tradition" that has done much to distort the dignity of Black lives.

When I encountered the Getty Museum Challenge during the coronavirus pandemic in 2020, I had already experimented with several ways to fill my enforced free time, having seen much of my singing work—operas and concerts—disappear overnight. Scrolling through social media, my feed was awash with people who had taken up the challenge, re-creating their favorite artworks using everyday items found at home. The submissions exposed the depressing truth that most of the so-called great artworks we choose to platform and celebrate do not tell the stories of people of color—the global majority. Here was an opportunity to take a new step in my dignity-restoring mission. I decided to revisit a search term I'd been compelled to explore at the very start of my opera career: "Black portraiture."

Back then I was looking for evidence to bolster my argument against "whiting up" for an opera production that required me to play the part of a French aristocrat. A message from the creative team had suggested I use a thicker layer of white makeup so as to create a more "uniform stage picture." I was the only person of color in the production. Regrettably, I tried it, once. I looked ridiculous. I subsequently trawled the internet, willing "Black portraiture" to find me an eighteenth-century Black French aristocrat I could show to upturn the narrow view that people of color from the time were all either enslaved or "savages." My search yielded a golden find in William Ward's copy of a portrait of Joseph Bologne, Chevalier de Saint-Georges, by Mather Brown (p. 84). Bologne was a champion fencer, a lauded classical composer, and a virtuoso violinist and conductor in eighteenth-century Paris. Armed with his likeness, I appeared at rehearsals with proof that the heavy white makeup I'd been asked to wear was not necessary. Here was a free Black man of high status portrayed in his own skin. I ditched the greasepaint and became Bologne in my short scene. The show's director and designer did not attain the "aesthetic uniformity" of powdered white faces, but I gained a greater sense of belonging and purpose during the performance. I was representing myself authentically as well as charting and acknowledging the diversity of European history.

Fast-forward to the COVID-19 lockdown of 2020. I was "the Negro" who would rediscover Black portraiture and make the Getty Museum Challenge a matter of representation. By re-creating as many Black figures as possible, using the stuff in my house and the camera of my iPhone 7, I would commit to rescuing their voices from oblivion—and in doing so, challenge how art history has been told.

As a singer, I breathe life into characters. My photographic re-creations of artworks draw on this discipline. They are performances. Although the lighting, set, costumes, and props are curated, many of the glances and poses happen in the moment. They capture a breath, or a beat, in the action of stepping into these historic paintings. To me, they are living operatic vignettes, each commenting on the scattered fragments—what the poet Derek Walcott called the "cracked heirlooms"—of the African diaspora. It is a process of finding the inherent lyricism within each Black figure I encounter, while at the same time meditating on the past, so I can process what I am seeing and construct a Black narrative on my own terms.

As photo re-creations on the page or onscreen, these performances do not involve my singing voice. But each represents a silent, disruptive howl. The Barbadian poet and academic (and distant relative) Edward Kamau Brathwaite spoke of a "howl" or a "shout" when he coined the term "nation language" to describe the nonstandard spoken English of the Caribbean and African diaspora. Brathwaite celebrated the fundamentally African shapes, sounds, and rhythms that underpin this way of speaking. It is a language based on environmental or natural experience, a language created by enslaved Africans transported to English colonies. It is "the experience of the hurricane," not of Salisbury Plain. As Brathwaite put it: "The hurricane does not roar in pentameters."[1]

Brathwaite identified nation language as a revolutionary force—an example of how enslaved Africans adopted, adapted, and resisted their colonial oppressors in order to create something that was wholly their own. Through this, as another critic described it, they found a way to "keep alive the memory of the freedom they had lost."[2] In other words, they made culture a site of resistance. These are ideas that are deeply personal for me. My mother grew up under British colonial rule on the island of Barbados, and her nation language is something I know intimately. Fifty years of living in the northwest of England have failed to erase the contours of her inherently revolutionary mode of speech. As for me, as a second-generation British Barbadian, I usually don't manifest nation language in my speech unless I'm naming my favorite Caribbean dishes or singing along to soca playlists in the kitchen. My own personal experience of the hurricane has been filtered through the Manchester mizzle and more than a splash of the fear of not fitting in. My portrait re-creations have, in that sense, represented a repossession of my Barbadian heritage.

I came to the Getty Museum Challenge having already spent a lot of time researching my ancestry. The result of this work is a family tree that stretches as far back as King Henry III, my great-times-twenty-five-grandfather. My lineage illustrates all the racial and socioeconomic complexities of the British Caribbean colonies. From my enslaved West African forebears at the bottom of the pecking order (recorded merely as property in registers that go back only as far as 1813) to my freed, mixed-race ancestors (sons and daughters of white enslavers and enslaved Black women, accorded some privileges on account of their racial heritage but denied most others) to representatives of the white "plantocracy" at the pinnacle of colonial society (some of them wealthy English Royalists who migrated to Barbados in the 1640s), my family tree includes all component groups of the hierarchy that helped cement the notion that a Black life was not a human life.[3]

One of the ways the white ruling class asserted its power was through culture. My enslaver ancestors commissioned artisans to carve marble monuments, create ornate silverware, and paint their portraits. When I look at my family tree, two hundred or so years of it are animated only by the faces of these men. Although I descend directly from them, their depictions do more to highlight the trauma and violence of plantation society than to ignite filial affection. The reality is that my Black ancestors generated the wealth to pay for these pieces of art. *They* endured the brutal system of enslavement on Barbadian sugar plantations. *Their* toil—against all odds—produced the "white gold" that made their Brathwaite enslavers some of the wealthiest humans on the planet. I bear witness to Black trauma when I look upon the so-called honorable generals I hesitate to call kin.

> Massa buy me, he won't killa me oh
> Massa buy me, he won't killa me oh
> Massa buy me, he won't killa me oh
> Before he kill me, he ship me regular.
>
> Ay, ay, ay, ay, ay, ay, ay-ay-ay . . .
> Ay, ay, ay-ay-ay . . . ay
>
> For I live with a bad man, oh la
> For I live with a bad man, oh buddah bo
> For I live with a bad man, oh la
> Before I would go to the riverside regular.[4]

I can only imagine what my enslaved ancestors might have looked like. My re-creations allow me to explore their submerged lives. I use my imagination as a rehabilitative tool, filling the blanks so that I can give agency back to my nonwhite ancestors and the Black sitters whose images I re-create.

A word about the structure of this book: I have chosen to present the portraits roughly chronologically, in three "acts." This sequencing shines a light on how representations of Black subjects have changed over time. Roughly speaking, Act 1 features Black figures drawn from life and also "imagined" Black identities; in many cases, the Black subject is marginal, an exotic accessory seen through a white supremacist lens. In Act 2, we witness the disruption of that status quo; Black figures are still subject to the white gaze, but they are portrayed as individuals. In Act 3, artists seize the genre of portraiture and create something entirely new, informed by the richly inclusive perspectives of both the makers and their subjects. This is not a book about creating a separate art history. It is about adding to and enriching the artistic canon we already know.

From our present vantage point in Act 3, I acknowledge that many of the Black sitters I have embodied in my re-creations are muted or marginalized. Some of them are completely anonymous, depicted by white artists solely to reinforce racist ideals. Stepping into the shoes of these long-muted Black figures has made space for me to chip away at and crack this Eurocentric edifice. I have adopted and adapted these works of art in the hope that by making these depictions completely my own, the lives of the individuals I portray might be unshackled, reimagined, and, most importantly, *seen*. Each of these Black figures has a distinctive nation language—their own particular contours, rhythms, and howls that speak to experiences of pain *and* joy. What interests me is whether finding and personifying these individuals can help bring justice to the portraits in question and perhaps even contribute to rehabilitating our colonized minds.

1 Edward Kamau Brathwaite, *History of the Voice: The Development of Nation Language in Anglophone Caribbean Poetry* (London: New Beacon Books, 1984), 10.

2 Dick Hebdige, *Cut 'n' Mix: Culture, Identity, and Caribbean Music* (London: Routledge, 2000), 26.

3 One of my ancestors, John Brathwaite (1722–1800), a colonial agent for Barbados, even contributed to a popular eighteenth-century manual on "slave breeding"; see Hilary McD. Beckles, *Britain's Black Debt: Reparations for Slavery and Native Genocide* (Kingston, Jamaica: University of West Indies Press, 2013), 125. The manual was titled *Instructions for the Management of a Plantation in Barbadoes, and for the Treatment of Negroes* (London, 1786).

4 Lyrics from the only known manuscript of a Barbadian work song/chant of the 1770s–80s, Lloyd-Baker Collection, Granville Sharp Papers, D3549/13/3/27, Gloucestershire Archives, England.

Act 1

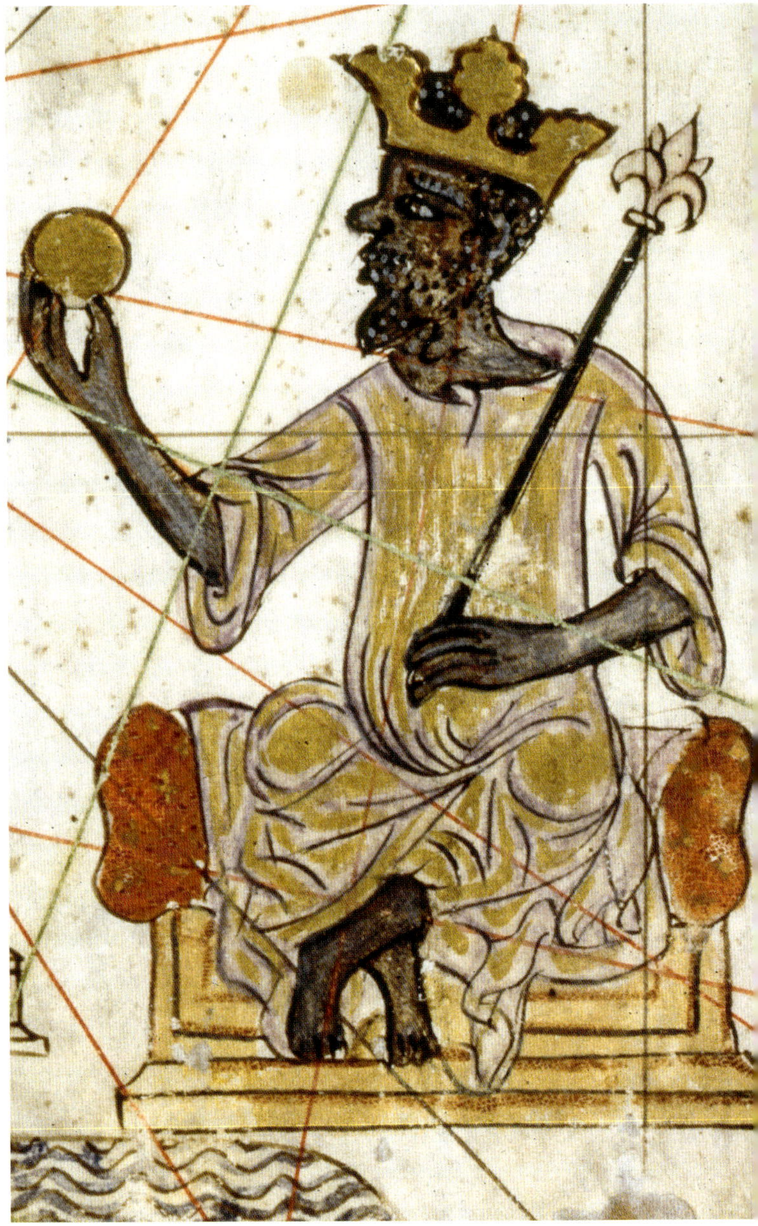

Mansa Musa

ca. 1375

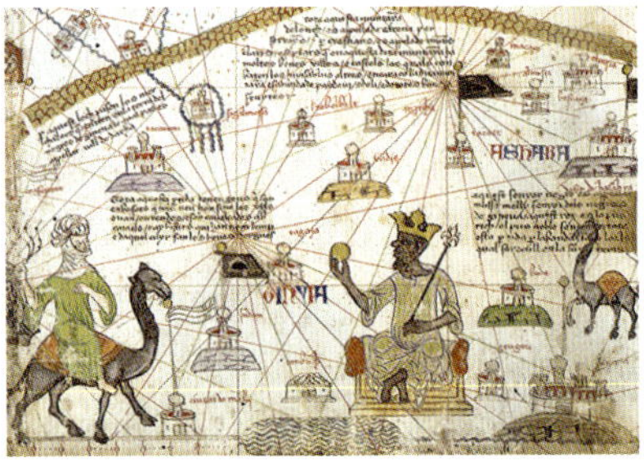

Abraham Cresques
Spanish, 1325–1387

In *Atlas of Maritime Charts* (*The Catalan Atlas*)
Illuminated parchment glued to board
Each panel: 64.5 × 25 cm ($25\frac{3}{8} \times 9\frac{7}{8}$ in.)
Paris, Bibliothèque nationale de France (BnF), Ms. Espagnol 30, fol. 3

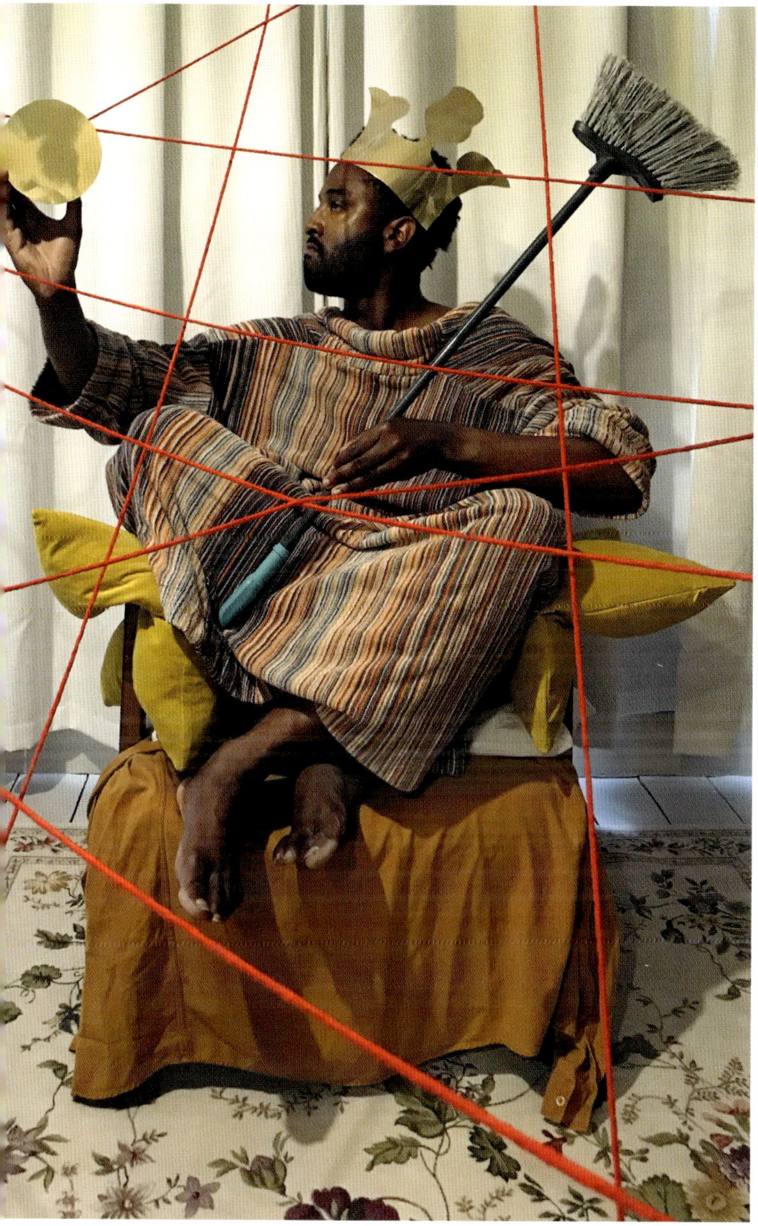

Act 1

At the center of a map showing trade routes in the Sahara sits a king with a golden orb, scepter, and crown. Reworked with cardboard, a bathrobe, a broom, and wool yarn. This is Mansa Musa, emperor of Mali and perhaps the richest man who ever lived. He developed Tombouctou and Gao into important cultural centers, making Mali a sophisticated seat of learning in the Islamic world. Legend has it that when Musa made a pilgrimage to Mecca in 1324, he brought a caravan of sixty thousand people, twelve thousand of whom were enslaved. His appearance on the map illustrates how indispensable West African gold had become to the rest of the medieval world. Yet topmost in mind during the making of my re-creation was the complexity of embodying the character of an enslaver.

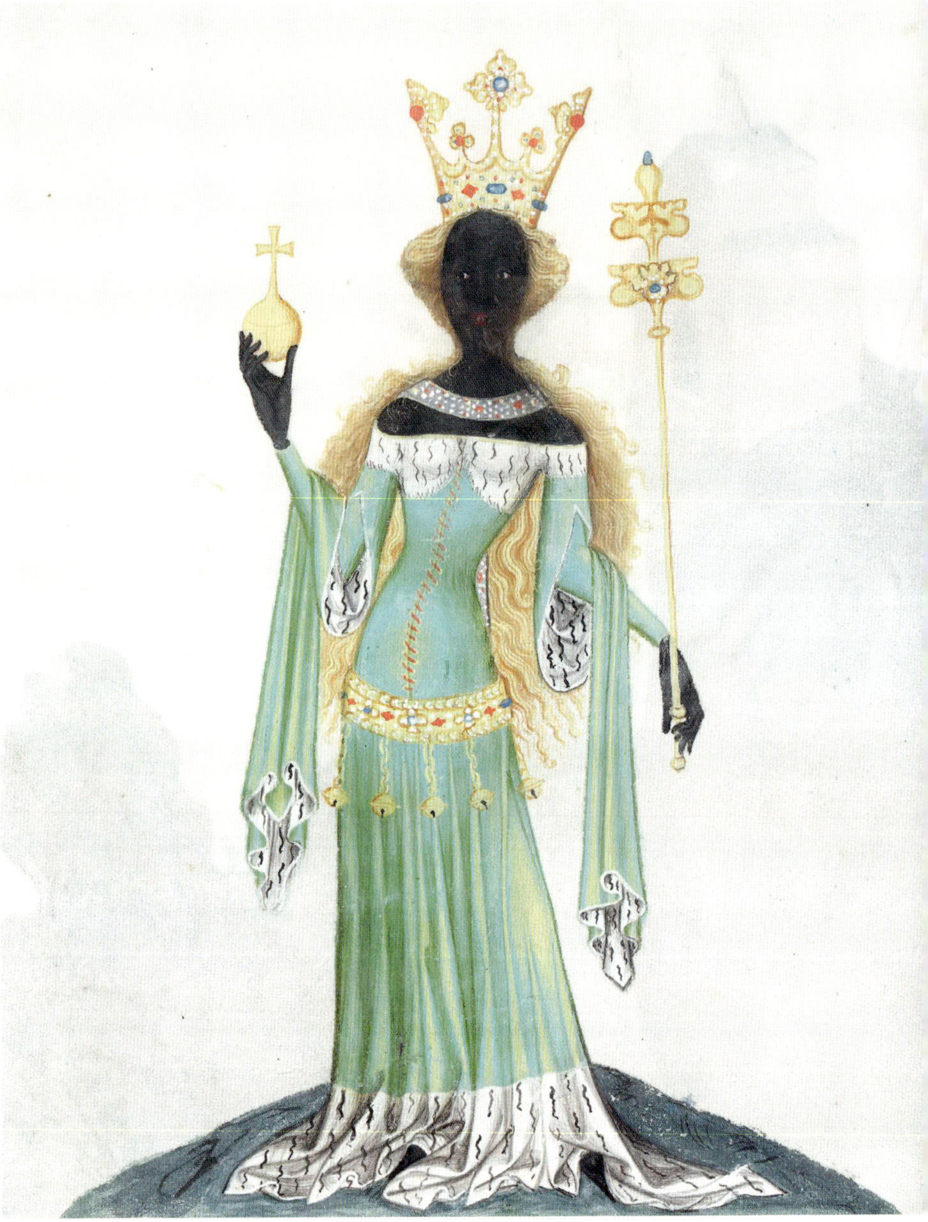

Queen of Sheba

before 1405

Konrad Kyeser
German, 1366–1405

In *Bellifortis*
Illumination and gilding
on parchment
32 × 24 cm
(12⅝ × 9½ in.)
Germany, Göttingen State
and University Library,
2 Cod. Ms. Philos. 63, Cim.,
fol. 122r

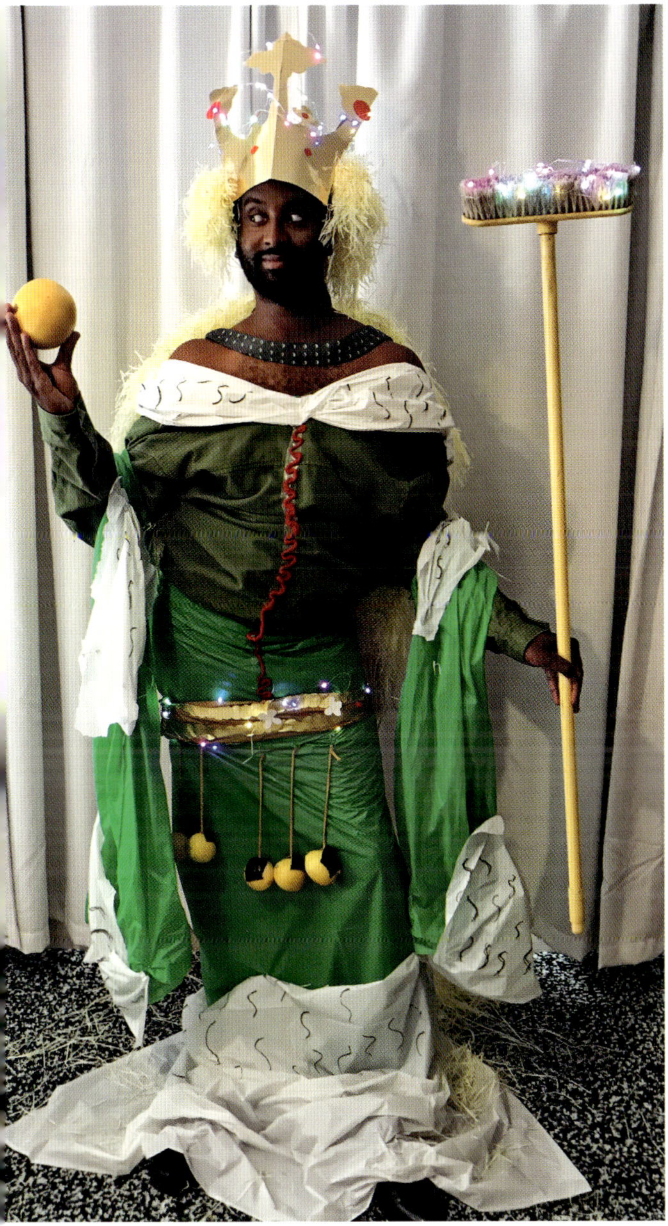

Act 1

Poised and majestic, the queen wears a luxurious gown with bells hanging from the waist. Reworked with lemons, grapefruit, fairy lights, and tissue paper. According to the Hebrew Bible, the queen of Sheba, or Saba' (spanning modern-day Ethiopia and Yemen), arrived in Jerusalem bearing gold, jewels, and spices and tested King Solomon's wisdom through a series of riddles. By the twelfth century, she had emerged as a symbol of the Catholic Church traversing the globe, typically depicted either alongside a person of color or as a Black woman herself. Here she is represented as a role model of sorts, a noble figure embodying the divine wisdom of Christianity. Scholars believe the hands and face in this rendering were darkened at a later date.

Gondolier [Miracle of the Relic of the Cross at the Rialto Bridge]

ca. 1496

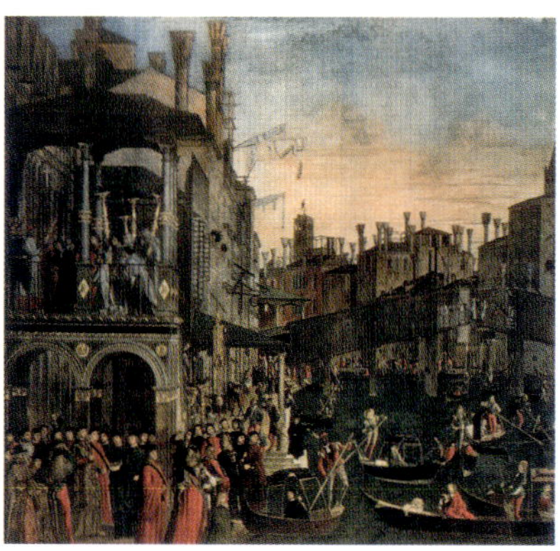

Vittore Carpaccio
Italian, ca. 1460–ca. 1526

Tempera on canvas
371 × 392 cm
(146 × 154⅜ in.)
Venice, Gallerie
dell'Accademia

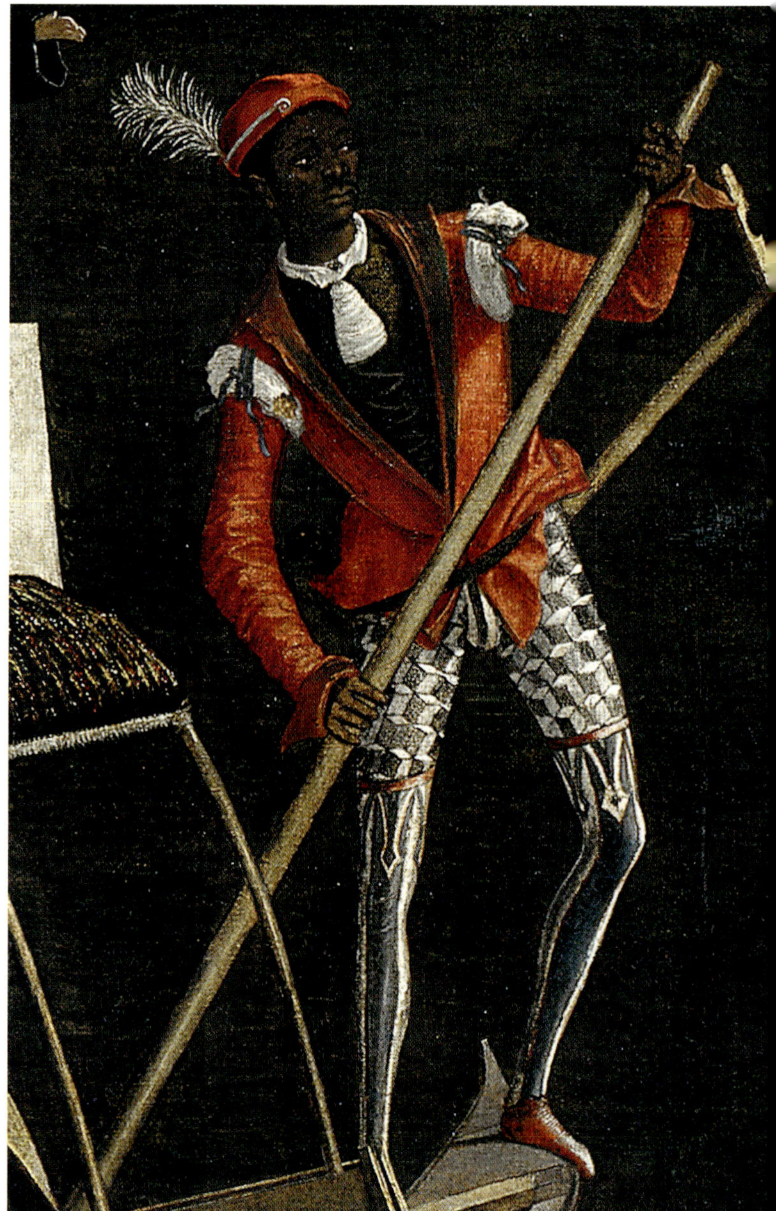

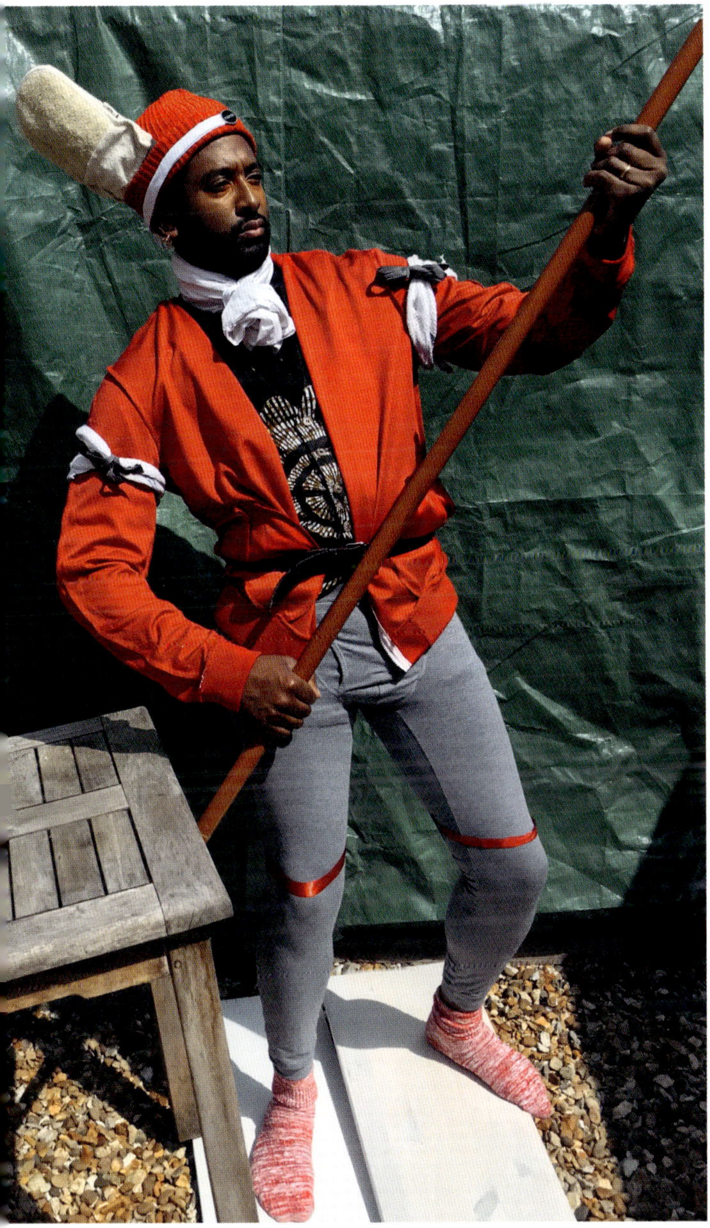

Act 1

Principal gondolier reworked with a "Purpose" pin from the National Museum of African American History and Culture on my hat and a Côte d'Ivoire print waistcoat. Though religious in theme, this painting confirms the presence of Black Africans in Renaissance Venice. The featured figure is one of two Black gondoliers in the scene. The men attract attention not just because of their skin color but also thanks to their flamboyant costumes. I have wondered whether the cube pattern on their stockings could signify that they came from North Africa, where Islamic art forms feature similar geometric designs. From the mid-1400s, growing numbers of enslaved peoples were trafficked from sub-Saharan and North Africa to Europe. The Black freedmen who ferried passengers in Venice rarely had families of their own, but membership in a gondoliers' association provided a ready-made kinship network.

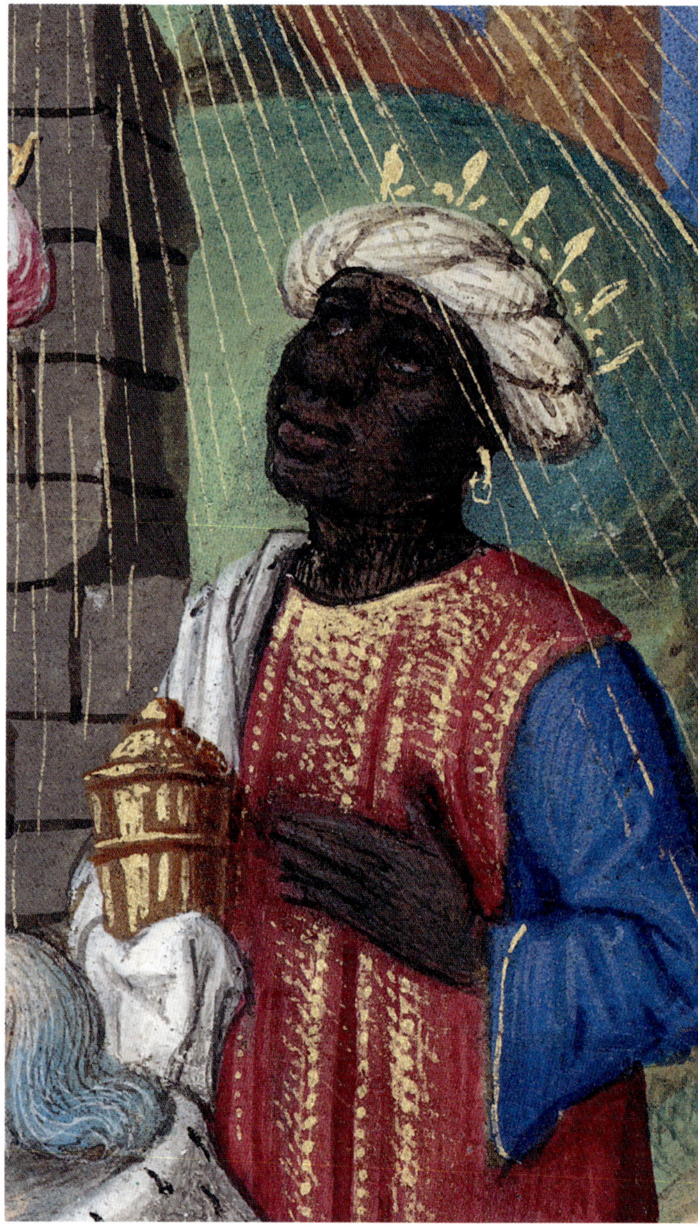

The Adoration of the Magi

ca. 1480–90

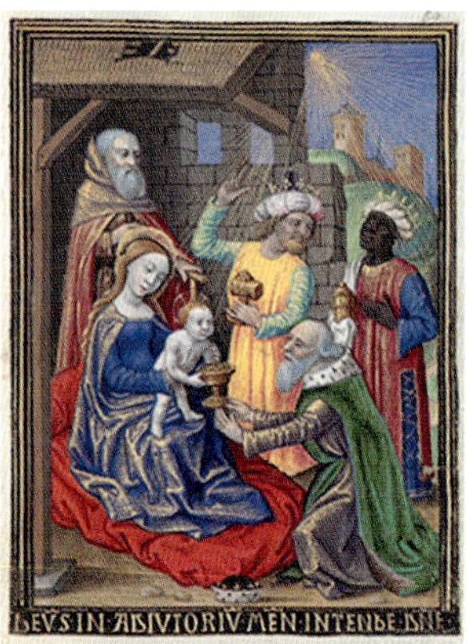

Georges Trubert
French, active 1467–1499,
died before 1508

In a book of hours
Tempera, gold leaf, gold
and silver paint, and ink
11.4 × 8.6 cm
(4½ × 3⅜ in.)
Los Angeles, J. Paul
Getty Museum, Ms. 48,
fol. 59

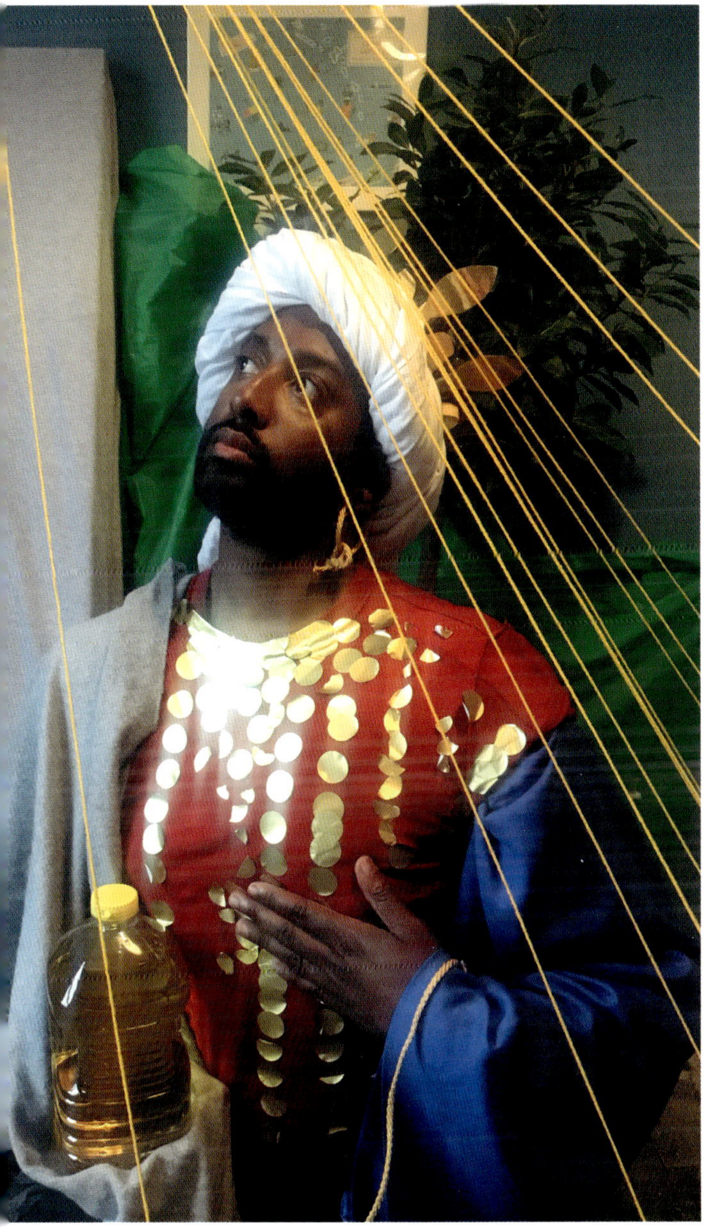

Act 1

The magus Balthazar reworked with a bottle of cooking oil and wool yarn. The Three Kings, like the Queen of Sheba, symbolized the global reach of the Catholic Church during the medieval period. Today, especially in Europe, it is widely accepted that one of the Magi was a Black king from Africa, but that did not become the norm until the fifteenth century. His emergence speaks to the presence of Black people in European cities during the mid-1400s, reminding us how the rise of trade with Africa, as well as the trade in African lives, influenced representations in art.

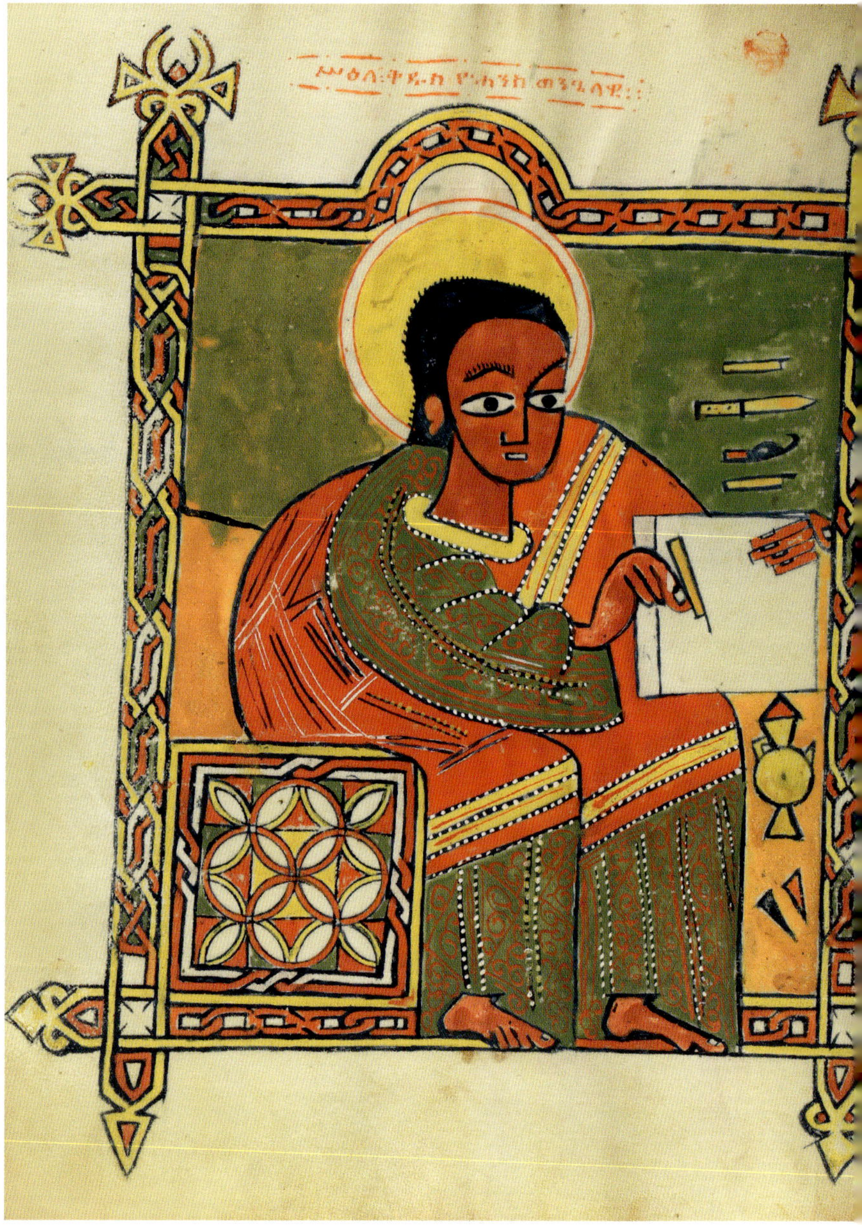

Saint John

ca. 1504–5

Unknown artist

In a gospel book
(Ethiopian)
Tempera
34.5 × 26.5 cm
(13$\frac{5}{8}$ × 10$\frac{3}{8}$ in.)
Los Angeles, J. Paul Getty
Museum, Ms. 102, fol. 215v

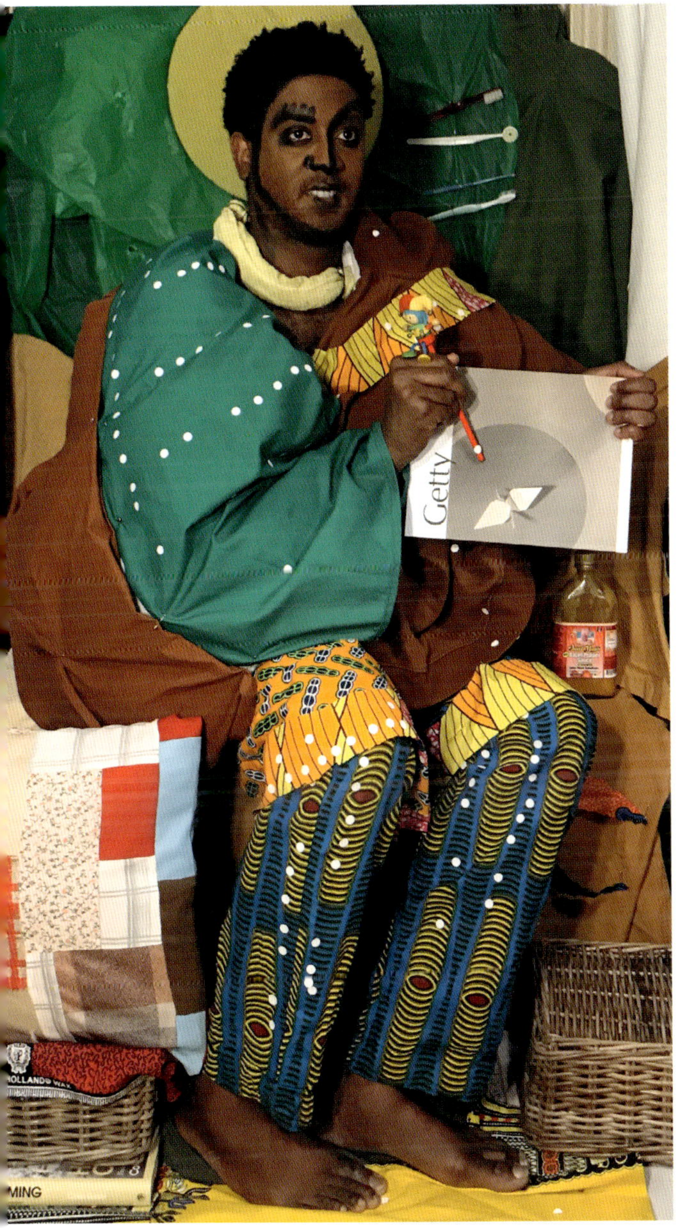

Act 1

The saint reworked with white dot stickers, a comforter, West African wax fabrics, face paint, Getty magazine, toothbrushes, and a bottle of Bajan hot pepper sauce. Christianity in Ethiopia dates back to the fourth-century kingdom of Aksum. This vibrant manuscript, dating from the early 1500s, shows the evangelist John bent over a table writing his Gospel. His rounded back, his almond-shaped eyes, and the dotted pattern on his clothing are hallmarks of Gunda Gundé, a geometric style named after a Stephanite monastery in the present-day region of Tigray.

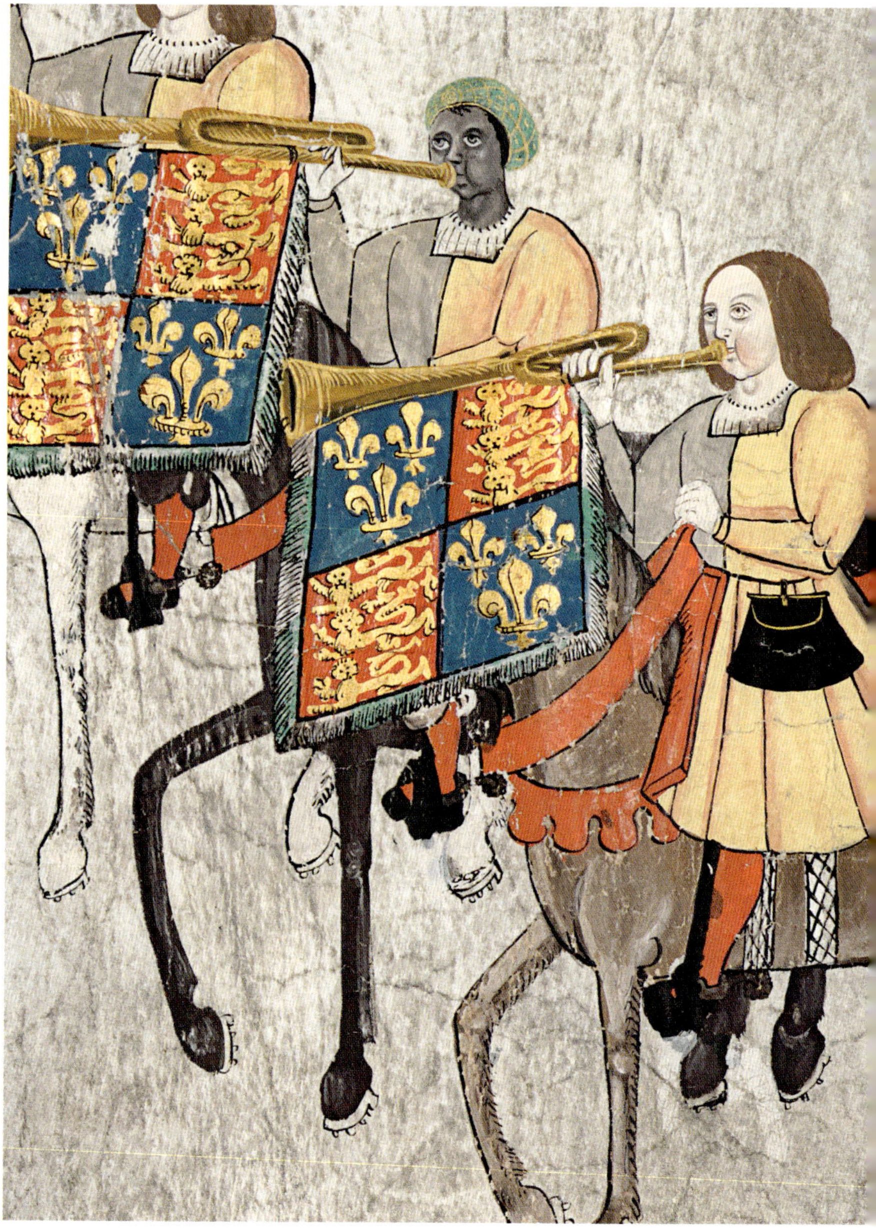

John Blanke

1511

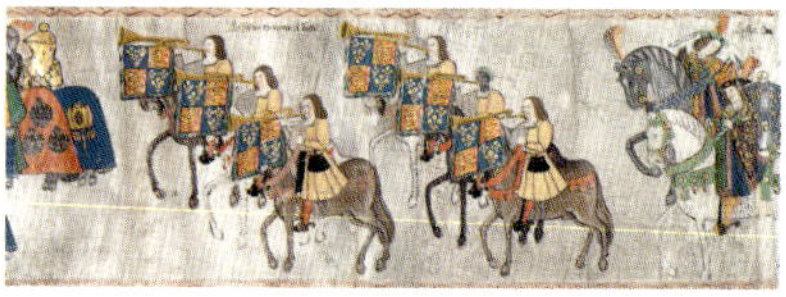

Unknown artist

In the Westminster
Tournament Roll
Paint on vellum
37.5 × 1813.6 cm
(14¾ × 714 in.)
London, College of Arms

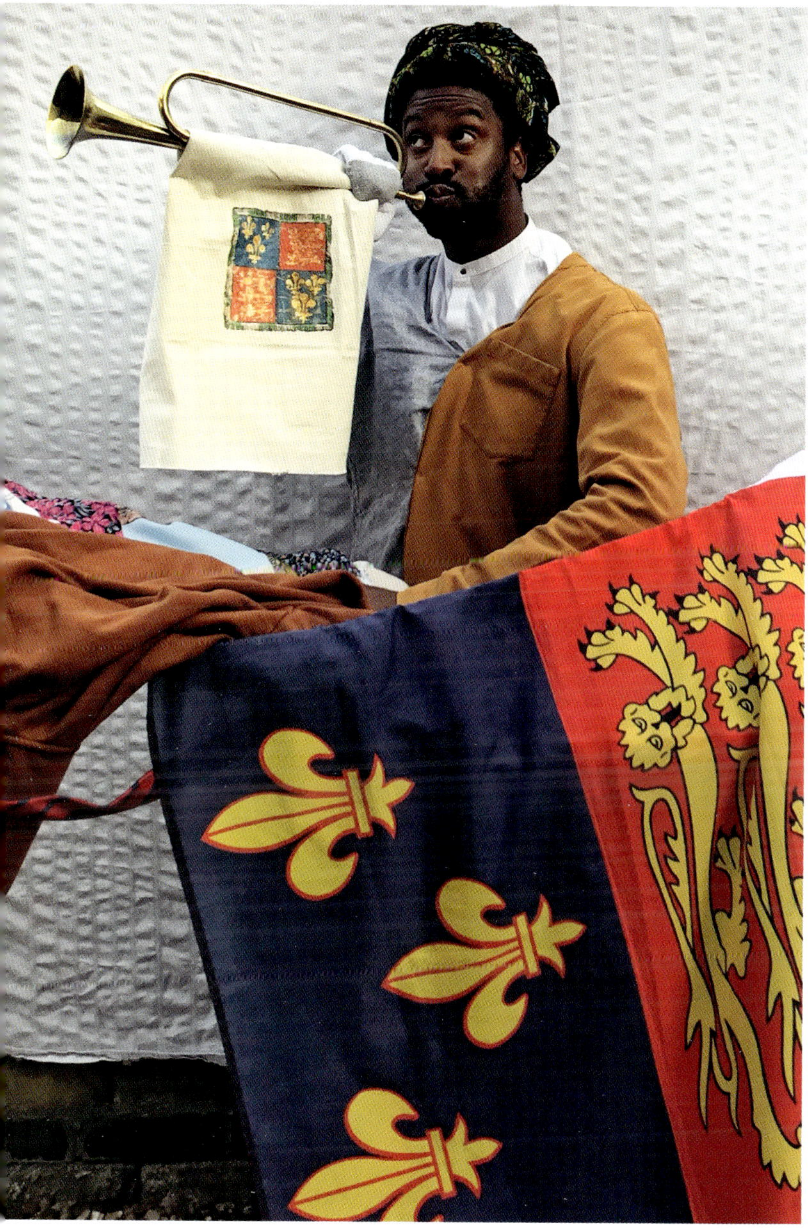

Act 1

John Blanke is the only Black Tudor for whom we have an attributable image. Reworked with a clotheshorse, a West African print headdress, and an upside-down trumpet and reproduction Tudor banner kindly provided by the John Blanke Project. Blanke is thought to have been of North or West African heritage, but further details are not yet known. As a court musician, he would have witnessed landmark moments in British history and played at many great performances of the Tudor period. This portrait is from the manuscript Henry VIII commissioned to record a joust staged after the birth of his son, Henry, to Catherine of Aragon; the entire work, unrolled, is almost sixty feet long. Blanke appears twice: once on the way from the court and again on the way back. He is dressed splendidly, instrument in hand—a Black artist in plain sight at one of the most prestigious events of his time.

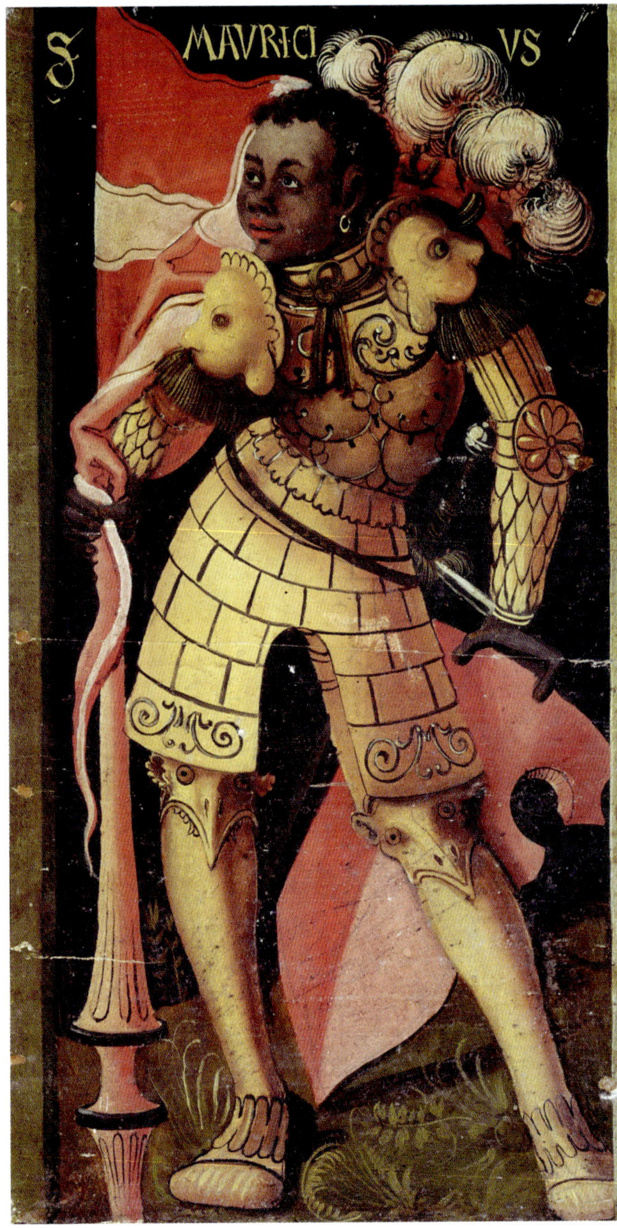

Saint Maurice

1517

Unknown artist

Oil on wood
77 × 43.5 cm
(30⅜ × 17⅛ in.)
Alterode Kirche, Germany

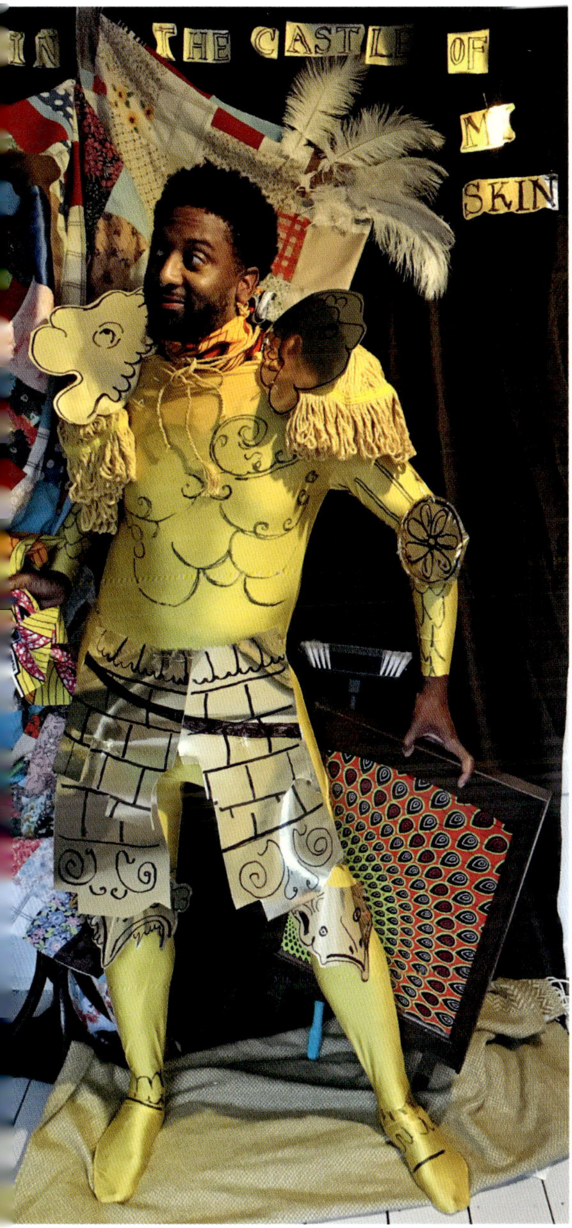

Act 1

A legendary martyred commander of the Theban Legion reworked with Granny's patchwork quilt, West African prints, mop heads, and the title of Barbadian writer George Lamming's acclaimed novel *In the Castle of My Skin* (1953). There is no evidence of Saint Maurice's heritage. As with the Black Magus, his Blackness emerged as a device to evoke cosmopolitanism and Christian universalism. From the thirteenth century, German rulers bolstered expansionist aspirations by commissioning images of a Black Saint Maurice in portraiture, sculpture, altarpieces, and stained glass. Here he is dressed in full German armor. With his cocked hip and jaunty smile, he seems an admirable Christian warrior—at home in the castle of his skin and worthy of veneration. The cult of Saint Maurice declined in the sixteenth century, which historians have suggested might be explained by the rise of the transatlantic slave trade.

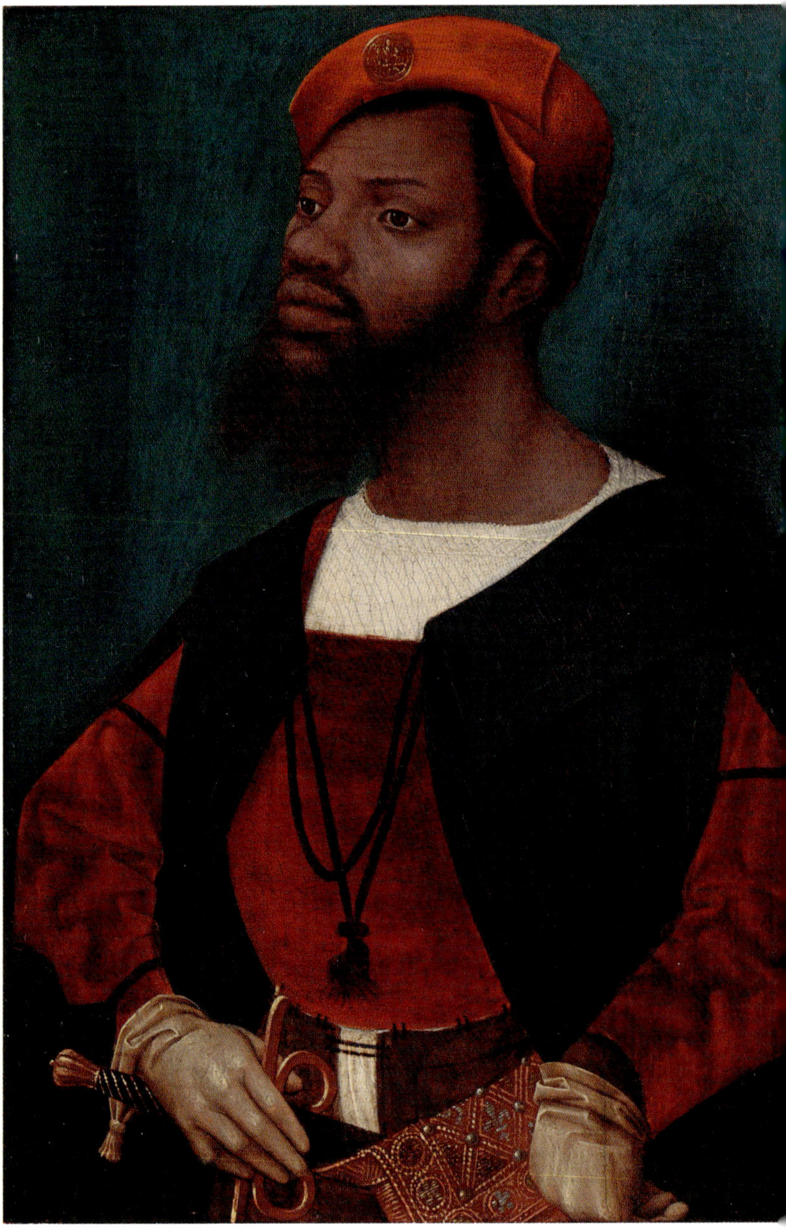

Portrait of an Unknown Man

ca. 1525–30

Jan Mostaert
Netherlandish,
ca. 1475–1555/56

Oil on panel
30.8 × 21.2 cm
(12⅛ × 8⅜ in.)
Amsterdam, Rijksmuseum,
SK-A-4986

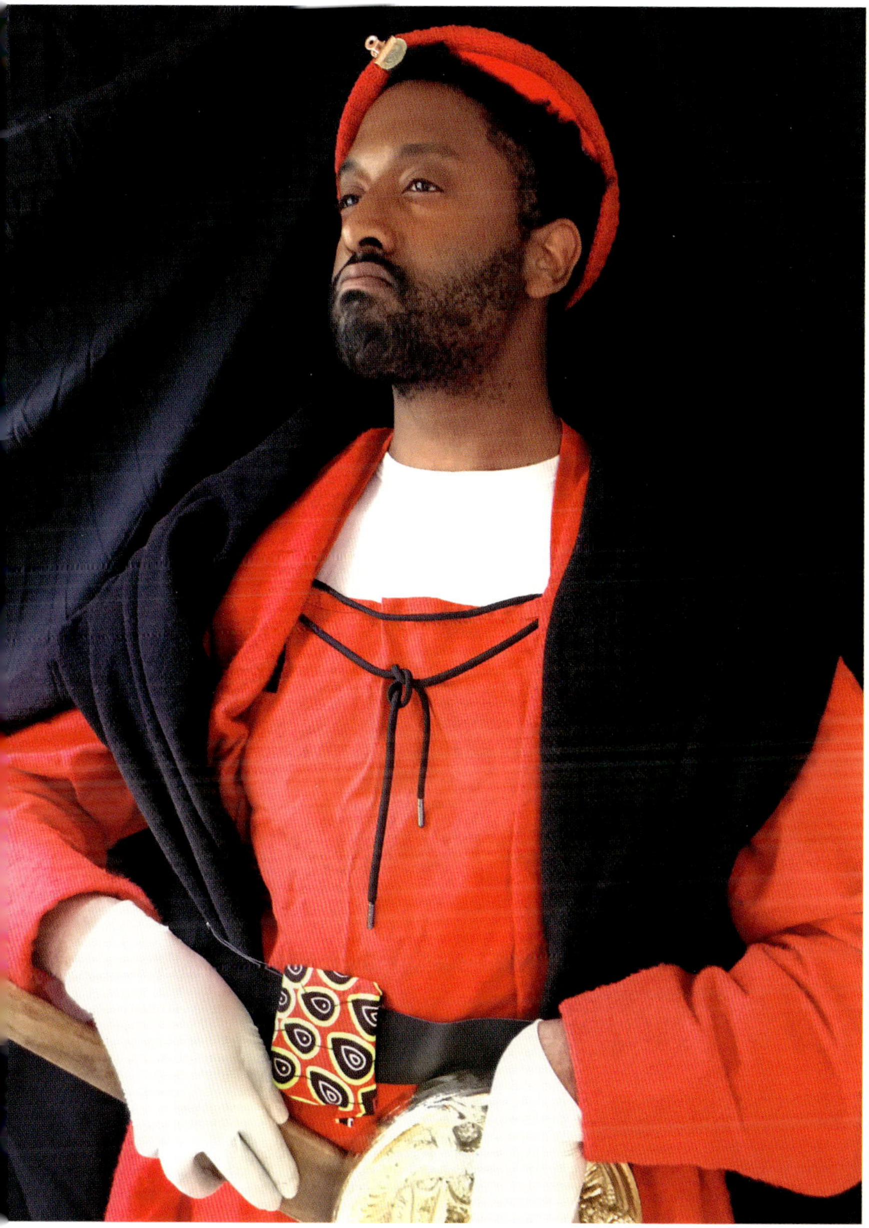

Act 1

Reworked with West African print fabric, surgical gloves, my grandfather's cou-cou stick, a wool hat, a coin, and a gold medallion. It has been proposed that this is Christopher the Moor, a Black archer who served as a bodyguard in the Brussels court of Emperor Charles V. The badge of the Virgin he wears on his hat is a souvenir from Halle in Flemish Brabant, a pilgrimage site favored by the Habsburg rulers. His beautiful attire helps to place him as a member of court society—as does, perhaps, his extravagant beard. The maintenance of tightly curled Afro facial hair can be a hassle owing to the ingrown hairs that commonly occur after shaving or trimming. Do his fashionable beard and unblemished skin signal that he had ample leisure time for an Afro-specific grooming regime?

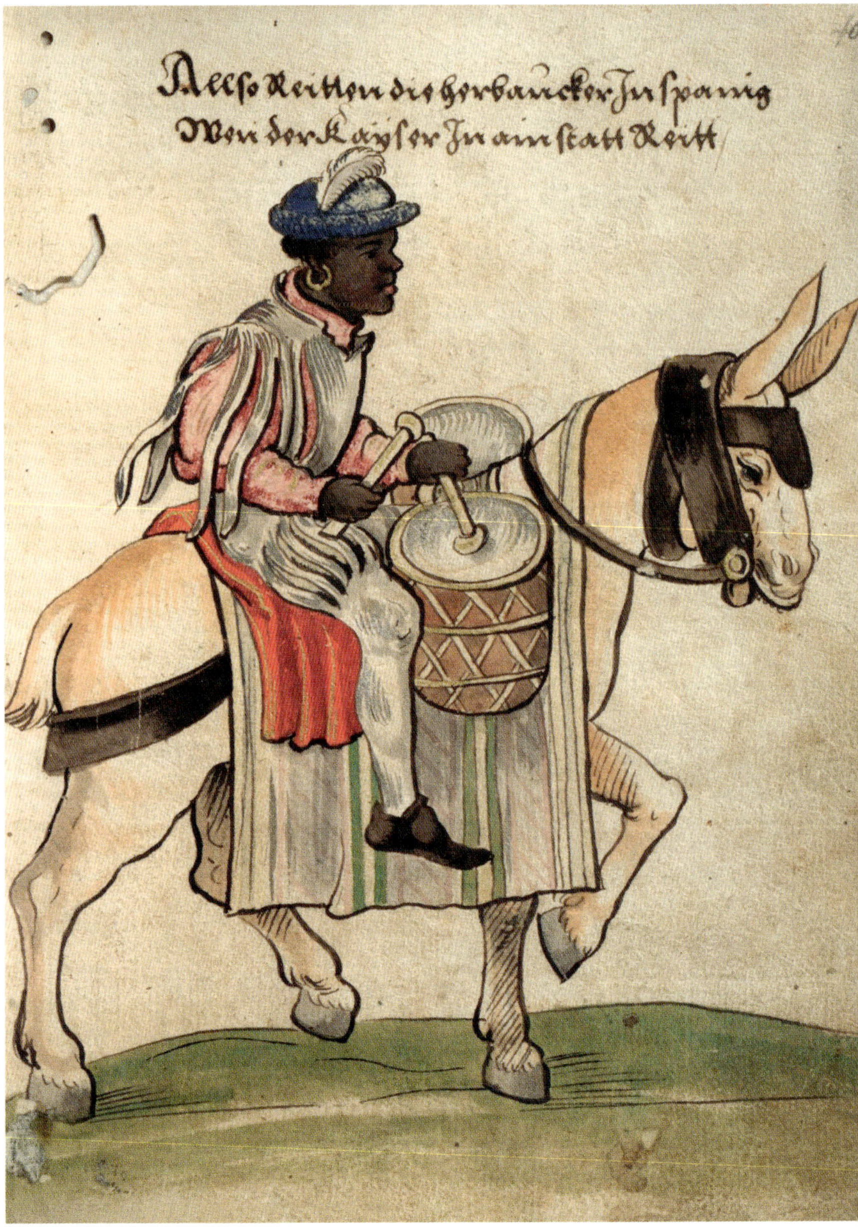

Drummer

1530–40

Christoph Weiditz I
German, ca. 1500–1559

In *Costume Book*
Ink on paper
19.8 × 15 cm
(7¼ × 5⅞ in.)
Nuremberg, Germanisches
Nationalmuseum, Hs 22474

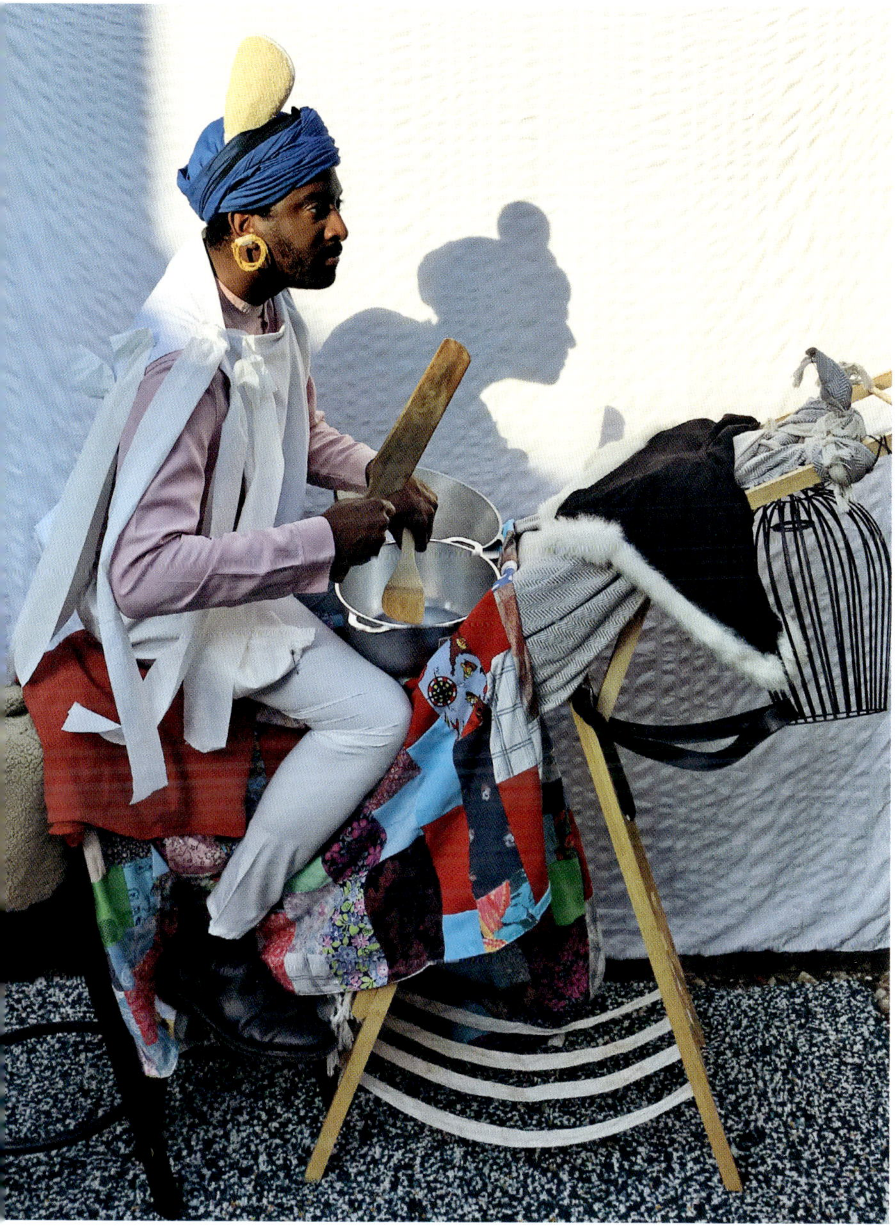

Act 1

A Black drummer playing at the ceremonial 1529 entrance of Emperor Charles V is taken from Weiditz's unpublished costume book. Reworked with toilet paper, Grandpap's cou-cou stick, Granny's quilt, and a clotheshorse. The inscription above the drummer says, "Thus ride the army drummers in Spain when the emperor rides into a city." Weiditz drew this Black drummer when he accompanied Charles V through Aragon and Catalonia. The subject's earring and plumage are incredibly expressive accessories that would have made this portrayal a noteworthy and "exotic" addition to a manuscript of cultural difference. By this time, African people were visible in cosmopolitan courts across Europe, particularly in the Mediterranean region. There was also an established tradition of Black musicians playing at European courts. Charles V's aunt, Catherine of Aragon, even brought Black trumpeters to England in her entourage.

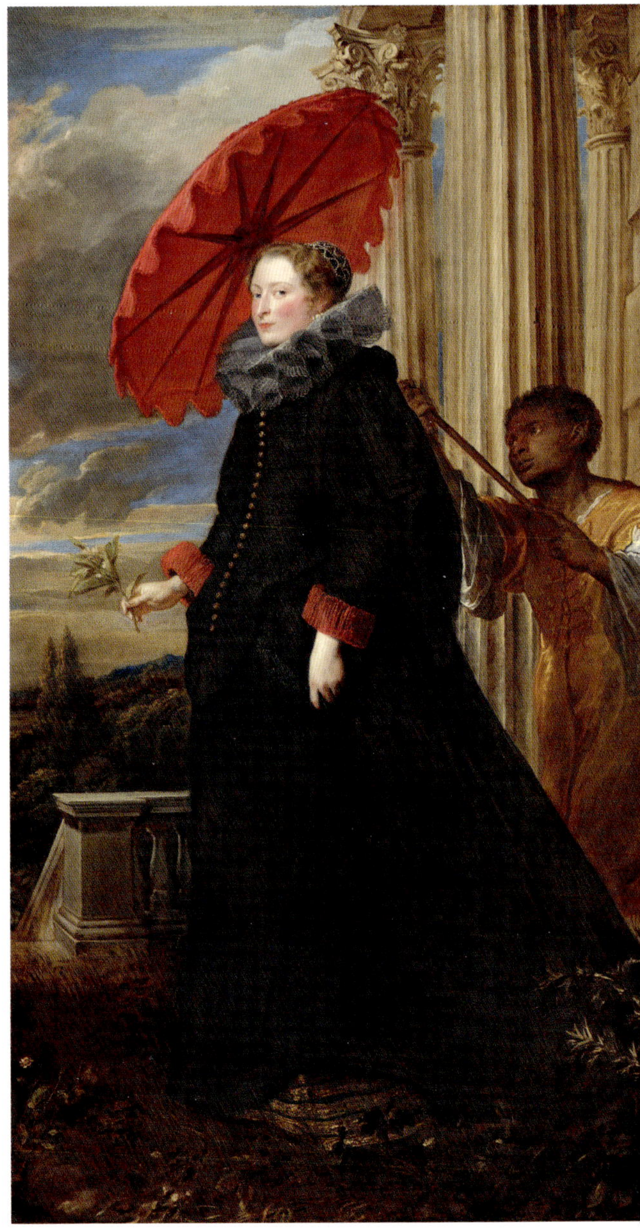

Marchesa Elena Grimaldi Cattaneo

1623

Anthony van Dyck
Flemish, 1599–1641,
active in England

Oil on canvas
242.9 × 138.5 cm
($95\frac{5}{8} \times 54\frac{1}{2}$ in.)
Washington, DC,
National Gallery of Art,
1942.9.92

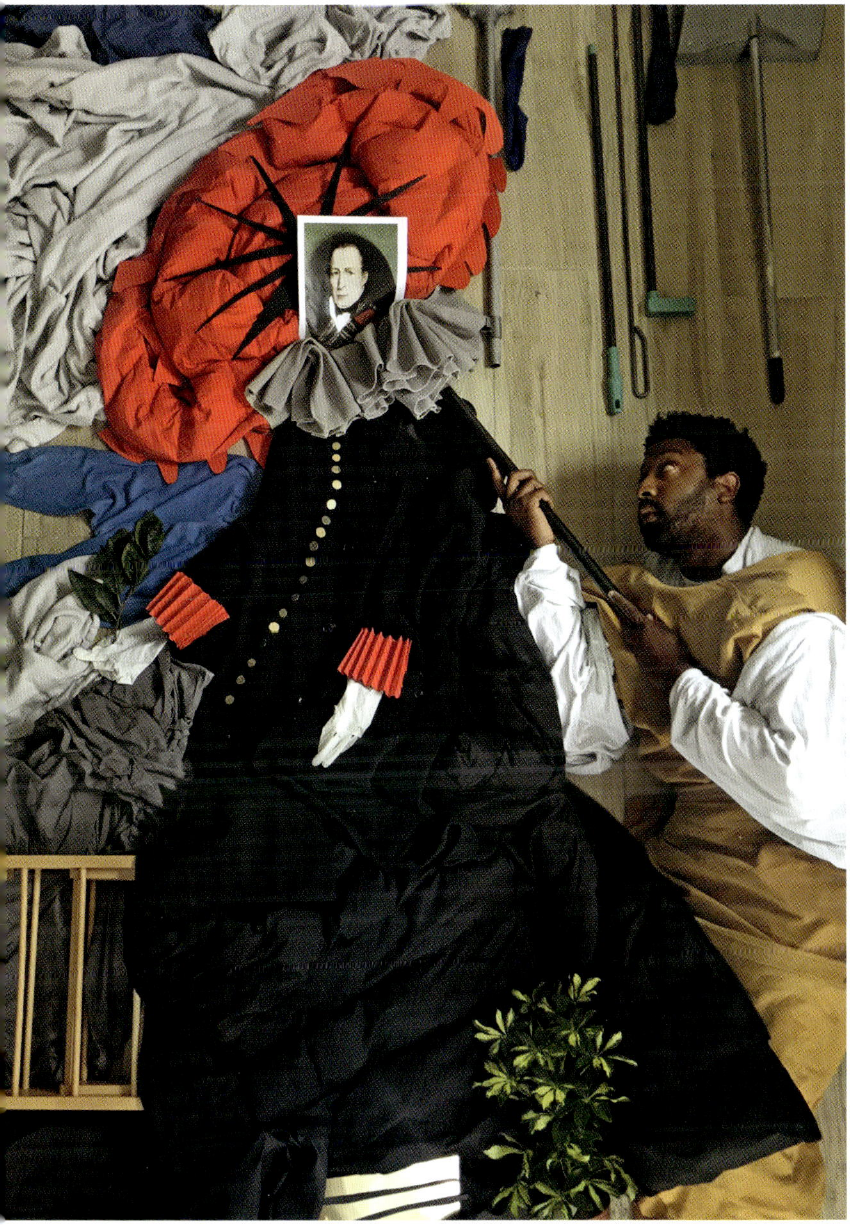

Act 1

Reworked with a portrait of my five-times-great-grandfather the Barbadian enslaver Miles Brathwaite II, a red puffer jacket, and a sprig from a plum tree. Every aspect of this image is meant to emphasize the marchesa's status. The young Black attendant is marginal and ambiguous while she is disproportionately taller—a saintlike figure with a flaming red halo. The parasol he holds up highlights his position not just beneath her but also beneath the viewer. Her red cuffs pull attention down to her hands, one of which clutches a sprig of orange blossom, a traditional symbol of chastity. The inclusion of a Black attendant is likely Van Dyck's nod to the Venetian artist Titian, who portrayed Black servants in a number of paintings. But his presence is also a poignant reminder of the active trade in Black lives from Africa to Genoa.

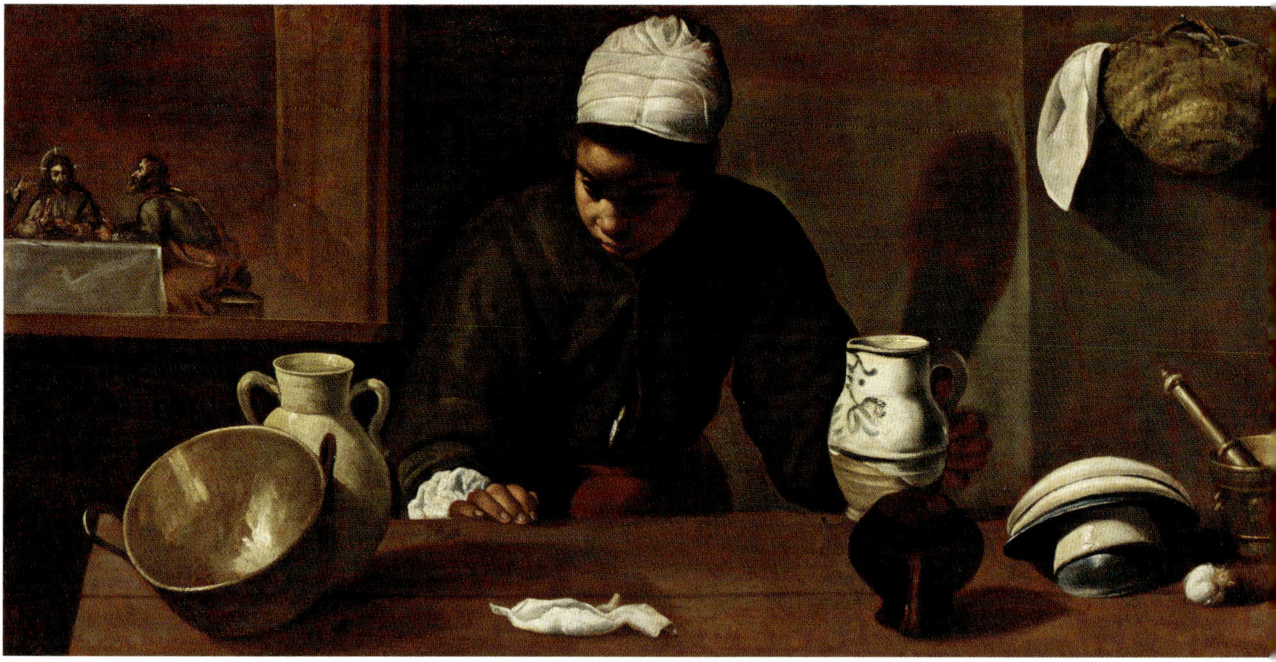

Kitchen Maid with the Supper at Emmaus

ca. 1617–18

Diego Velázquez
Spanish, 1599–1660

Oil on canvas
55 × 118 cm
(21⅝ × 46½ in.)
Dublin, National Gallery
of Ireland, NGI.4538

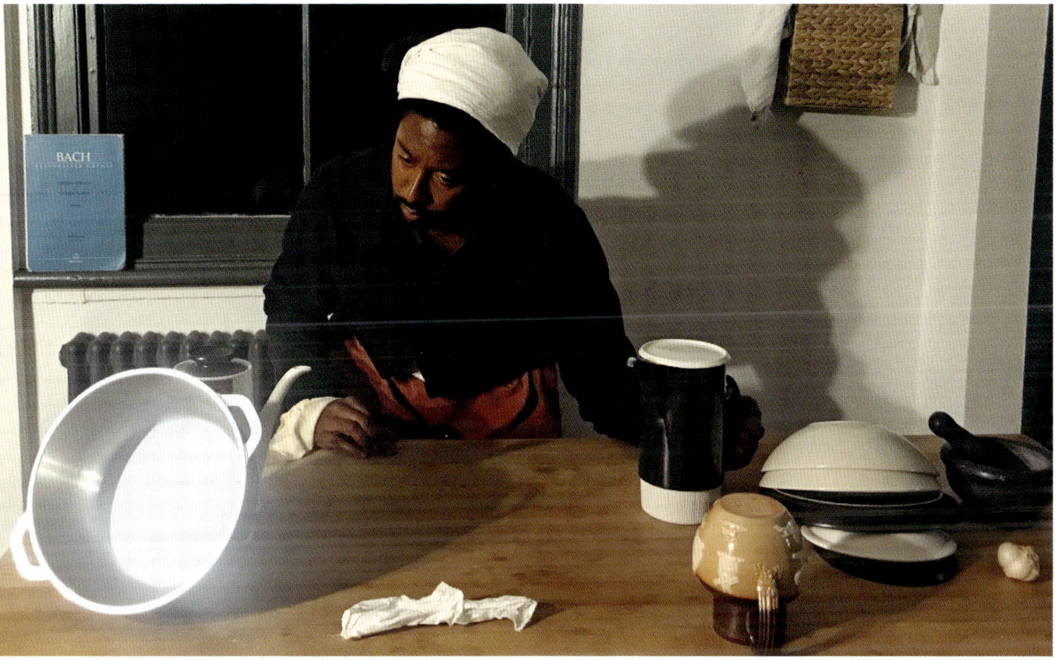

Act 1

In the foreground of Velázquez's earliest known work, we see a kitchen worker at the inn where Christ and two disciples have stopped for their evening meal. The biblical scene (reworked with a score of Bach's *Saint John Passion*) is tucked away in the background at left. This work is traditionally described in Spanish as *La Mulata*, a violently offensive term for someone of mixed race. Does the white jug reflect the subject's white self? Is her Blackness represented by the dark, upside-down vessel? We know that Velázquez owned enslaved people, but it is difficult to ascertain whether this painting is amplifying or subverting white supremacism. Its religious content further complicates matters; in Catholic societies, baptism was a tool of colonial governance and enslaved people were all, in theory, baptized Catholics.

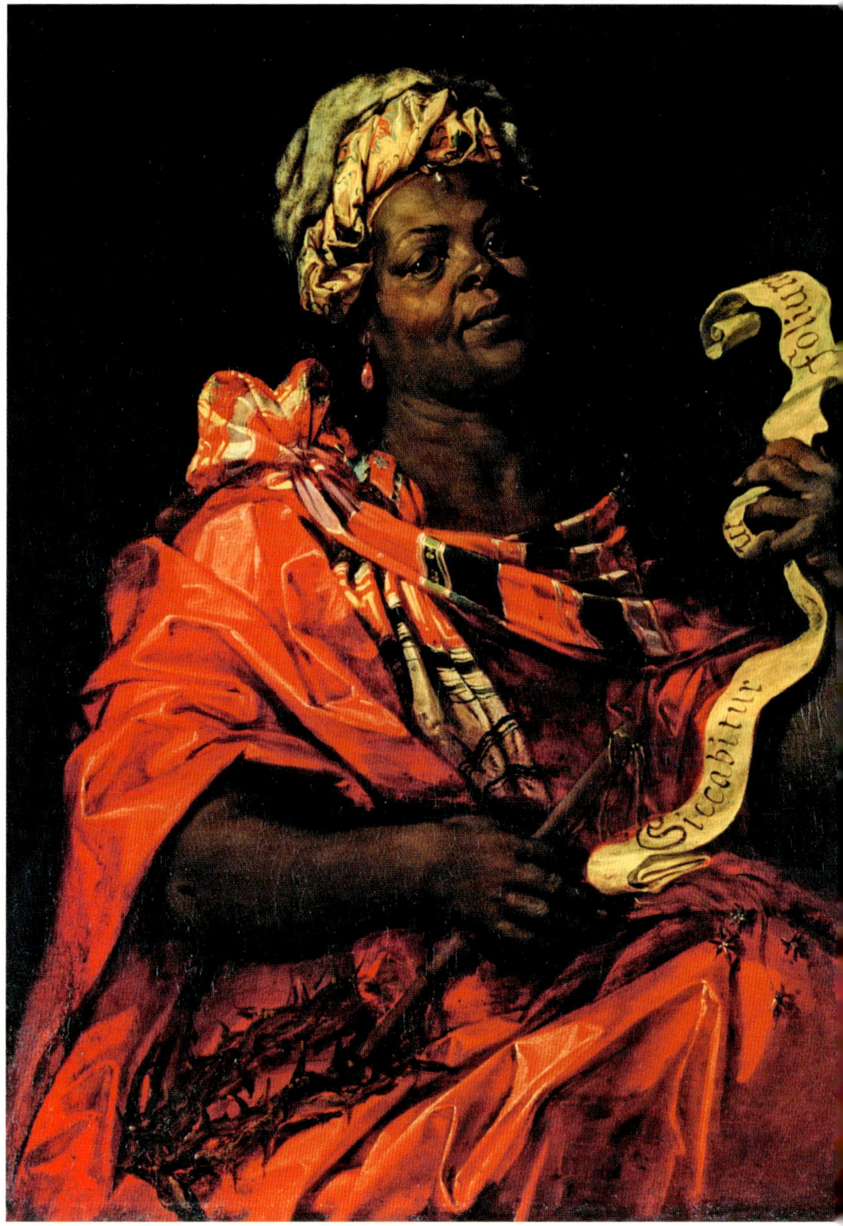

The Sibyl Agrippina

ca. 1630

Attributed to
Jan van den Hoecke
Flemish, 1611–1651

Oil on canvas
106.5 × 80 cm
(42 × 31½ in.)
Düsseldorf, Germany,
Kunstpalast, mkp.M 125

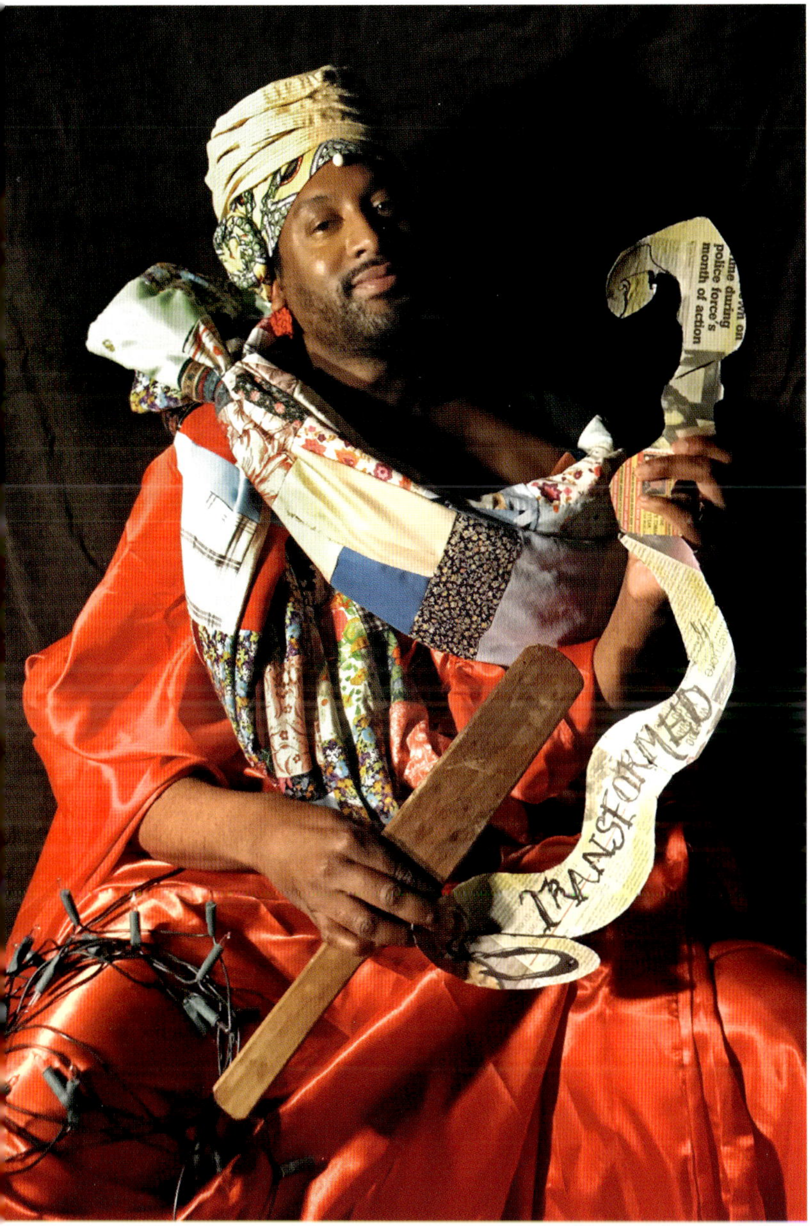

Reworked with Grandpap's cou-cou stick, Granny's patchwork quilt, and fairy lights. The Sibyls were oracles, or priestesses, in ancient Greece. One of a series of Sibyls by the Flemish painter Hoecke, this depiction of a Black woman as the "Egyptian" Sibyl follows a tradition in Western art but also speaks to the increased availability of Black models in the Netherlands as a result of the growing trade in enslaved Africans. The figure's whip and crown of thorns allude to the suffering of Christ at the Crucifixion. The inscription on the banner reads *Siccabitur ut folium* ("He will shrivel like a leaf"). It is likely that this representation would have been understood, in its time, against the backdrop of debates surrounding the Christianization of enslaved communities.

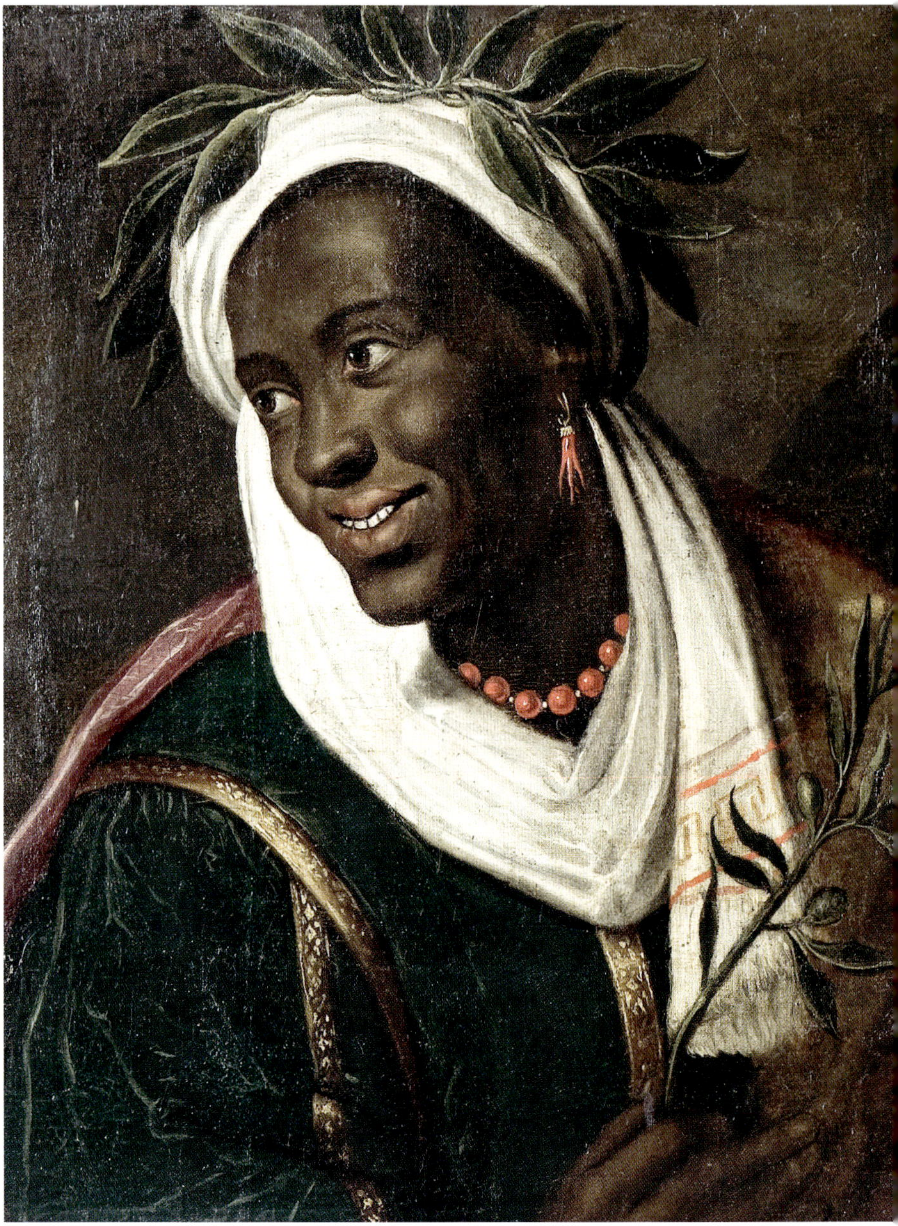

Portrait of a Man Crowned with Laurel

seventeenth century

Circle of Albert Eckhout
Dutch, ca. 1610–1666

Oil on canvas
55.8 × 44 cm
(22 × 17$\frac{3}{8}$ in.)
Whereabouts unknown

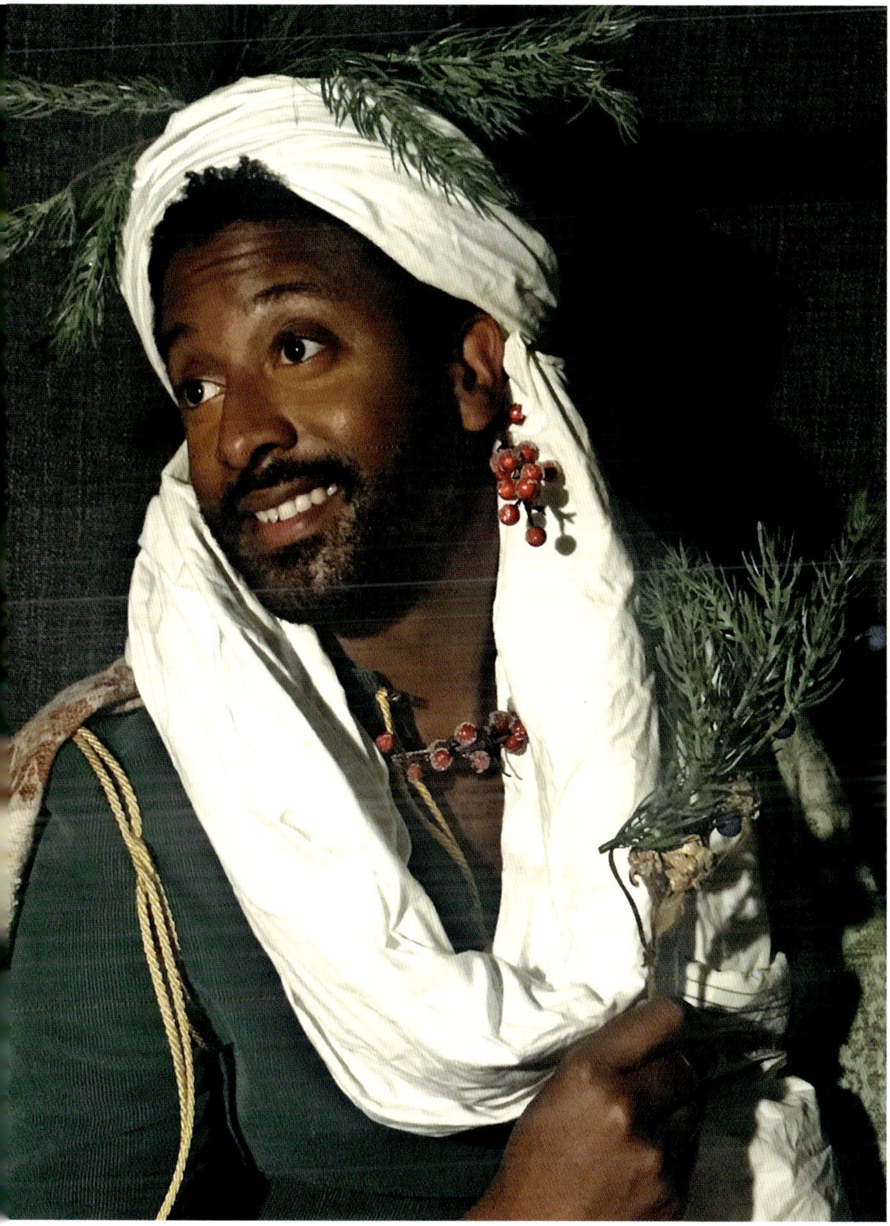

Act 1

Reworked with Christmas decorations. Very little is known about this work, which is attributed to a follower of the Dutch painter Eckhout. The figure wears a laurel wreath and holds an olive branch, ancient Greek symbols of victory. Given these attributes, the painting could be meant as a meditation on the rewards and costs of glory for people of color. Yet the liveliness of the sitter's smile and the glint in his eyes give the impression that this work captures a specific milestone in the life of an actual person. His pose is such that it spotlights his jewelry, which seems to be carved from precious red coral. The proposed date of the portrait coincides with the rise of red coral jewelry production in the Italian town of Torre del Greco, near Pompeii. Might this image depict a man garlanded for achievements in the region's niche industry?

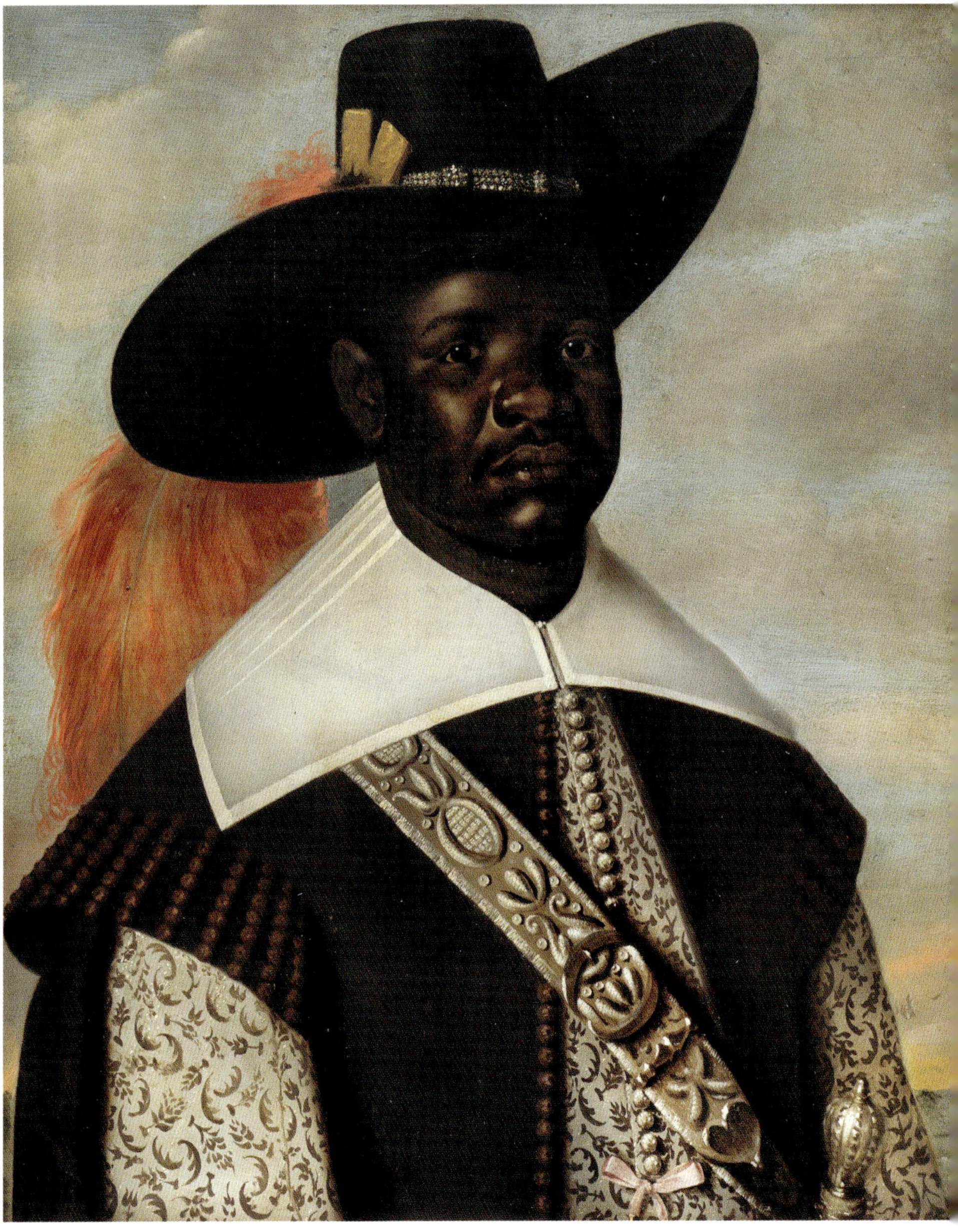

Don Miguel de Castro: Emissary of Kongo

ca. 1643

Jasper Becx
Dutch, d. 1647

Oil on panel
75 × 62 cm
(29½ × 24⅜ in.)
Copenhagen,
Statens Museum for
Kunst, KMS7

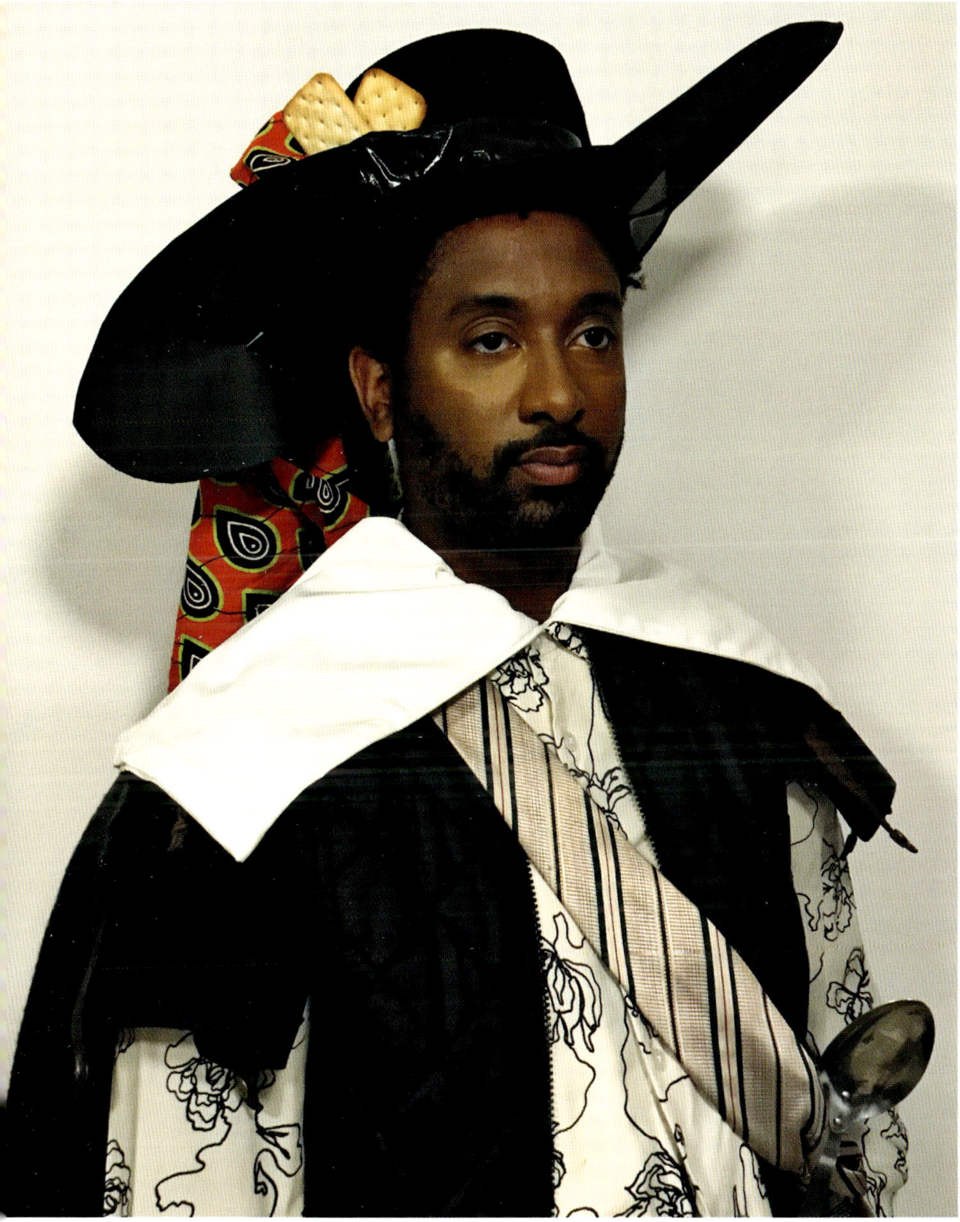

Reworked with West African fabric, cream crackers, and a serving spoon. Don Miguel and his attendants, Pedro Sunda and Diego Bemba (p. 104), traveled to the Netherlands via Brazil as part of an ambassadorial party seeking Dutch intervention to help resolve internal conflict in the kingdom of Kongo. Becx probably received the commission while the delegation was in Brazil. The portraits illustrate a turning point in the representation of Black people in European art, as we begin at last to see identifiable individuals depicted as central figures. Don Miguel's appearance in noble Portuguese attire sends a powerful political message: here is an African man who is adept at negotiating elite European society.

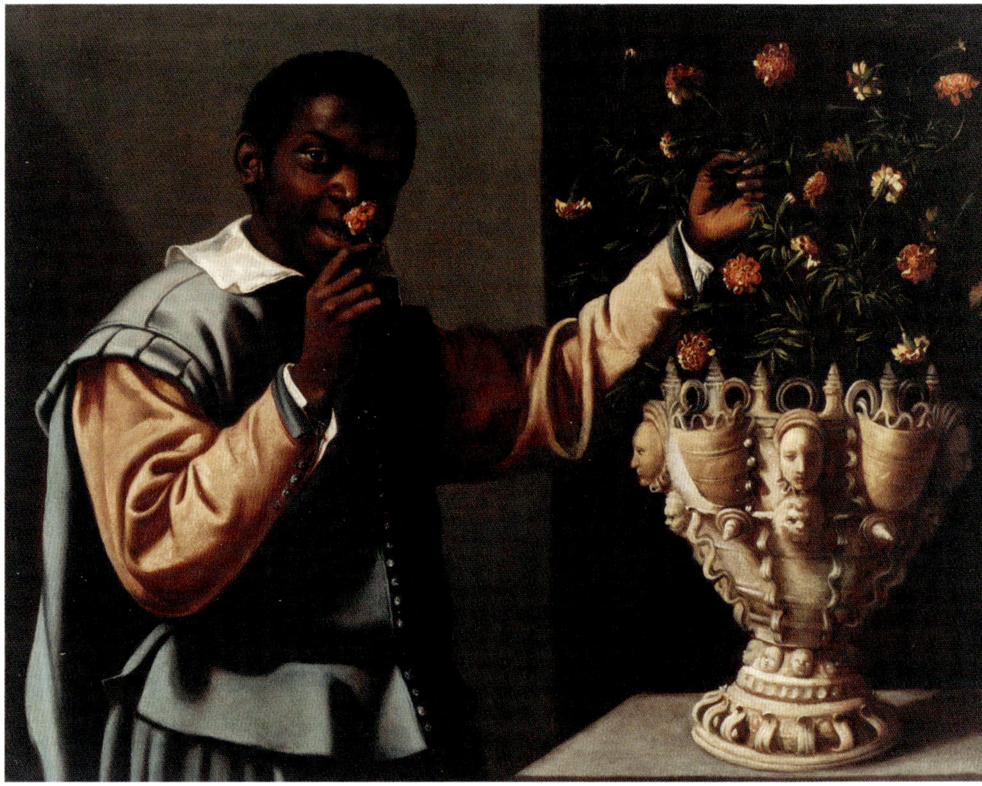

Allegory of the Sense of Smell

early seventeenth century

Follower of
Bartolomeo Passarotti
Italian

Oil on canvas
71.8 × 96.5 cm
($28\frac{1}{4}$ × 38 in.)
Houston, The Menil
Collection, CA 6804

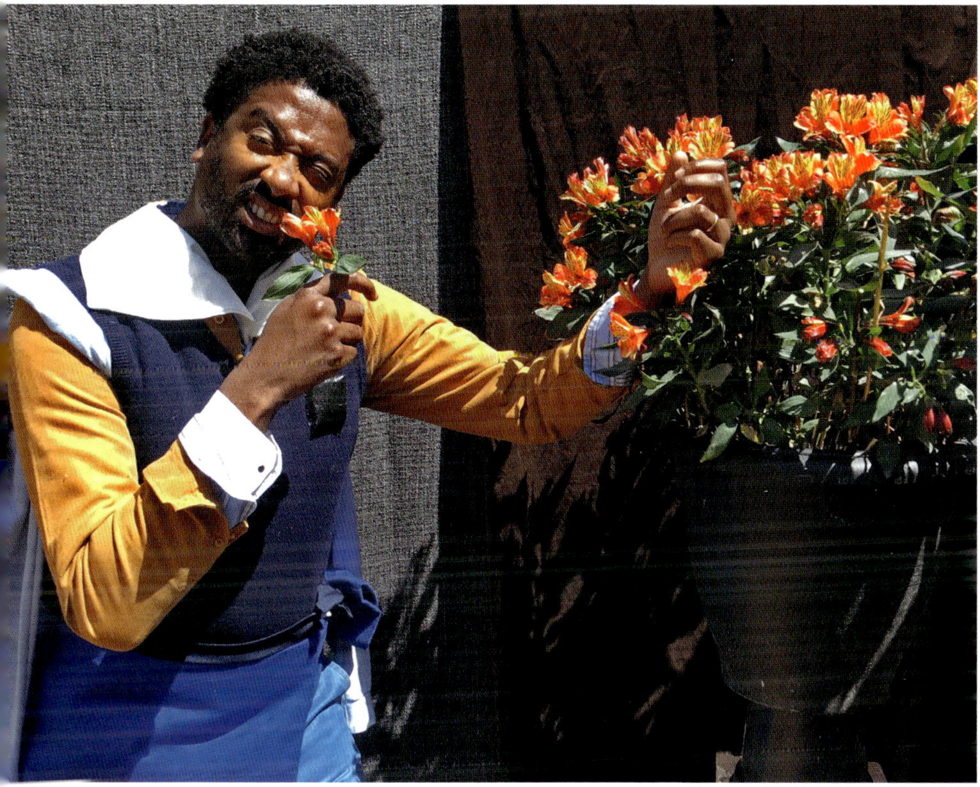

Act 1

This is probably from a suite of paintings representing the five senses. Reworked with an alstroemeria plant. Robed in blue and orange, a young Black man savors a blossom he has just picked, becoming an embodiment of the sense of smell. His appearance in this picture speaks to the presence of Africans in Renaissance European society. Note how he grabs the plant with his left hand, becoming one with the flora. Does his frown suggest recognition that his exotic "otherness" would prompt both disdain and fascination on the part of the viewer?

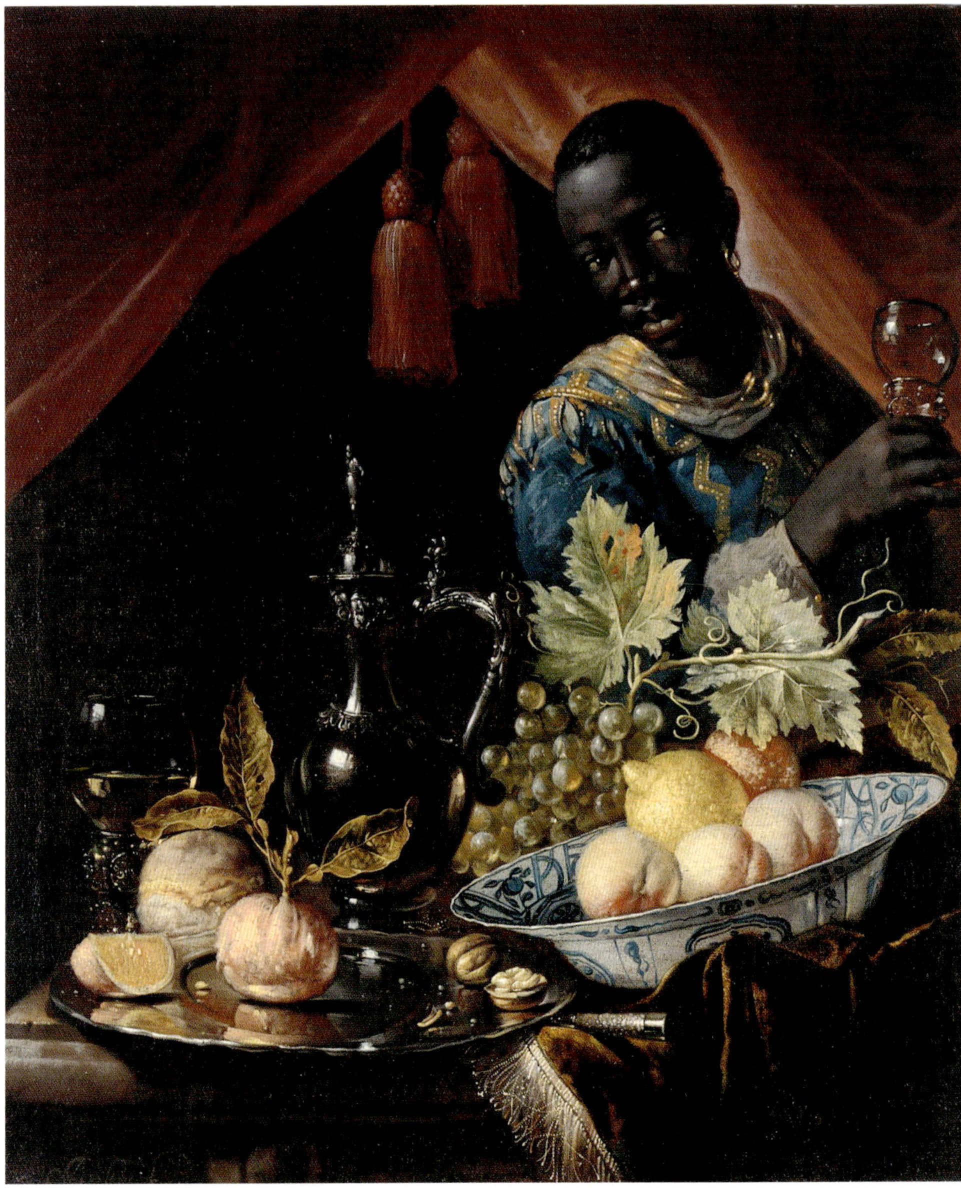

Still Life with Peaches and a Lemon

mid- to late seventeenth century

Juriaen van Streeck
Dutch, 1632–1687

Oil on canvas
90.5 × 80 cm
(35⅝ × 31½ in.)
Whereabouts unknown

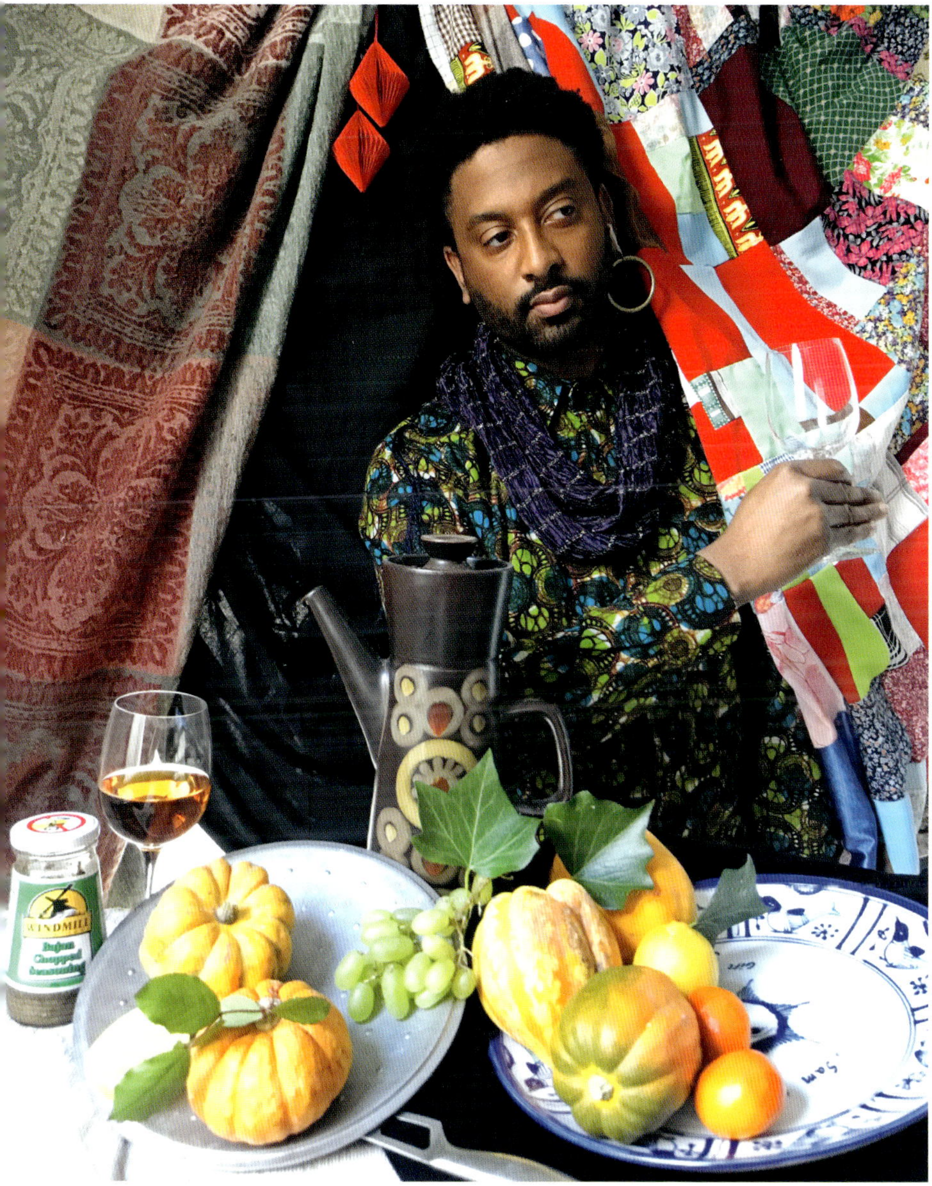

Act 1

Reworked with African print, Granny's patchwork quilt, and Bajan chopped seasoning. Dressed in gold-embroidered blue velvet, a young man emerges from behind a curtain. He holds an empty silver-gilt goblet and looks off to the side, as if responding to a request for more wine. Like the peaches and citrus spilling onto the table before him, his presence in the scene points to extravagant luxuries afforded by the expansion of the Dutch Empire—specifically Mediterranean fruit and Black people as property. In seventeenth-century art, the motif of the Black servant was a marker of wealth whether the patron was an enslaver or not. Restaging this portrait today opens possibilities for remembering and understanding the conditions of enslaved lives.

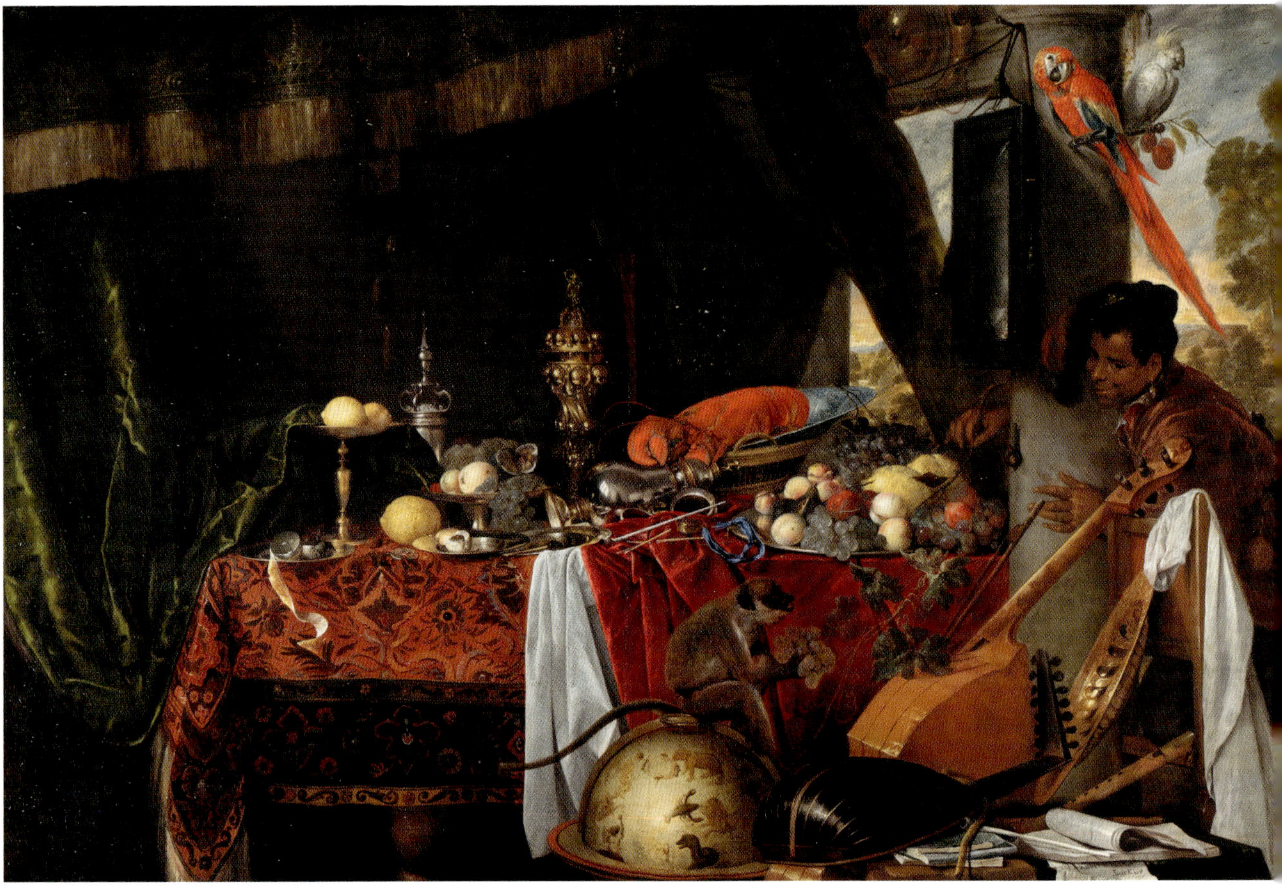

Still Life with Servant and Parrot

1641

Jan Davidsz de Heem
Dutch, 1606–1684

Oil on canvas
171 × 262 cm
(67$\frac{3}{8}$ × 103$\frac{1}{8}$ in.)
Brussels City Museum,
K.1878.5

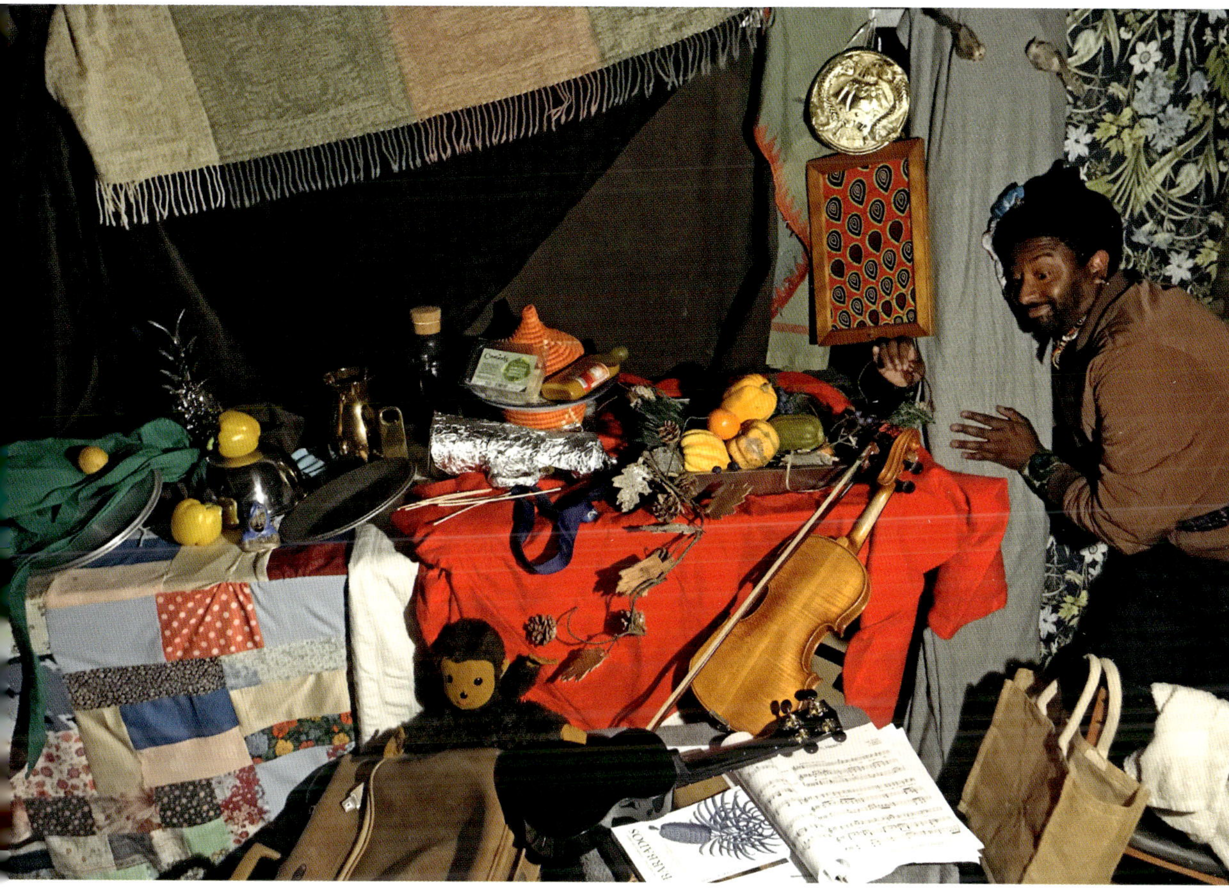

Act 1

Reworked with feather bird clips, Granny's patchwork quilt, salted cod, hot pepper sauce, a bottle of homemade sorrel (a traditional hibiscus Christmas drink from Barbados), an Othello candle snuffer, and a copy of Richard Ligon's *A True and Exact History of the Island of Barbadoes* (1657). Stylized and ornately dressed, this Black figure is dehumanized. Like the exotic parrot and monkey and the lavish display of lobster, pomegranates, figs, and lemons, his presence signifies wealth. The work's original title identified him as a "Moor," a word derived from the Latin *Maurus* that was used to describe Berbers and other Muslim peoples from the ancient Roman province of Mauretania in what is now North Africa. Renaissance Europeans used "Moor" and the related word "blackamoor" to describe any nonwhite person. Today the term is considered racist and culturally insensitive.

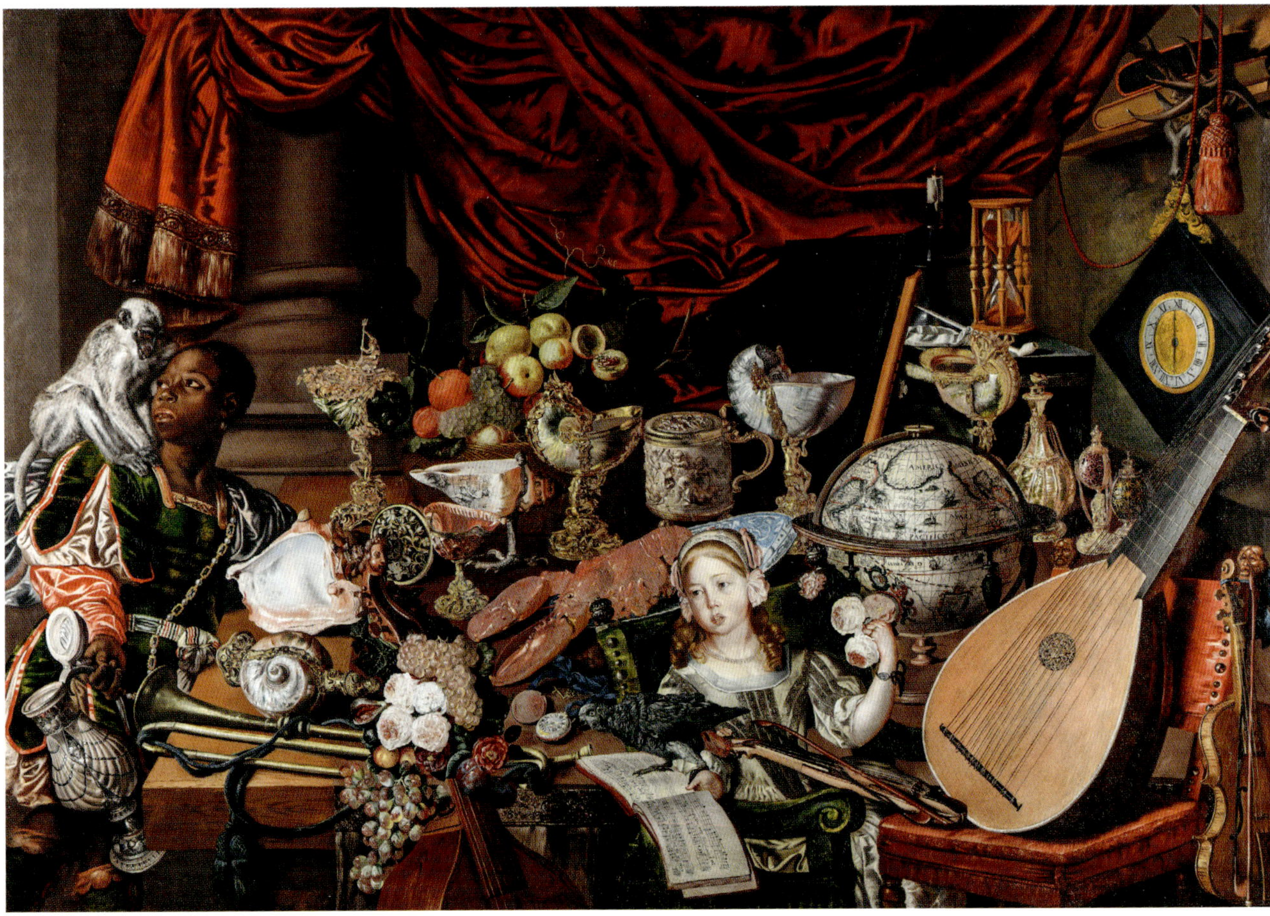

The Paston Treasure

ca. 1665

Unknown artist

Oil on canvas
165 × 246.5 cm
(65 × 97 in.)
England, Norwich Castle
Museum and Art Gallery,
Norfolk Museums, 1947.170

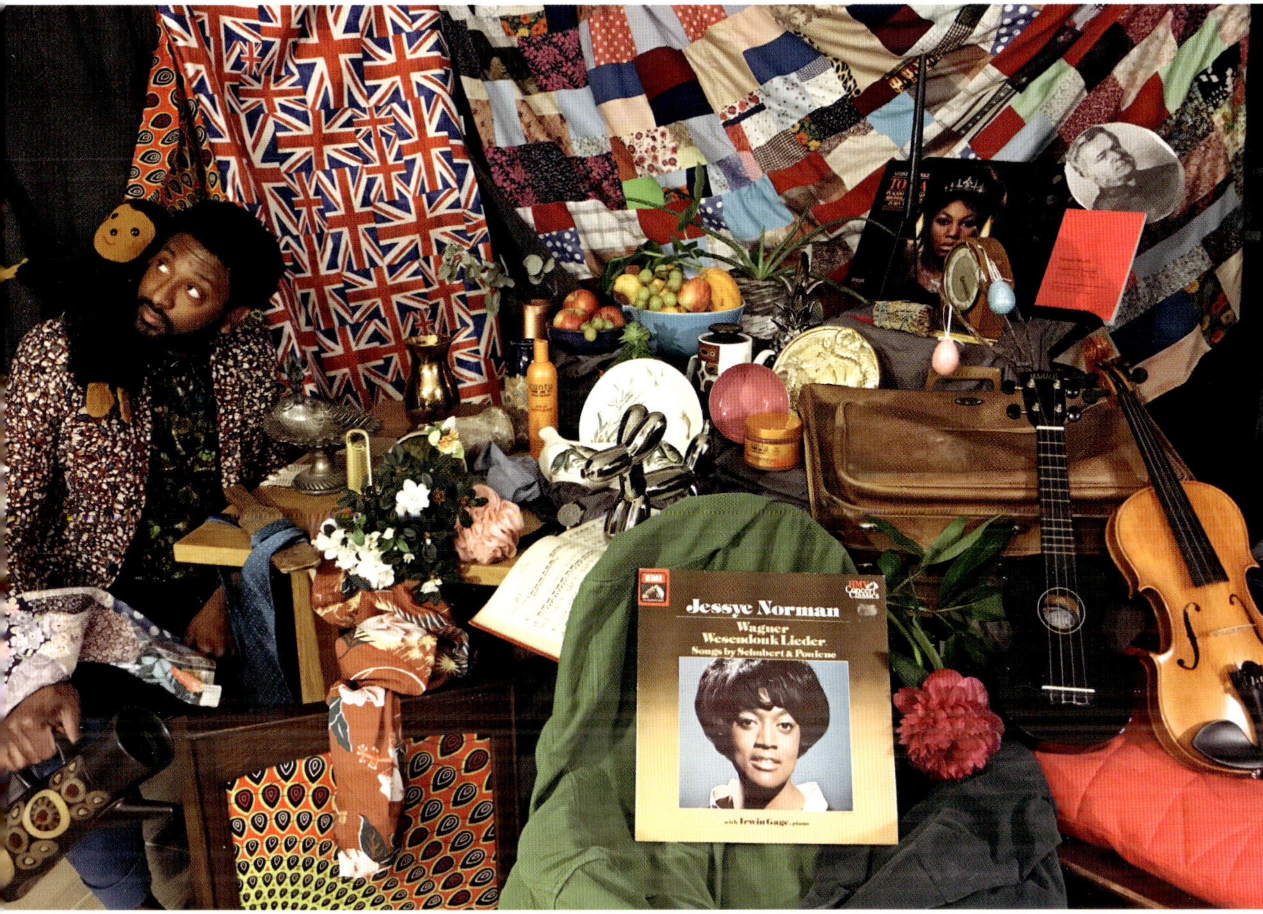

Act 1

Reworked with Afro hair products, Côte d'Ivoire prints, Granny's patchwork quilt, Jessye Norman and Leontyne Price records, and luggage from my family's arrival in the United Kingdom. This painting, which is thought to have been commissioned by Sir William Paston, depicts just a fraction of the treasures scooped up during the Paston family's extensive travels, including tropical fruit, exotic animals, priceless curiosities, and a Black man exquisitely clad in velvet and silk. His flesh tones are finely rendered, but is he even really there? His presence is all that visually links this display of wealth to the brutal conditions of chattel slavery. His depiction, to me, represents a process of being dehumanized twice over—first as a piece of property, and then again because this scene is so far removed from his actual reality. My re-creation asks what it means to take up space as a Black man.

We thrive in networks.
Time, space, blood, bones, ocean, trees, air, data.
Viral, and storied.
Meshed.
Rooted and rerouted.
Here, there, everywhere leaving dust trails
in our wake.
We reach out for affinities: mining, linking,
calibrating.
Querying and questioning source codes.
Pacing, across databases, to find relations,
fragments, clues; shards of delftware.

Feeling in the Dark

Rediscovering Black Portraiture as Speculative Metadata

Temi Odumosu

Or an empty record, a nook, an erasure, a defacement.
A periwinkle flower for an unmarked grave.
A nebula, in the lines of an open palm, (imagine, the hand as endless sky).
We search and we search, trailing and tracing, scrolling and scrying, for some kind of groove.

Courting Algorithms

Recently I searched Google using the terms "Black boy portrait." In preparing for this essay, I thought it was important to know where we stand—what happens in summer 2022 when US-based internet users also attempt to travel Peter Brathwaite's journey of art historical discovery. And to do so in that messy way we sometimes do online, when we're not really sure what we're looking for specifically, but there is a question we want to unfold, vulnerabilities for which we need a little assistance and recognition.

I had some hesitation over this information seeking, knowing that search engines are fundamentally designed not with historical recovery and identity expression in mind but rather marketing and sales. I was also unsure because we know by now that these algorithms (these instructional formulas), making decisions about where our searches go, are not neutral. Designed and then sustained by weary, biased humans, they tend to follow our flaws.[1] And the more we feed them our habits and imperfections, the more they mirror and intensify them. When the internet studies scholar Safiya Noble searched for "Black girls" one weekend in 2011 to find inspiring activities for her young stepdaughter and nieces, the demeaning and stereotypical content the internet produced revealed how racial and gender bias is very much embedded in the technological present. Over a decade has passed since her initial search, which eventually led to the book *Algorithms of Oppression* (2018), a critical provocation sensitizing tech companies to these problems. And now, just like Noble, I negotiated with myself about the issues of coding. On the one hand, it's important that our expressions and ideas are present in these information systems, but on the other hand, are we unintentionally nourishing the beast with our identity searches—giving Google analytics another racialized code, to repeat historical lines of thinking? An internet search for Black presence courts continuous risks of negation, of being "thingified," to use Aimé Césaire's term,[2] which is why I used the word "portrait" and not just "image," "boy" instead of "servant." I agree that this is also faulty logic, but is there a right way to search for lost kin? Is conscientious internet participation really possible?

Google search is not meant for navigating the pathways of the heart. But I did the search anyway. Because some data haunts and other data can heal.

The first page of search results was interesting (right). At the top, I was immediately confronted by a grid of Google-generated images of Black children, mostly color photographs of them facing the camera directly, some looking serious, others smiling—stock photos that might be used to illustrate advertisements or articles. Who/whose *were* all these children? And what does it mean that Black body images are the "stock" (the cultural and creative asset) for ubiquitous storytelling? More importantly, who uses these assets, and why? Pinterest, Getty Images, and other photo sites provided mostly professional and positive representations, with associated metadata keywords such as "beautiful," "sad," "handsome," "cute," "serious," "smiling," even "magical" and "zen." For the most part, the internet understood my search for "Black boy" as meaning African American, although one or two continental African children did appear. And Etsy's marketplace, as the leading result, provided a whole range of positivist merchandise, including religious imagery, uplifting affirmations, images of children reading, and the repeated use of a crown for adornment. These corrective images (or counterarchival messages) seemed to register a pronounced cultural shift, but I was also curious as to whether the algorithm had been following my representation research and reading my emails, and was now somehow addressing my sensibilities directly. It is sometimes hard to tell when the internet is statistical and when it is personal.

The first art historical link in the results was to a familiar artwork in the National Portrait Gallery in London: *A Black Boy*, a mezzotint

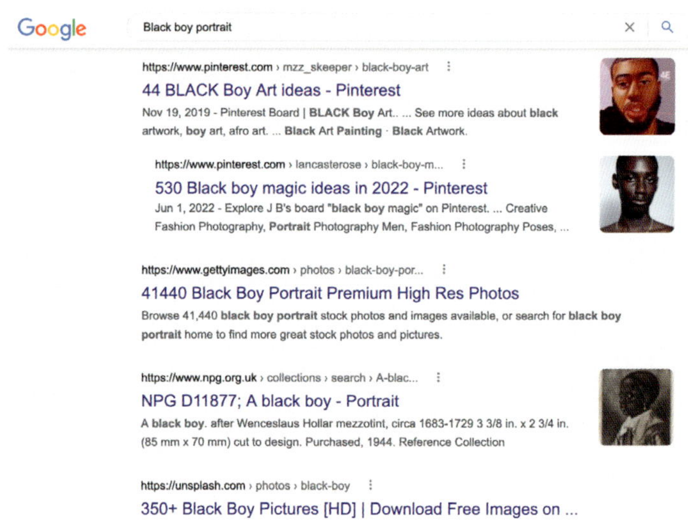

▼ Screenshot of the author's Google search results for "Black boy portrait"

▸

After Wenceslaus Hollar (Bohemian, 1607–1677, active in Germany, Flanders, and England), *A Black Boy*, ca. 1683–1729. Mezzotint, 8.6 × 7 cm (3⅜ × 2¾ in.). London, National Portrait Gallery, NPG D11877

▾

E. A. Burbank (American, 1858–1949), *Portrait of a Young Black Boy*, n.d. Chalk, 50.8 × 40.6 cm (20 × 16 in.). Massachusetts, Davis Museum at Wellesley College, 2018.27

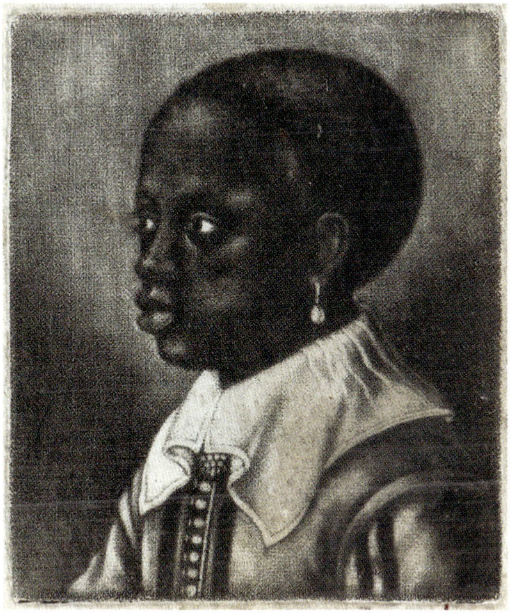

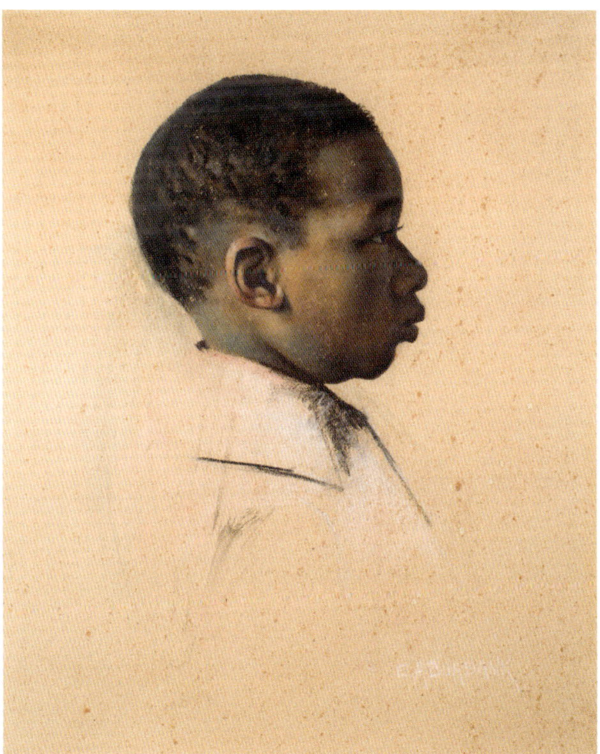

engraving made in the late seventeenth or early eighteenth century after a 1645 portrait by Wenceslaus ("Wenzel") Hollar (top left). This anonymous child was granted presence in the space of art through an emergent European print culture transformed by intersecting foreign influences: Hollar, an immigrant artist born in Prague, meeting, or responding to, an African presence in the Netherlands, and evidencing the encounter. Scholarship has not yet determined whether this child was a specific person or a type created by the artist for deployment in other contexts. With several versions of this print in different collections (at least seven variations reside in the British Museum alone) as well as another widely reproduced image made by Hollar of a Black woman, we really don't know whose lives and stories are cited in (and by) these faces.[3] Seventeenth-century French reworkings of these images, naming the woman Hyanisbé and the boy Hyempsal, are likely references to characters in literature.[4] Anonymous figures such as these—elusive, unmoored, malleable—can be moved between functions, telling different stories based on context. So, what might we name these two people now?

Back to Google. After the Hollar print, on page 2 came a nineteenth-century chalk drawing of another anonymous child in profile, this time by the US painter Elbridge Ayer Burbank, in the Davis Museum collection at Wellesley College (below left). I had not seen this work before, so I paused, then softened, observing the artist's attempts to register subtleties in skin tone and his precise engagement with the child's hair-growth pattern and texture. This human-to-human contact across time and media, the

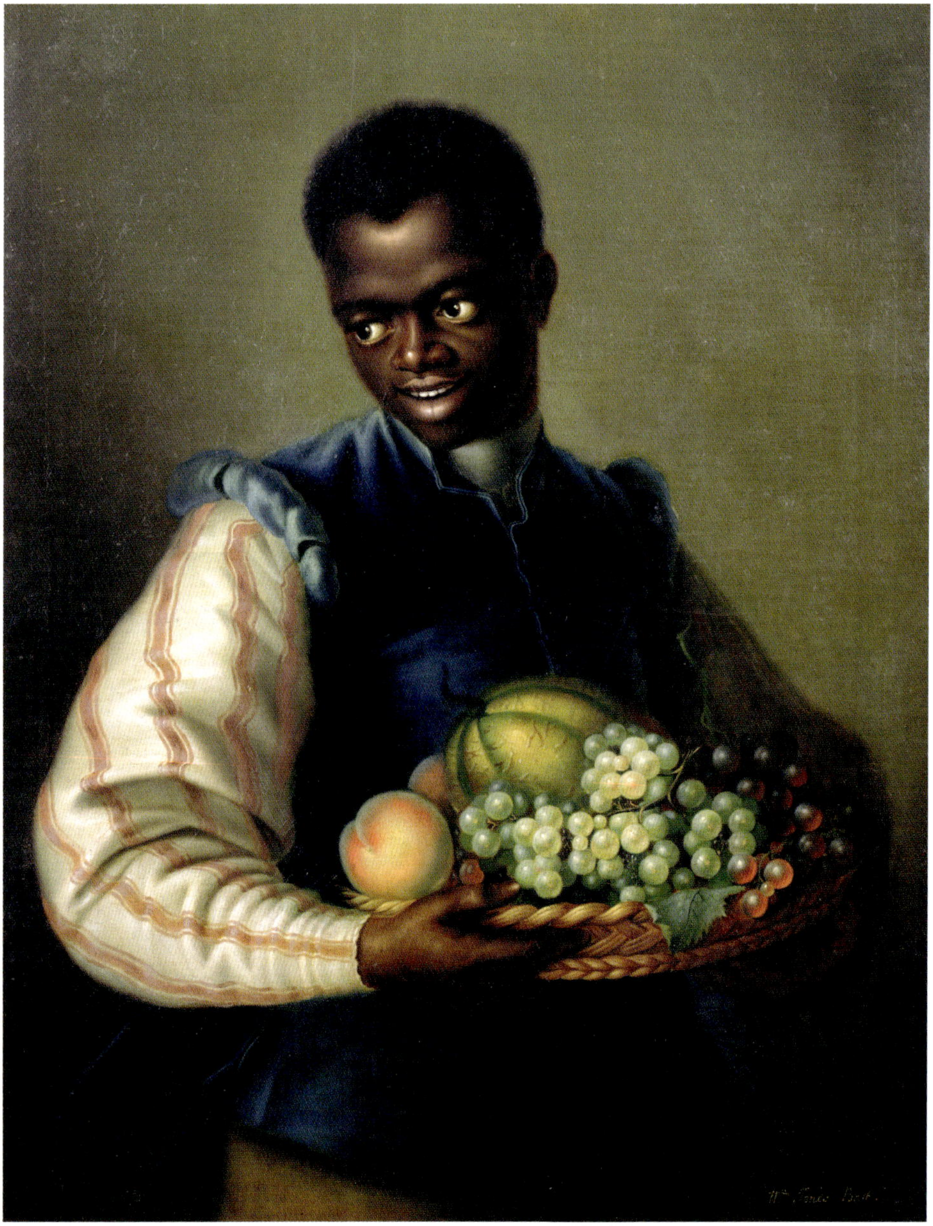

◄
William Jones (British, active 1764–75), *The Black Boy*, ca. 1769. Oil on canvas, 89.5 × 70 cm (35¼ × 27½ in.). Bath, England, Victoria Art Gallery and North East Somerset Council, BATVG : P : 1980.1

delicate meeting between my eyes and this child's face, momentarily paused my professional conditioning. I ignored the ethnographic tone of the artist's oeuvre as described in the museum's descriptive text. And I resisted the urge to scale up and seek out Burbank's works in other collections. Because what if this sketch is all we have as a register of this child's presence on the US landscape? He deserved my attention.

I saved the page link and returned to the Google search results once more.

Scrolling across multiple pages with a focused intensity, I noticed how history fluttered, coming in and out of focus: more stock photo websites, Carrie Mae Weems's stunning photograph *Blue Black Boy* (1997), stock photos again, an Amazon link, a reference to Richard Wright's memoir *Black Boy* (1945), and so it continued. Hidden away at the end of page 3 was another artwork I had spent some time with before, namely a portrait called *The Black Boy* (ca. 1769, p. 54) by William Jones. Jones was a British artist based in Bath, a spa town that in the eighteenth century was a country retreat for royalty, rich city merchants, and politicians. Jones usually painted still lifes, but he was evidently taken by this young man (who people anecdotally say worked in the local pump house) and invited him to a portrait sitting. Perhaps I am rewriting the scenario, but I say "invited" as the most generous way to describe how an African person would sit for an early modern portrait. How did this young man come to appear in this painting?[5] Through sittings in the studio, as the result of a quick sketch, or from memory? Of his own volition, or at the behest of his master (the person responsible for the silver chattel collar around his neck)? And was the smile a genuine expression or an invention—an eighteenth-century deepfake, a posthumous imposition to convey a stereotypical image of a compliant African?[6] For this young man, and the two children before, there is much we can only infer using the imagination in fusion with contextual research. Still, at least the questions themselves insist on a former "wholeness in the object," as Erskine Peters poetically put it—an insistence that there was a real person behind the paint and the varnish (somewhere, someplace).[7] Asking granular, peculiar questions is an attempt to break the matter-of-factness of these artworks by refusing lopsided power perspectives on history. Such questioning refuses "the terms of diminished subjecthood."[8]

My Google search made from an internet router in the US Pacific Northwest yielded limited historical results, in the sense that the three words with which I chose to query the system did not produce the kind of imagery that emerges when using other constellations of terms. Perhaps the generalizing word "portrait," with its assertion of representing known individuals or those who once lived, was unable to intervene in established logics determining Black (in)visibility.[9] Other search terms, however, provided more historical sources. For example "Black servant painting," which offers up colonial-era family portraits with peripheral African attendants who perhaps meet established expectations of Black people in Western art. Or "slave art history," which deepens engagement with colonial violence through representations that include images of torture and other forms of dehumanization. This is not to say that my search was in any way neutral. It contained frictions and biases, by necessity and design. It was also conducted in the United States, thereby adding a localized twist to the results. What would such a search call up in Germany, in Dakar, in Cape Town, in Dubai, in Hong Kong? One key issue that was affirmed by the internet results, at least, was typological anonymization—an annoying, inherited habit of decontextualizing Black subjects so that they are not wholly accounted for within a network of loving human relations, on- and offline. Quite often they are just "there"—Black children, heads, bodies floating in cyberspace but signifying, tethered to publishing power structures such as museums, image banks, and e-stores, which generate the searchable data and set the terms for encounter and contact.

Recoding Code

In searching for Black presence (tailwinds of the African diaspora), the internet raises many questions while intensifying old but still fresh wounds. It confronts us with a varied spectrum of visibilities, and many absences that are thick with meaning. Which is why Peter Brathwaite has so poignantly described his own journey navigating Google in search of people of African descent in art as "feeling in the dark": an apt way to explain a delicate commitment to processing complex histories within coded structures and algorithmic black boxes in order to find glimmers of soul connection.[10] This *feeling* is the tentative inquiry of an extended hand that reaches out—typing, scrolling, zooming in on collections databases, and making contact. At the same time, *feeling* (or feelin') is deep sensation—a powerful attraction that registers kinship (like a warm hand moving across bare skin)—or an intuition, a haunting awareness that "something happened" here, even when information is limited or absent, or when there is uncertainty about an image's veracity as "portrait." As Avery Gordon writes about these liminal experiences: "The ghost makes itself known to us through haunting and pulls us affectively into the structure of feeling of a reality we come to experience as a recognition. Haunting recognition is a special way of knowing what has happened or is happening."[11] Brathwaite's *feeling* (data/presence) in the dark is therefore trusting that art history's unnamed, untitled, or little-known Black subjects are a "bridge to the dead" who are still vital for the living.[12]

I want to begin to consider Brathwaite's intimate re-creations of historical artworks for the Getty Museum Challenge on social media as speculative metadata, by which I mean an intentional double practice of re-signifying the cultural web while imagining worlds/histories/relations/time otherwise. Metadata that makes propositions. Librarians, archivists, and museum collections cataloguers generally work with a concept of metadata as "data about data," or descriptive information that explains the content and context of a particular digital record: scanned or photographed documents, artworks, objects. Metadata is both embedded in the back end of digital records and visible in the front-end experience, for example through keywords, location, or provenance information.

Useful metadata emphasizes the record's place and meaning, not just within the collection but also in the wider cultural and sociopolitical context. Overall it helps internet users better find and access records while contributing to a more cohesive and open cultural commons online. But producing metadata is hard work and not easily automated. It requires the detailed labor of migrating existing information about the physical collections online and then considering how this information might be edited, developed, and adapted as more knowledge unfolds, or as the need arises for different kinds of descriptive practices and storytelling about the records.[13] This whole process is challenged, and can be delayed, by thorny issues of trust, privacy, consent, and ownership, which trouble digital reproductions because they are often unsettled in the physical collections. Brathwaite's practice emerges from and confronts this methodological intersection—the transfer of meaning from sensitive historical matter into big data.[14]

Brathwaite's affective mapping of lesser-known Black presences in Western art history extends the possibilities for how we might think about metadata practices online. By repeating postures and redesigning artworks to include references to his own heritage, family, and biography, Brathwaite personalizes and becomes entwined with museum records, producing new image metadata (meta-images) that reformulates the artworks. Twinned and entwined, they travel around the web together, creating a new context of meaning. Think, for example, of Brathwaite's grandmother's handmade quilt, which features in many of his re-creations (see pp. 45, 67, 93). Could the presence of an elder's careful handiwork be the necessary visual and narrative key for asking viewers, *and* collections, to stop and consider the "love that reassembles the fragments" (to invoke Derek Walcott)?[15] As Brathwaite describes it, his re-creations seek "to rub away at the edifice," to move past an artwork's surface meanings. In editing the established record by way of his own Black-body-image, his intention is to change (or redirect) the proposed subject of the original painting such that instead the Black subject's "culture could shine, amaze, and be treasured"—something only possible through radical acts of aesthetic confrontation.[16]

We could call this digital-to-analog-to-digital practice spiritual tagging, or perhaps simply re-mattering the dismembered. We could also describe these re-creations as "imagined records"—an expressive, social, and counter-archival practice that challenges erasures and provides "a trajectory to the future out of a particular perspective on the past."[17] Either way, Brathwaite reclaims these digitized artworks as spaces for historical reckoning, for accessing and altering what researchers like to call primary source data (in digital form). What I am suggesting here is that the image re-creations work in two directions: as performed data that questions sources (artworks) housed in museum collections as well as the language and descriptive practices used to communicate online, and at the same time as data that seeks to reconfigure the more fundamental code—those languages developed over centuries for establishing who and what has value. This is data that haunts *and* heals.

1 In this line of thinking, I am indebted to the work of scholars such as Safiya Noble, Simone Browne, and Ruha Benjamin. See Safiya U. Noble, *Algorithms of Oppression: Data Discrimination in the Age of Google* (New York: New York University Press, 2018); Simone Browne, *Dark Matters: On the Surveillance of Blackness* (Durham, NC: Duke University Press, 2015); and Ruha Benjamin, *Race after Technology: Abolitionist Tools for the New Jim Code* (Cambridge: Polity, 2019).

2 Aimé Césaire, *Discourse on Colonialism*, trans. Joan Pinkham (New York: Monthly Review Press, 2000), 42.

3 The challenges of identification in Hollar's print of a Black woman are discussed in Kim Hall, "Object into Object? Some Thoughts on the Presence of Black Women in Early Modern Europe," in *Early Modern Visual Culture: Representation, Race, Empire in Renaissance England*, ed. Peter Erickson and Clark Hulse (Philadelphia: University of Pennsylvania Press, 2000), 346–77.

4 Versions are housed at the Bibliothèque nationale de France, Paris; the Bibliothèque municipal de Rouen, France; and the New York Public Library.

5 For some important reflections on this question of appearance, see Nicholas Mirzoeff, "Decolonizing Appearance: A Curatorial Introduction," in *Decolonizing Appearance*, ed. Tone O. Nielsen and Yannick Harrison (Copenhagen: CAMP/Center for Art on Migration Politics, 2018), 9–13.

6 For a reading of the portrait as a racialized fantasy, see Catherine Molineux, *Faces of Perfect Ebony: Encountering Atlantic Slavery in Imperial Britain* (Cambridge, MA: Harvard University Press, 2012), 56–57.

7 Erskine A. Peters, "Stereotyping: A Movement against Consciousness," in *Ethnic Notions: Black Images in the White Mind*, ed. Janette Faulkner et al. (Berkeley: Berkeley Art Center, 1982), 23. In this essay, Peters confronts the dehumanizing role of racist anti-Black Jim Crow objects (money boxes, cookie jars, postcards) and asks us to consider who is trapped in/by these demeaning images.

8 Tina Campt, "Black Visuality and the Practice of Refusal," *Women and Performance: A Journal of Feminist Theory* 29, no. 1 (2019): 83.

9 For an important and nuanced discussion with regard to historical artworks, see Marcia Pointon, "Slavery and the Possibilities of Portraiture," in *Slave Portraiture in the Atlantic World*, ed. Agnes Lugo-Ortiz and Angela Rosenthal (Cambridge: Cambridge University Press, 2013), 40–69.

10 Peter Brathwaite in conversation with curator Sonya Dyer on the subject of "Illuminating Black Histories" for the online conference "From De-colonial to Anti-colonial: What's Next for Museum Interpretation?," held November 26, 2020, and available at https://youtu.be/fOWF1l4_Sm8.

11 Avery Gordon, *Ghostly Matters: Haunting and the Sociological Imagination* (Minneapolis: University of Minnesota Press, 2008), 63.

12 Saidiya Hartman, "Venus in Two Acts," *Small Axe: A Journal of Criticism* 26 (June 2008): 5.

13 See, for example, Mia Ridge, ed., *Crowdsourcing Our Cultural Heritage* (London: Routledge, 2017).

14 After years of enthusiastic scanning and information sharing online, museums are now reconsidering pathways of connection to digitized cultural resources. They are also finding ways to challenge silences, gaps, and blind spots in museum data, which are themselves the products of inequitable and sometimes violent histories. I have explored these concerns and possibilities in Temi Odumosu, "The Crying Child: On Colonial Archives, Digitization, and Ethics of Care in the Cultural Commons," *Current Anthropology* 61, no. 22 (2020): 289–302; and Mette Kia Krabbe Meyer and Temi Odumosu, "One-Eyed Archive: Metadata Reflections on the USVI Photographic Collections at the Royal Danish Library," *Digital Culture and Society* 6, no. 2 (2020): 35–62.

15 Derek Walcott, "The Antilles: Fragments of Epic Memory," Nobel lecture, December 7, 1992, https://www.nobelprize.org/prizes/literature/1992/walcott/lecture/.

16 These statements are taken from "Five Amazing Lockdown Recreations of Black People from Historical Portraits," https://www.bbc.co.uk/programmes/articles/1bQTPtGBpdNsDv8jH5PsjLj/five-amazing-lockdown-recreations-of-black-people-from-historical-portraits, which offers an overview of Peter Brathwaite's five-part series for the BBC Radio program *The Essay*.

17 Anne J. Gilliland and Michelle Caswell, "Records and Their Imaginaries: Imagining the Impossible, Making Possible the Imagined," *Archival Science* 16, no. 1 (2016): 61.

Act 2

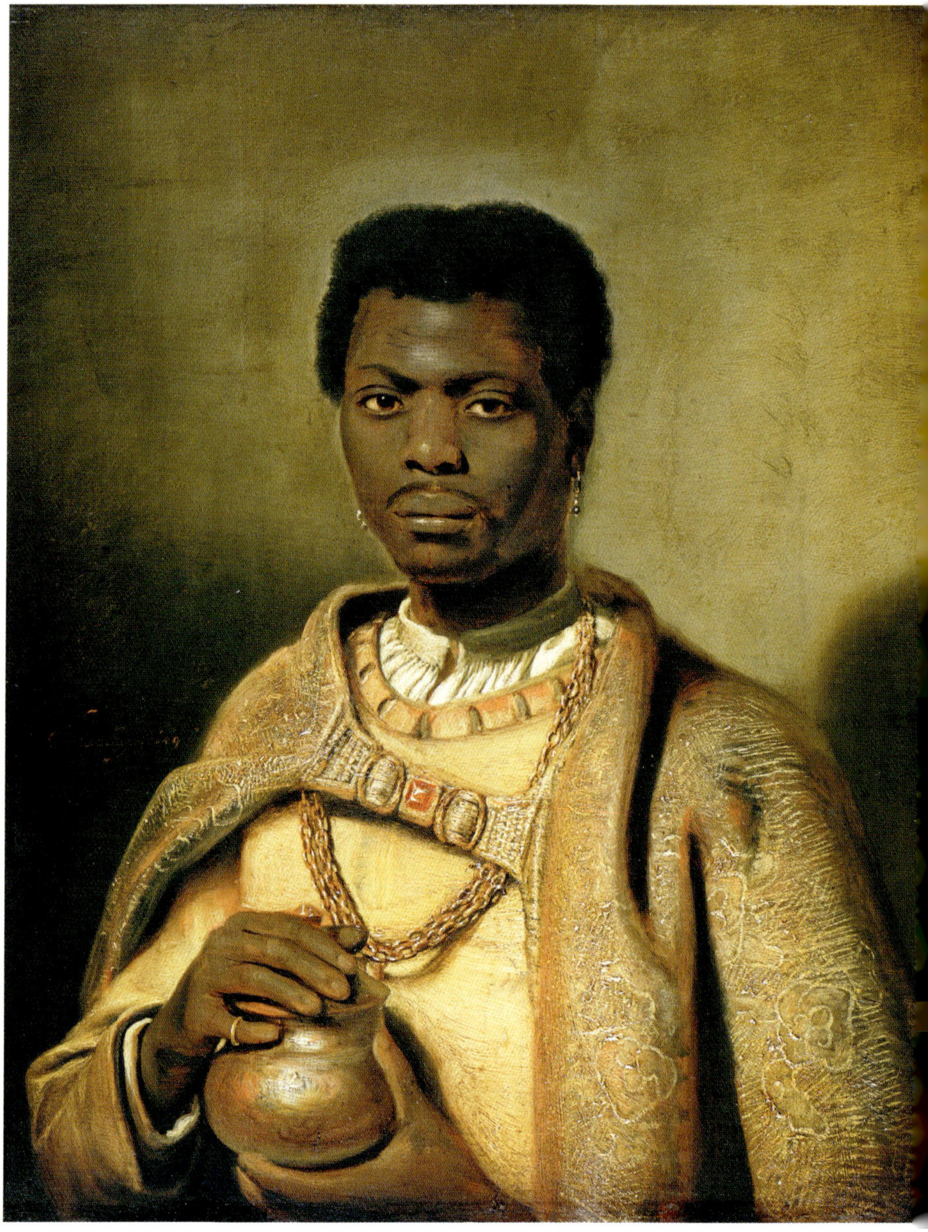

The African King Caspar

1654 or 1659

Hendrick Heerschop
Dutch, 1620/21–ca. 1672

Oil on canvas
74.8 × 60.5 cm
(29½ × 23⅞ in.)
Berlin, Gemäldegalerie

A resplendent King Caspar, one of the three biblical Magi, reworked with an upturned gold-colored vase, cardboard, gold piping trim, a yellow blanket, and a West African print in the fastening (note the reflection in the vase). Although the identity of Heerschop's sitter is not known, by the time his likeness was painted, Amsterdam had a Black community in and around Jodenbreestraat, a street near the residence of the famed painter Rembrandt.

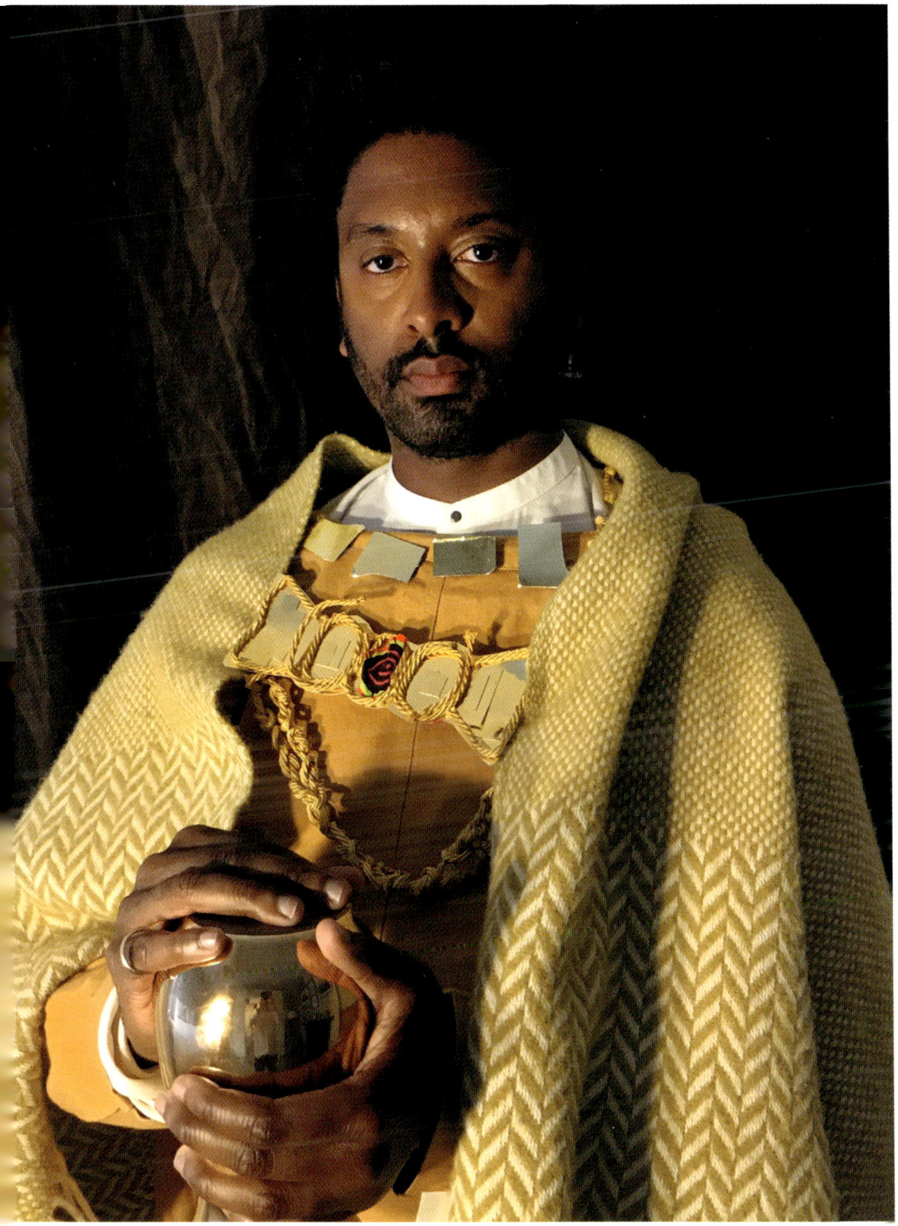

Act 2

Intriguingly, slavery did not technically exist on Dutch soil, but Black people were nevertheless trafficked to the Netherlands through the networks of the Dutch, Portuguese, and Spanish colonial empires. None of those who arrived in the Netherlands were called enslaved, but some remained bound to their oppressors while others lived independently. This unappropriated community provided models for increasing numbers of Dutch paintings that started to include Black subjects. What might the backstory of Heerschop's opulently dressed model be? Was his a life of comfort, or was he eking out a living on very little? Restaging this portrait was, for me, a meditation on the dignity in the sitter's forthright gaze.

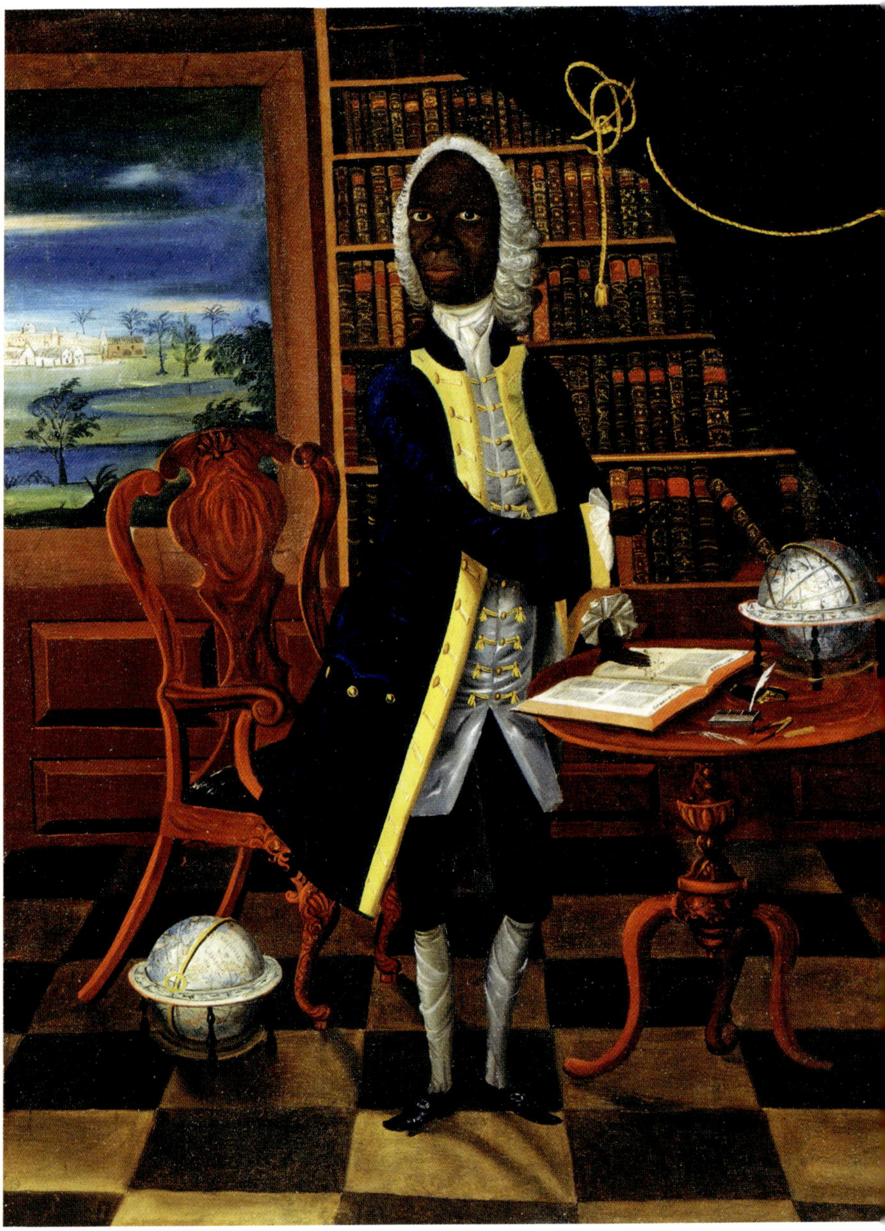

Francis Williams, the Scholar of Jamaica

ca. 1745

Unknown artist

Oil on canvas
66 × 50.1 cm
(26¾ × 19¾ in.)
London, Victoria
and Albert Museum,
P.83&A-1928

The first recorded Black writer in the British Empire, reworked with a Santa beard and a volume from *The Image of the Black in Western Art* (2011). Within ten years of having been freed, Francis Williams's father was wealthy enough to secure property in Jamaica (including enslaved people) and an education for his sons. Williams is believed to have been the first Black student to attend the University of Cambridge and is known to have

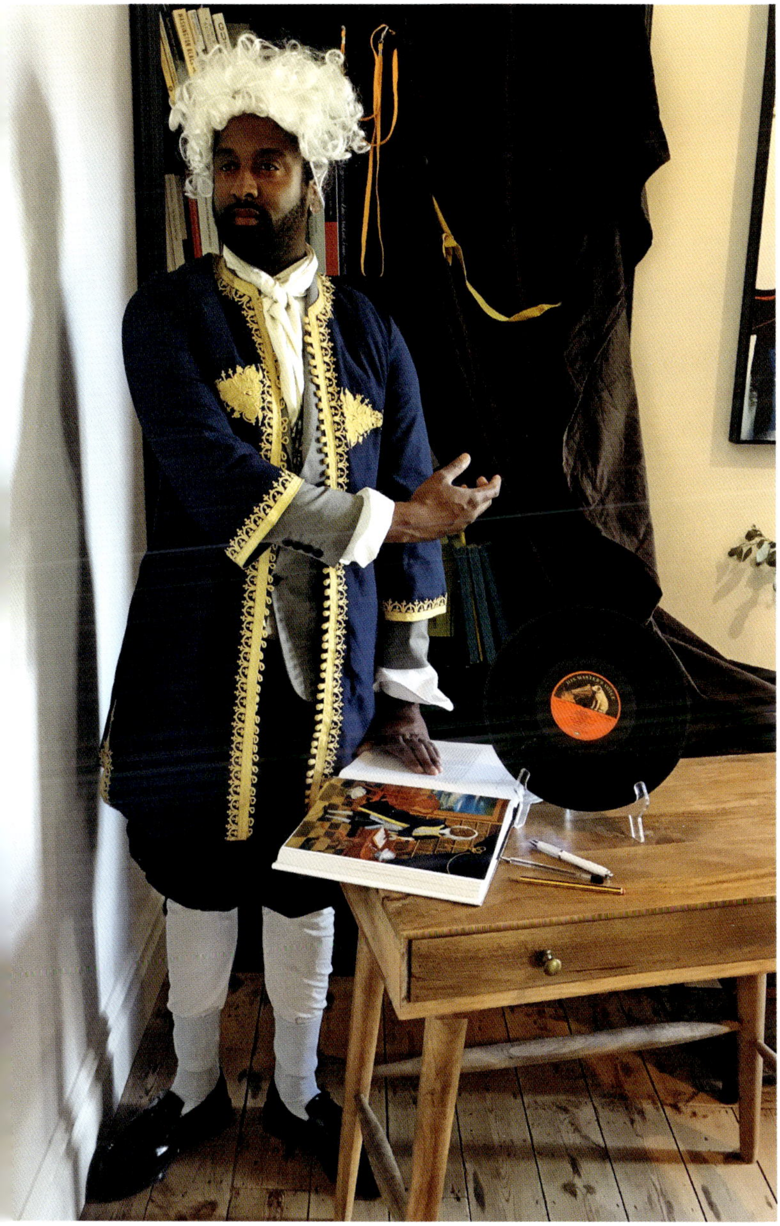

Act 2

belonged to Lincoln's Inn, a prestigious association of London barristers. He returned to Jamaica upon the death of his father and opened a school for Black children. This full-length portrait shows him in his study, gesturing toward the books behind him. The globes and mathematical instruments are symbols of academic achievement, and the quill and ink denote his talent as a writer. His feet straddle two tiles, one black and one white, perhaps indicating that despite his freed status, wealth, and intellectual prowess, he occupied an ambiguous position within Jamaica society.

Portrait of a Man in Livery

eighteenth century[?]

Godfrey Kneller or follower
British, 1646–1723

Oil on canvas
111.1 × 83.8 cm
(43¾ × 33 in.)
Bridgetown, Barbados
Museum and Historical
Society

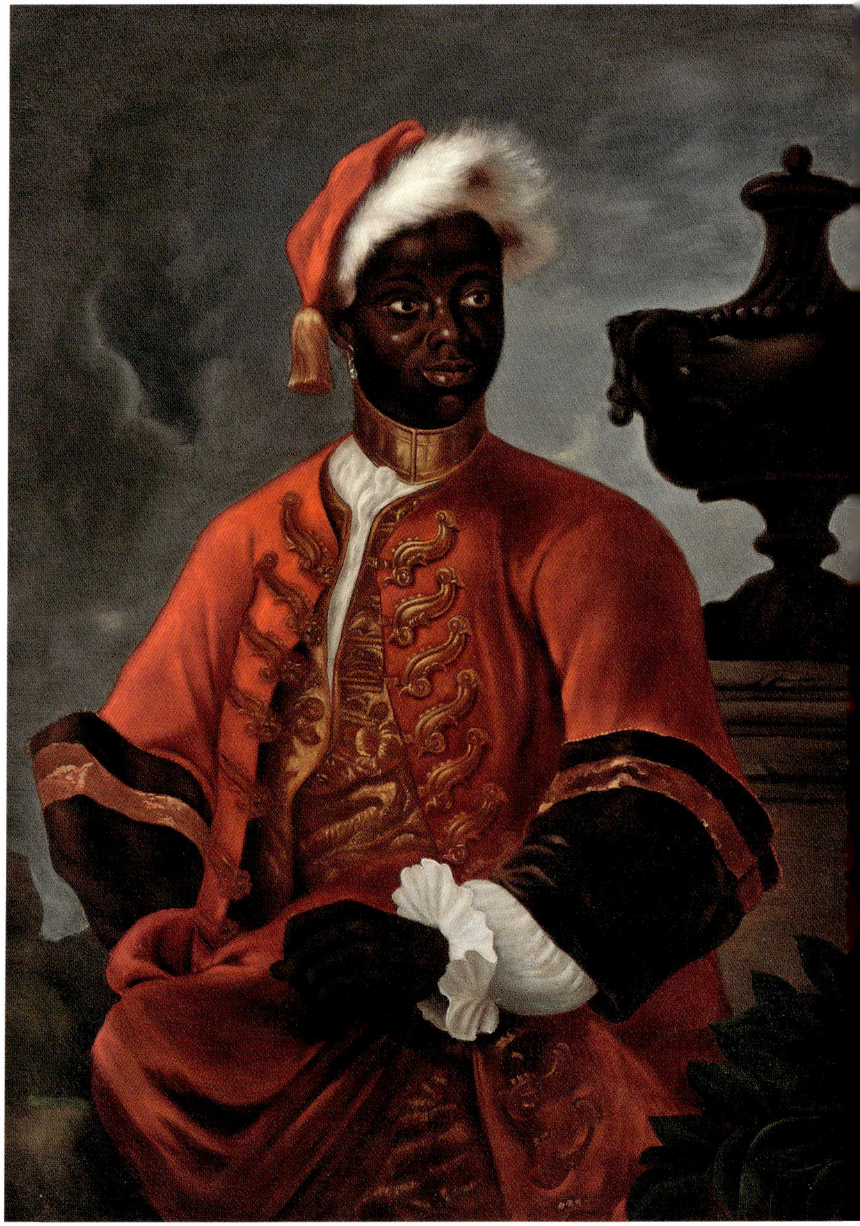

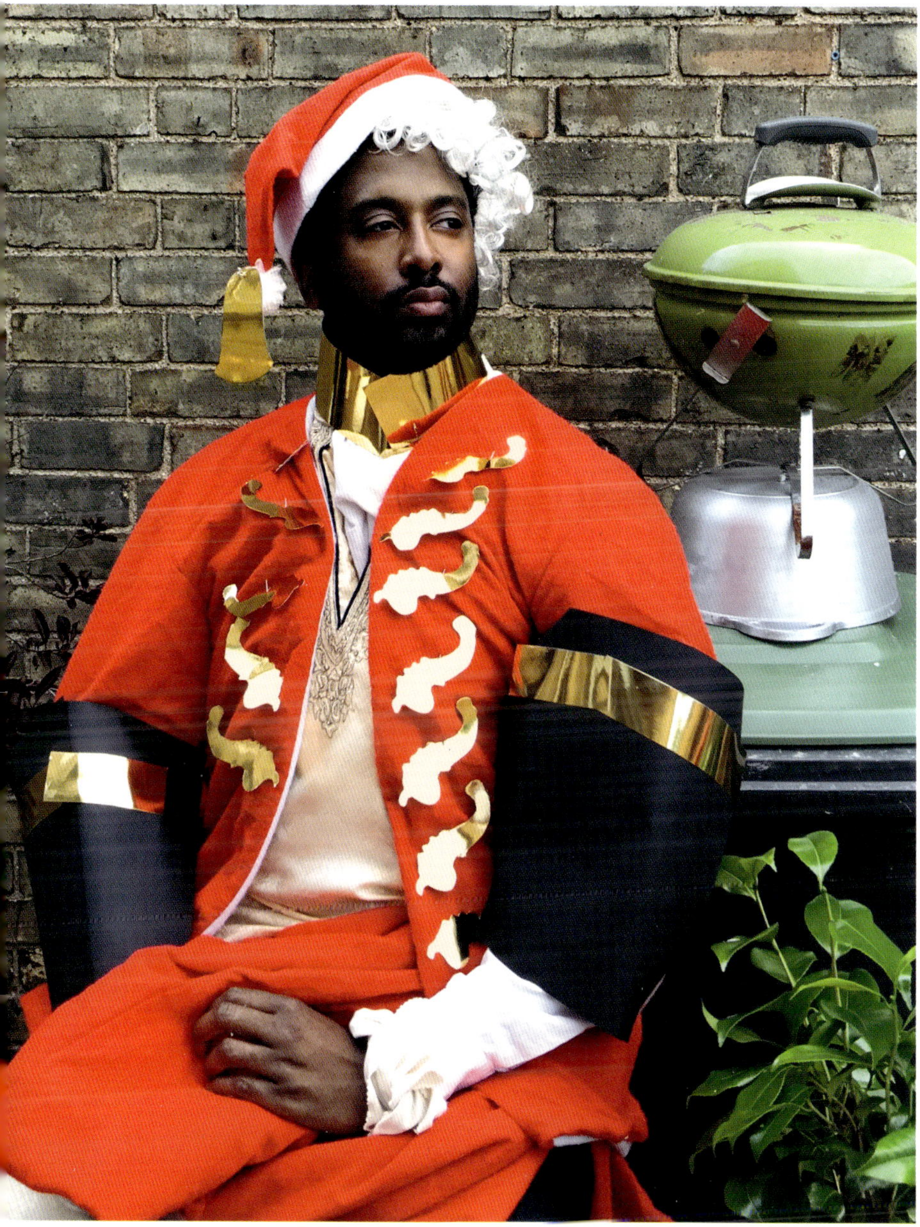

Act 2

A Black man in livery wears a collar of enslavement. Reworked with a Santa suit, a barbecue, and a West Indian buck pot given to me by my mother. This painting is remarkable for its bold use of color: the deeply saturated red velvet, the rich gold brocade, the bright-white details of linen and fur. Yet the burnished collar padlocked around the sitter's neck and the brooding storm clouds beyond seem to embody the powerful forces that bore down on enslaved people and inflicted violence upon them. This is a sizable and intricate work, and the man's pose is typical of prominent figures in contemporary portraits. There is confidence in his bearing and expression, but also vulnerability. What status had he truly achieved?

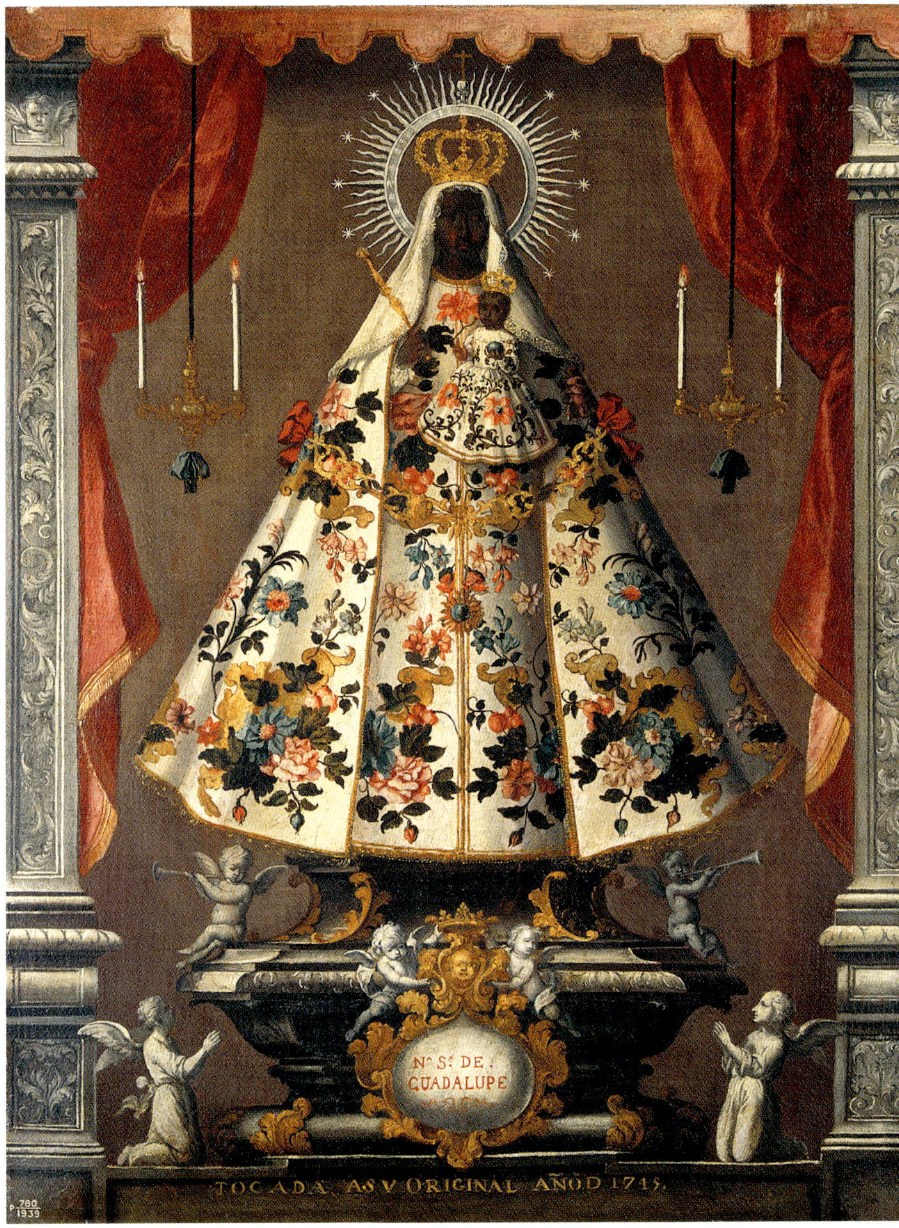

The Virgin of Guadalupe

1745

Unknown artist
Spanish

Oil on canvas
106 × 84.5 cm
(41¾ × 33¼ in.)
London, Wellcome
Library, 44828i

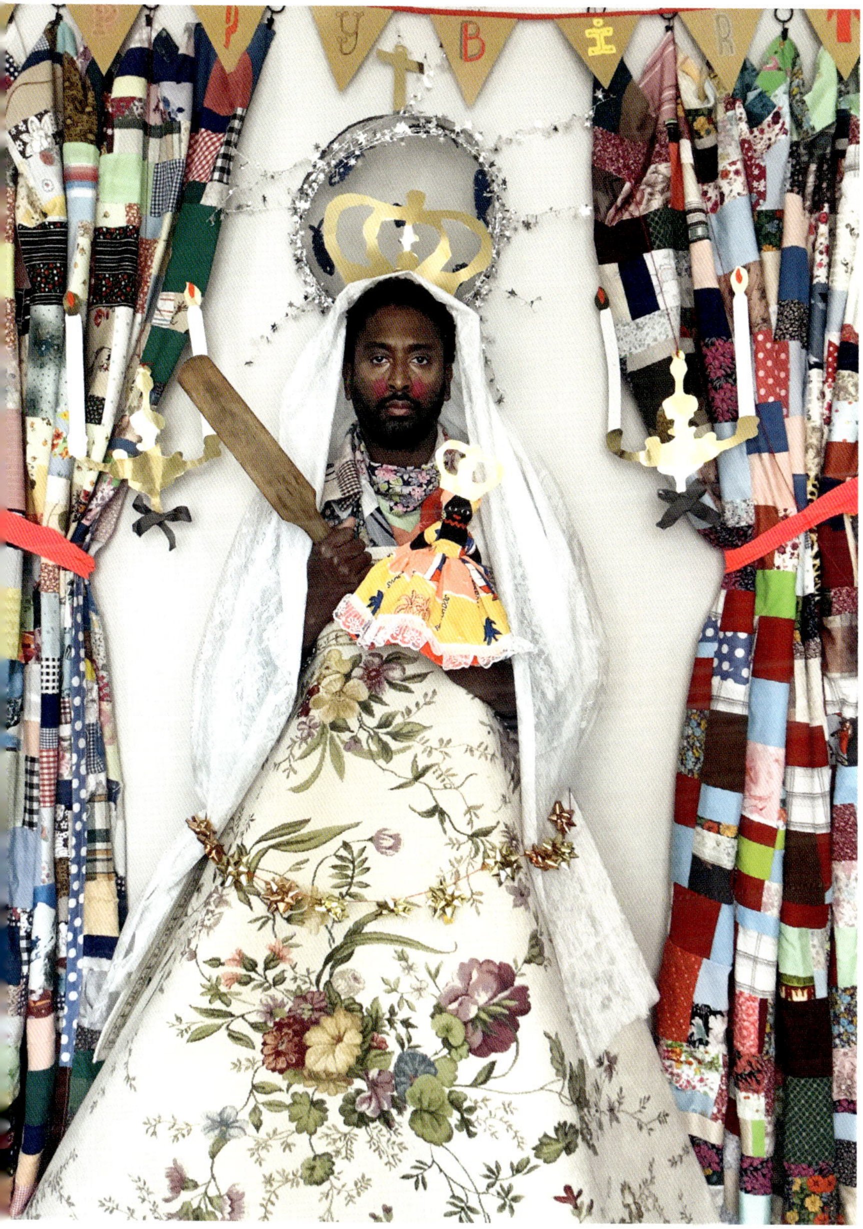

Act 2

The Virgin of Guadalupe of Extremadura, Spain, reworked with Granny's patchwork quilt, Grand-pap's cou-cou stick, tinsel, and a rag doll from Barbados. Paintings and sculptures of Black Madonnas are found in Catholic churches across Europe and Latin America, many dating from the medieval period. One controversial theory has it that the figures turned black through centuries of accumulated soot from incense and candles. A more likely possibility is that the Black Madonna is connected to pre-Christian worship of female divinities symbolizing fertility. In Mexico, where seventeenth-century missionaries reframed the Virgin of Guadalupe as a creolized blend of colonial and local iconography, the Black Virgin reflects how Indigenous communities resisted the process of assimilation.

Musician [Captain Lord George Graham, in His Cabin]

ca. 1745

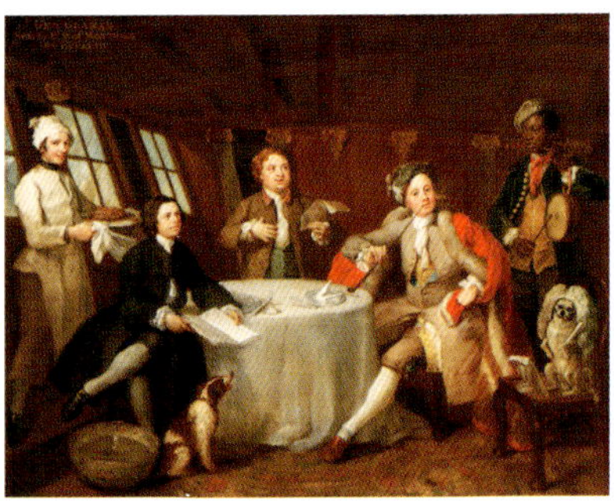

William Hogarth
British, 1697–1764

Oil on canvas
68.5 × 88.9 cm
(27 × 35 in.)
London, National Maritime Museum, BHC2720

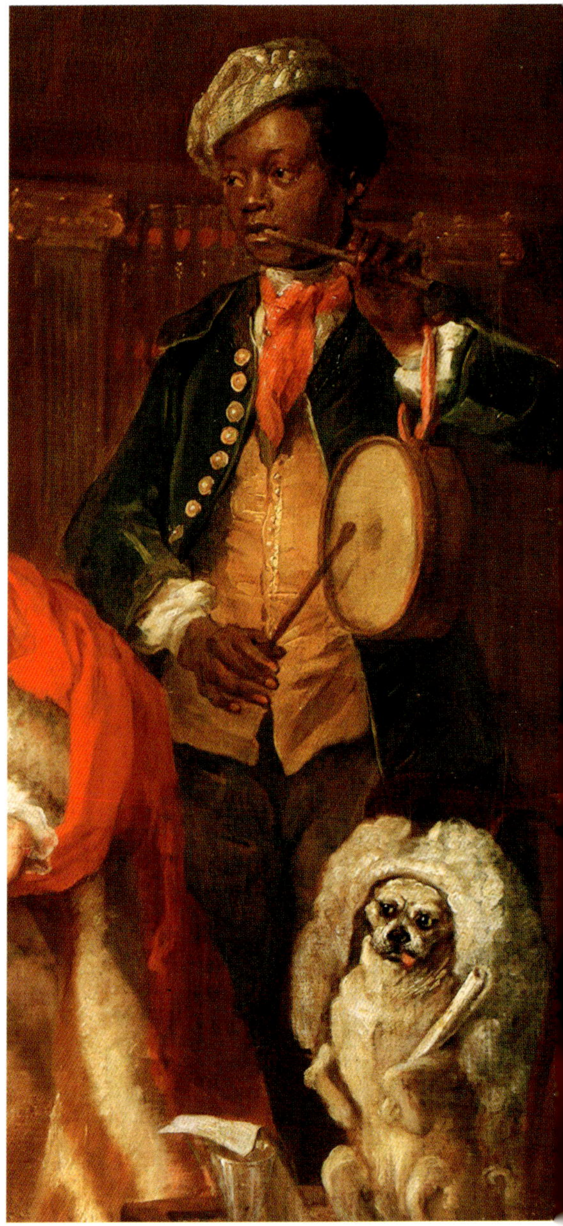

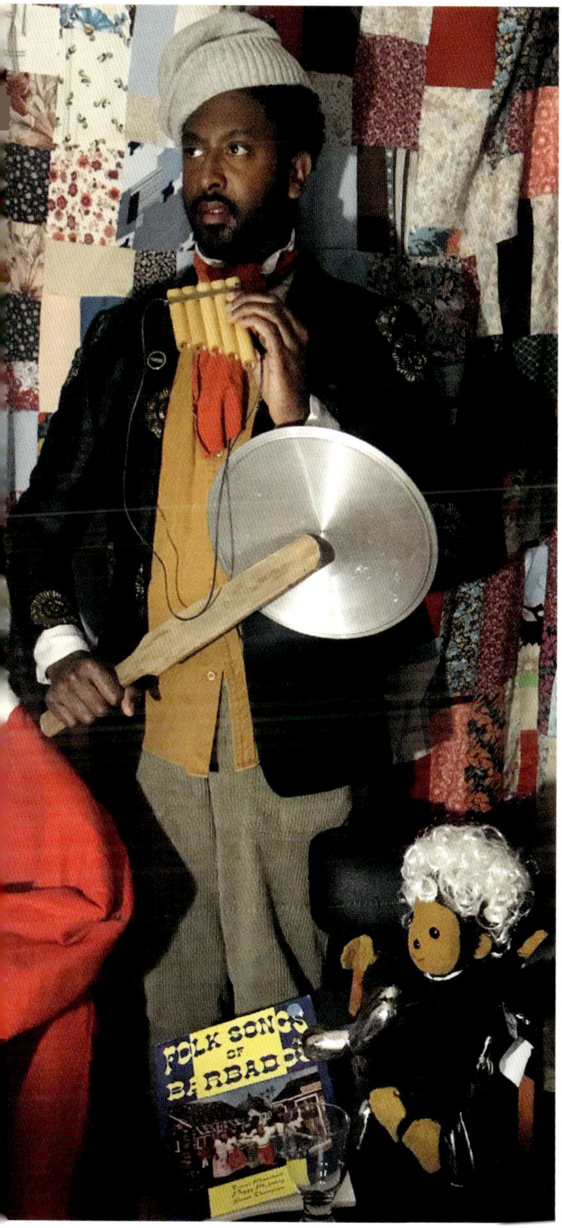

Act 2

Captain Lord Graham and his dinner guest are attended by a cook, a singer, and a Black musician playing a pipe and a tabor. Reworked with Granny's patchwork quilt, Grandpap's cou-cou stick, the lid of a buck pot, and a book of Barbadian folk songs. The fife-and-drum music the young man appears to be playing speaks to the British militia's use of enslaved musicians in the Caribbean colonies. In eighteenth-century Barbados, the contributions of enslaved musicians led to the development of a unique tradition that blended African and European elements and is known today as tuk. Behind the mask of European instruments, the enslaved were able to perpetuate West African musical traditions that had been suppressed under the Barbados Slave Code. I like to think of this musician's rebel sounds going unnoticed in the captain's cabin.

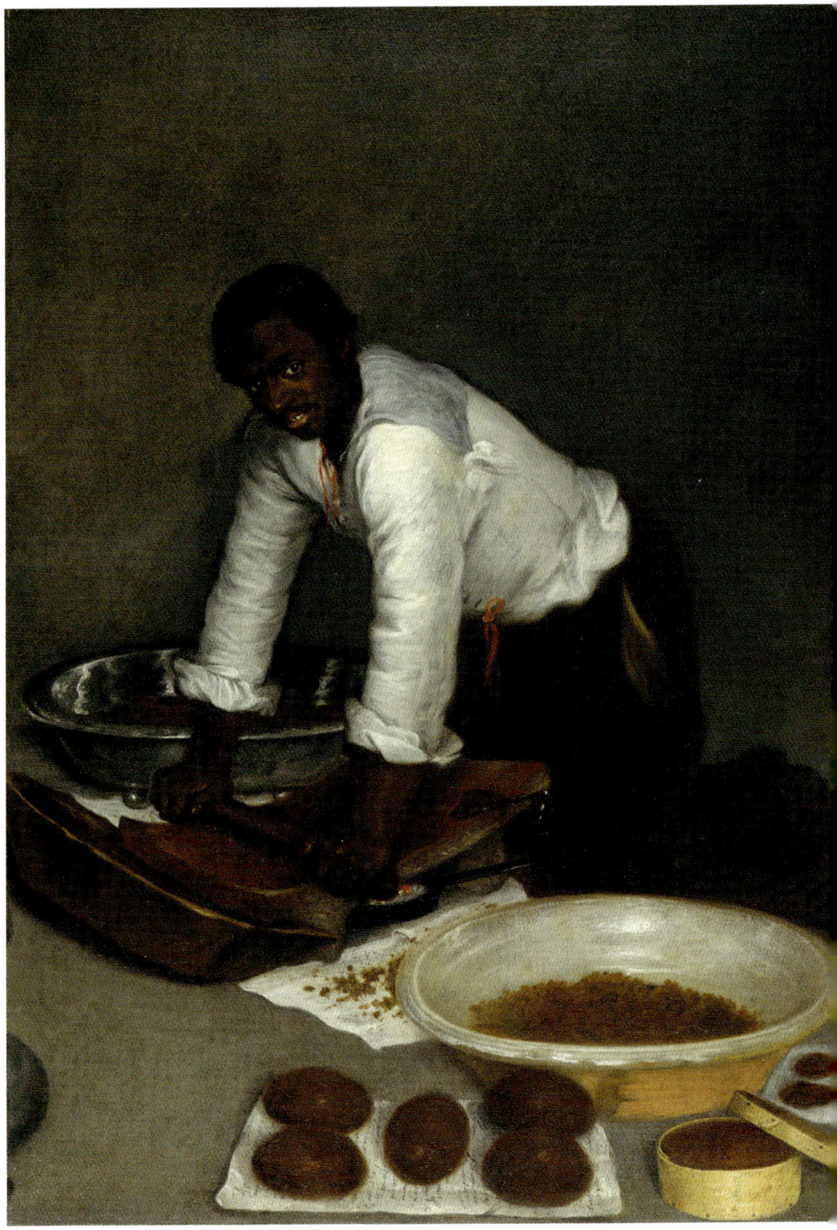

A Man Scraping Chocolate

ca. 1680–1780

Unknown artist
Spanish

Oil on canvas
104.1 × 71.1 cm
(41 × 28 in.)
Raleigh, North Carolina
Museum of Art, G.69.20.1

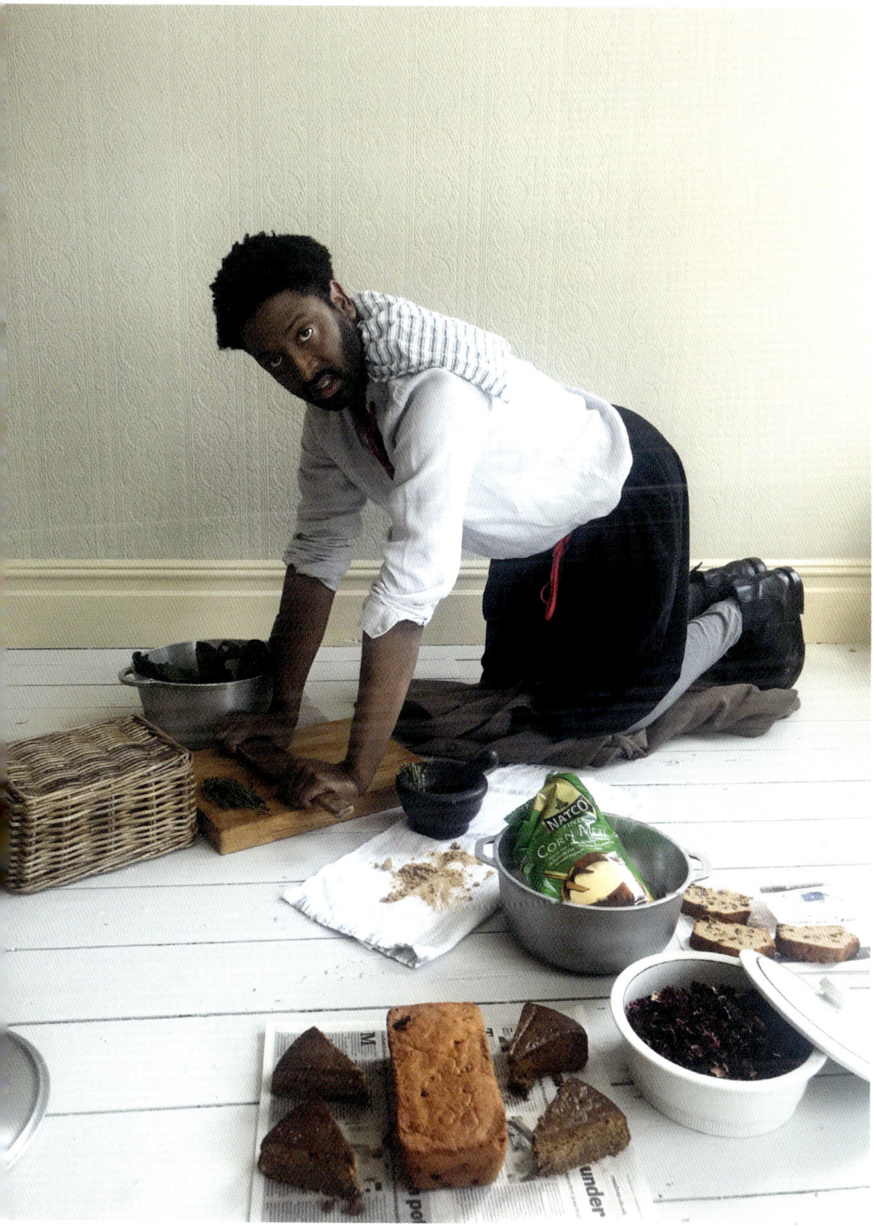

Act 2

Reworked with tools and ingredients of Barbadian cuisine: West Indian buck pots, cornmeal, dried sorrel, muscovado sugar, Mum's coconut bread, and Grandpap's cou-cou stick. Chocolate was among the first foods to travel from the New World to Spain during the 1500s. This painting depicts a man grinding cacao nibs with a metate, a curved stone widely used in Mexico and Central America. A cast-iron skillet holding smoldering coals provides heat to soften the resulting paste. The large bowls of raw ingredients and the array of treats displayed suggest that this man is an artisanal chocolate maker. It is unclear whether he is free or enslaved. We do know, however, that increasing numbers of enslaved Africans were transported to support cacao production as chocolate's popularity spread across Europe.

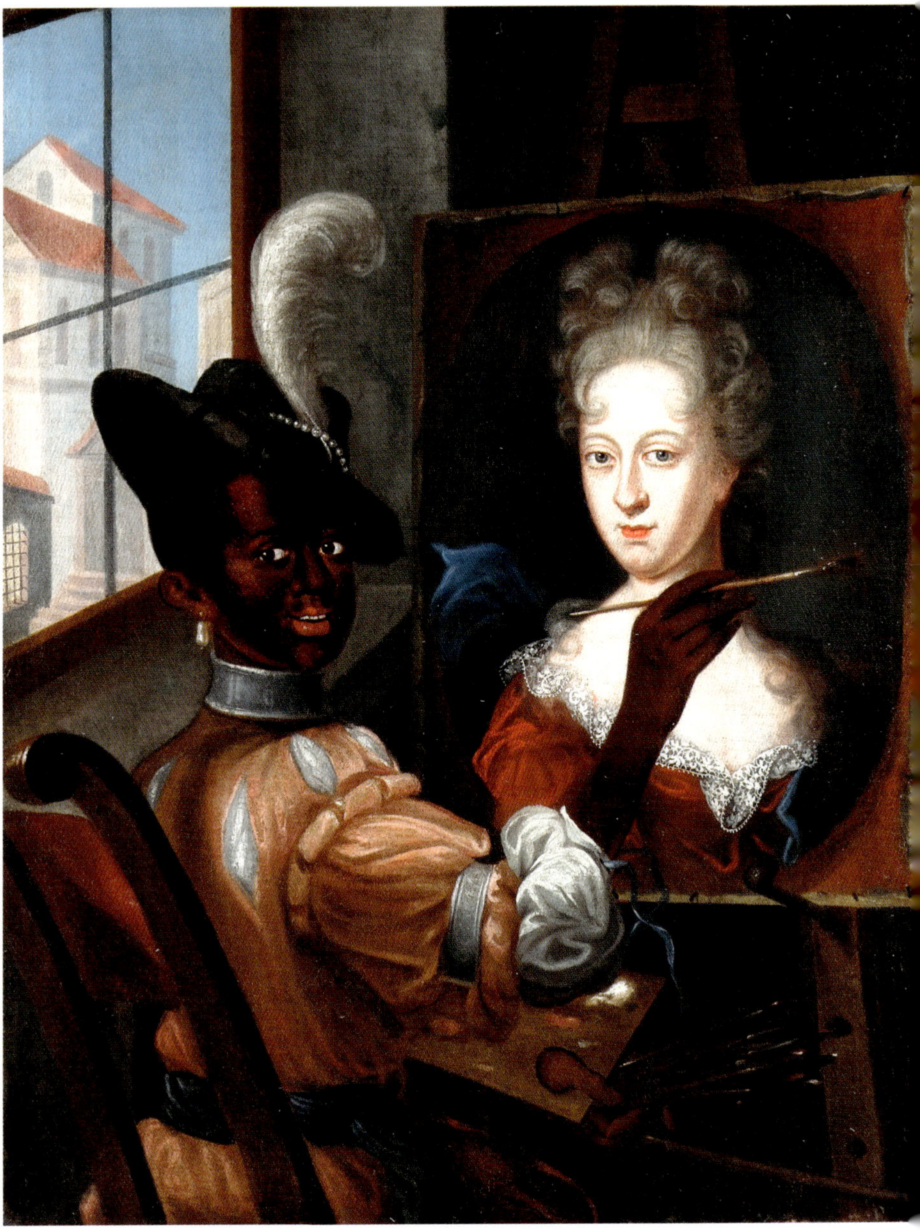

Artist Completing a Portrait of Maria Anna of Austria

first half of the eighteenth century

Unknown artist

Oil on canvas
104.1 × 82.6 cm
(41 × 32½ in.)
Courtesy Carlton Hobbs LLC

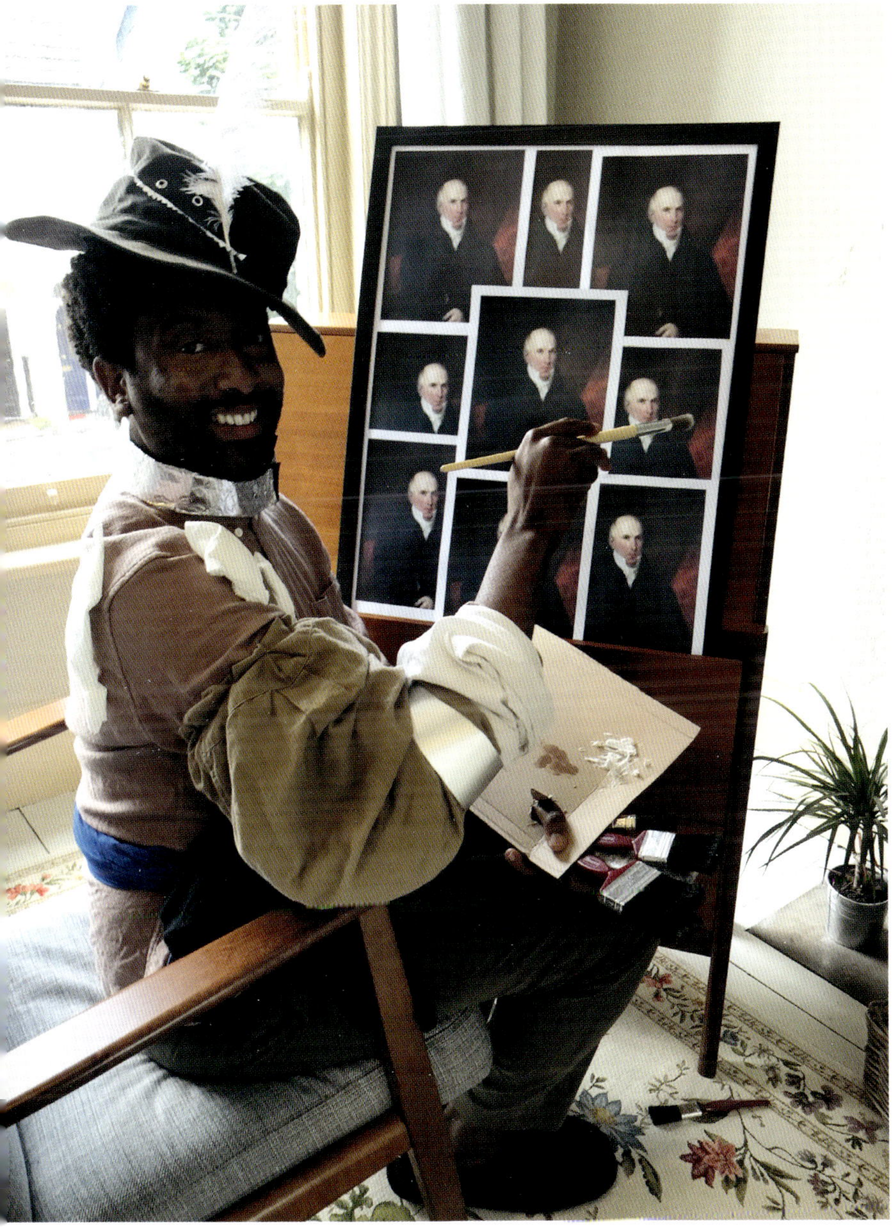

Act 2

Reworked with my ancestor Henry W. Grasset's portrait and a collar of aluminum foil. An elegantly dressed artist is completing a painting of Portugal's queen. Beyond the window, clear blue skies and limewashed buildings suggest a sun-kissed Mediterranean cityscape. The artist's metal collar and arm shackle would typically have been worn by enslaved men, but the pearl earring is a common motif in images of Black women. Is this an eighteenth-century representation of nonbinary gender identity? The artist looks out at us directly, eyes sparkling with laughter. Could this be a self-portrait by an enslaved Black artist? To me, this seems a person with agency, subservient to no one.

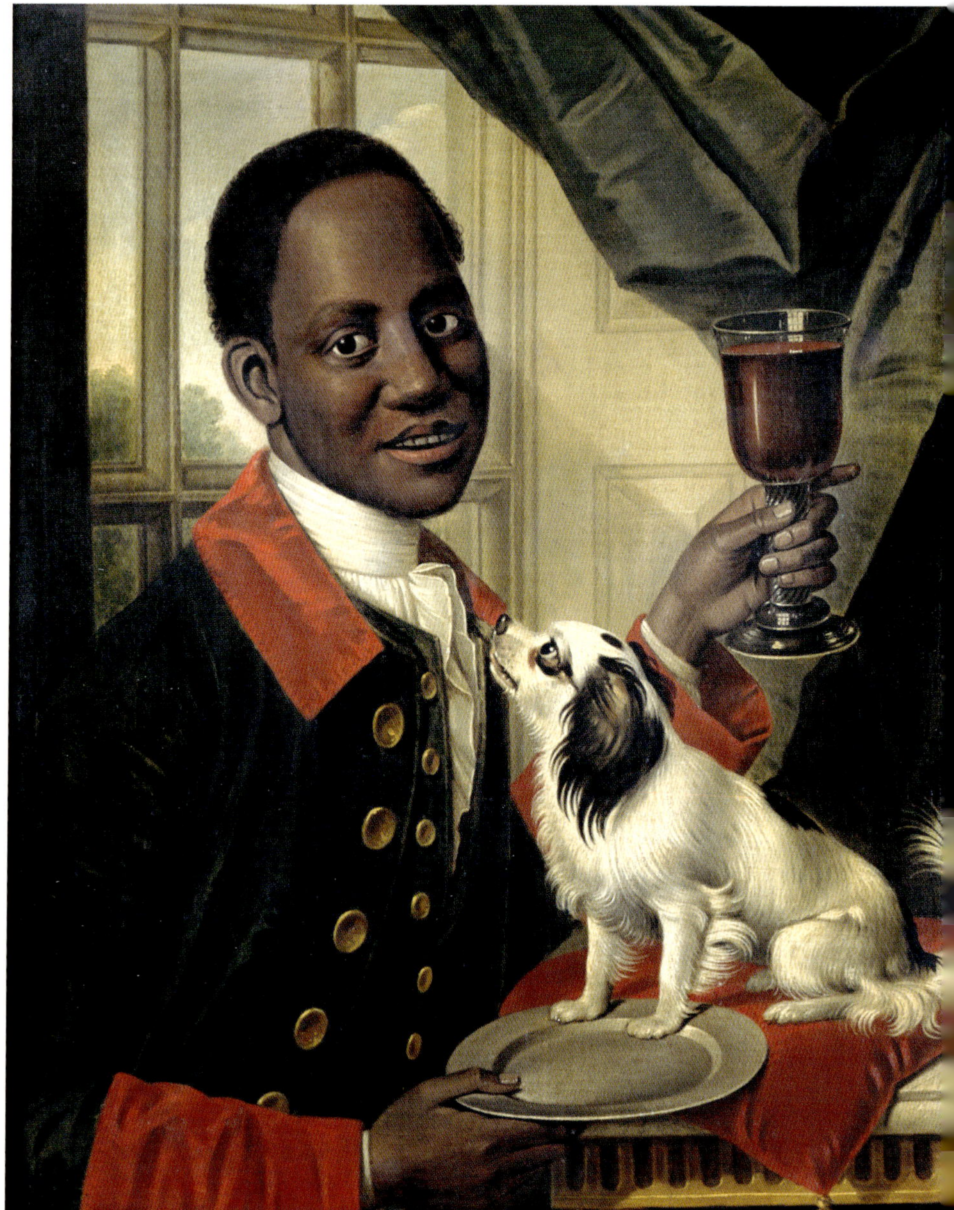

A Servant

ca. 1770

Unknown artist

Oil on canvas
76.2 × 63.5 cm
(30 × 25 in.)
Private collection

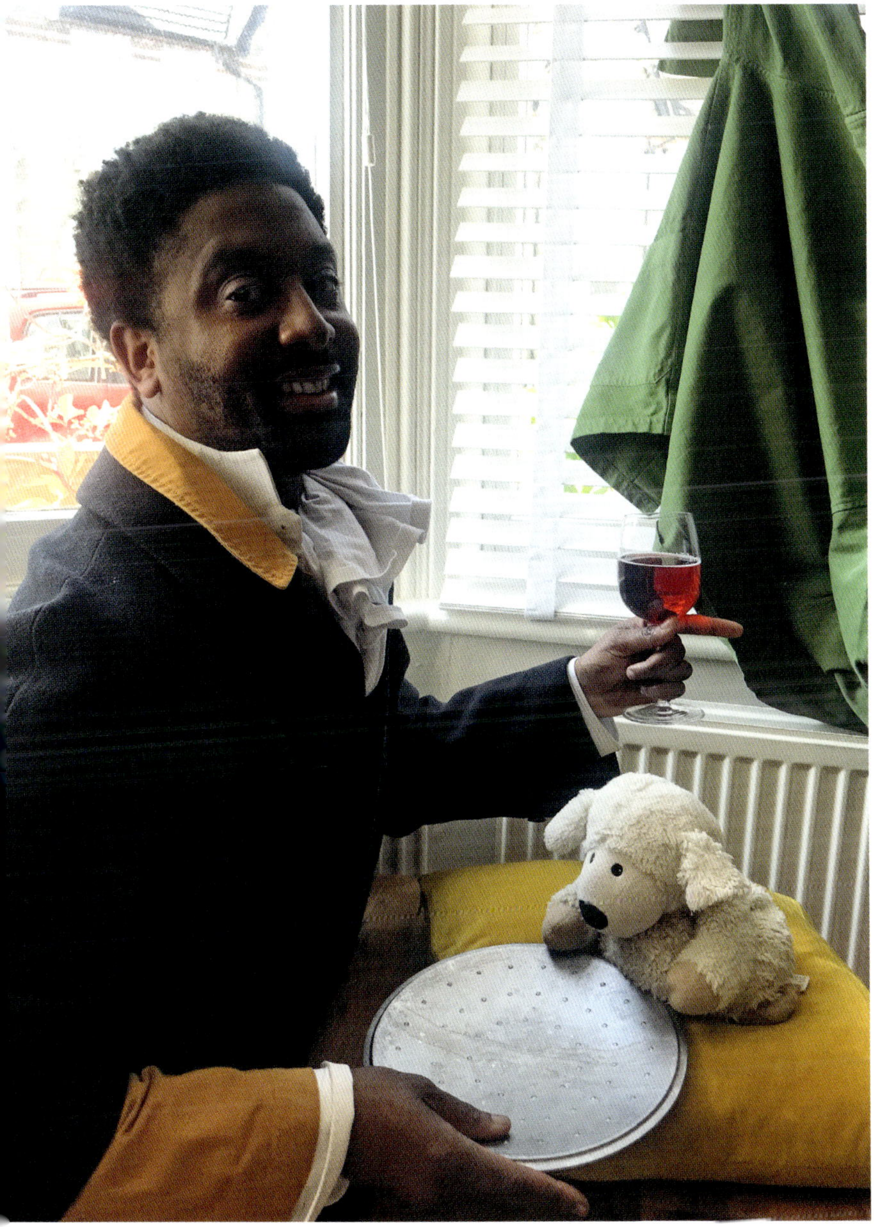

Act 2

A Black servant before a window, possibly in England, reworked with a West Indian buck pot lid, a toy sheep, and a glass of fruit juice. By the latter part of the eighteenth century, the majority of England's Black population worked in domestic service, both paid and unpaid. In aristocratic households, Black children were seen as status symbols and as investments for the future, but that did not mean they were not regarded as property. A sense of movement in this work implies that we have interrupted a game between the boy and the dog. The affection between them is clear. But which of the two is the more valued member of the household? The inclusion of the lapdog and the expensive glass and silverware accentuates the relationship between commodities and enslavement.

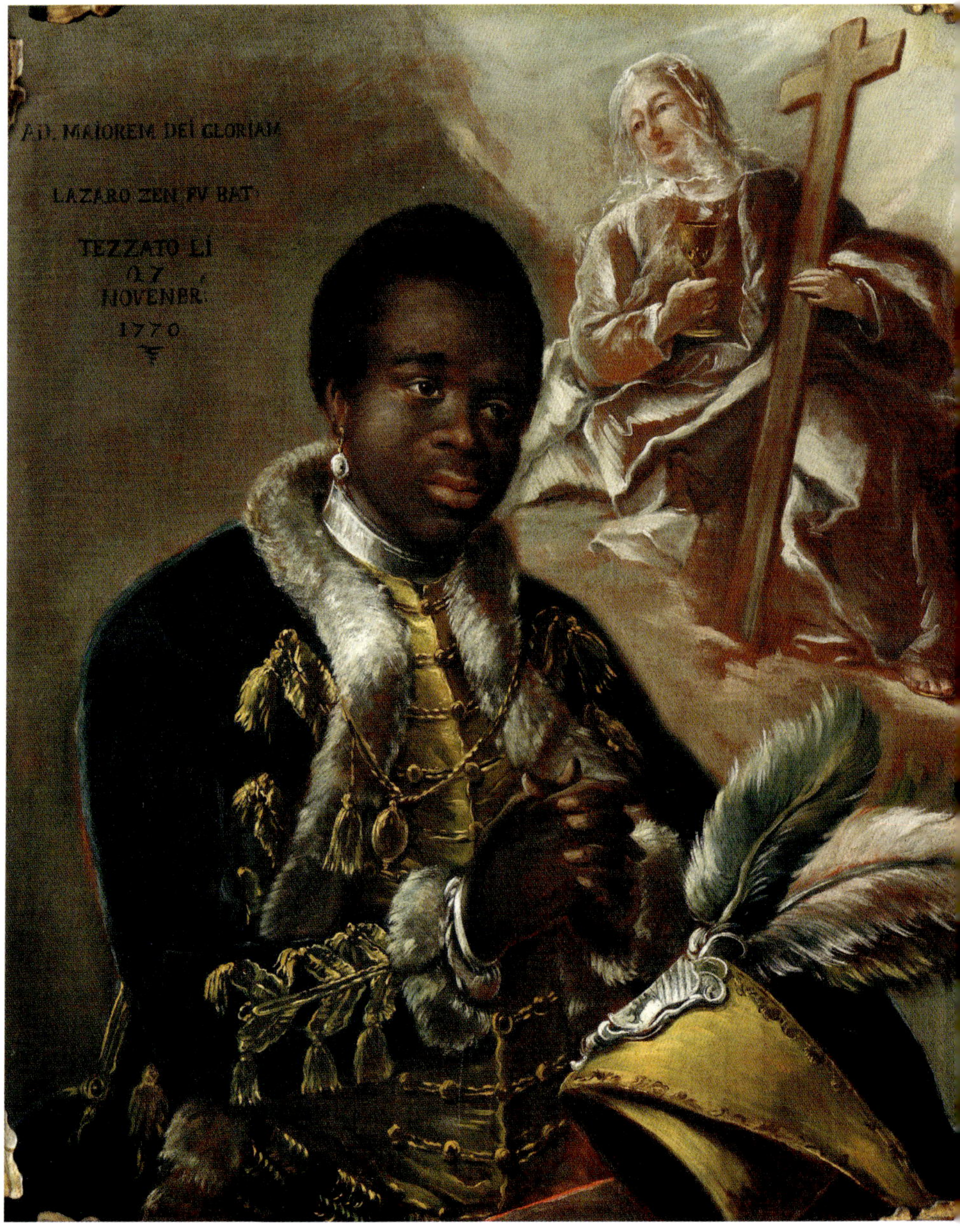

Votive Portrait of Lazzaro Zen

1770

Francesco Guardi
Italian, 1712–1793

Oil on canvas
93 × 77 cm
(36⅝ × 30⅜ in.)
Venice, Istituzioni di Ricovero
e di Educazione

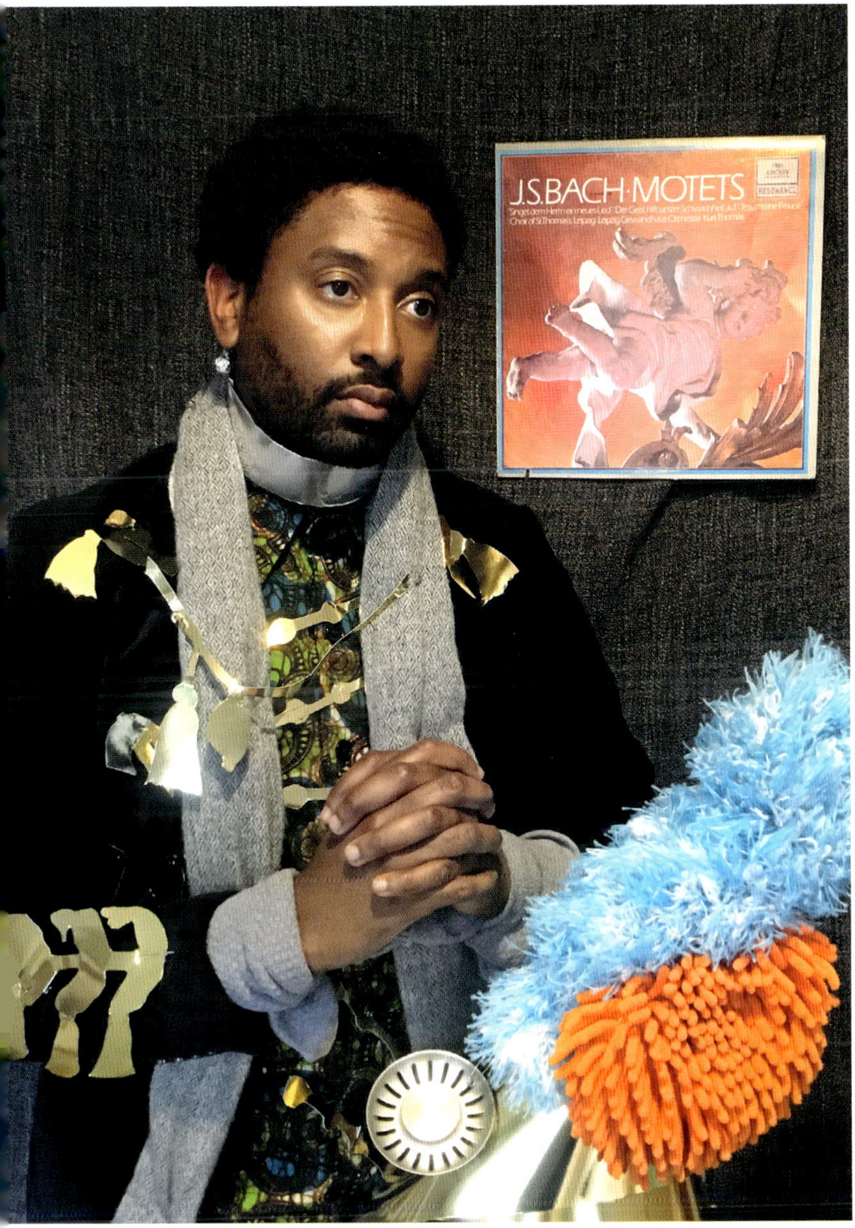

Act 2

Reworked with household dusters, a drain plug, a West African print, and an album of Bach's motets. Originally named Ali, this Guinean man arrived in Venice, probably enslaved, during his twenties. He entered the city's institute for catechumens, Christian converts preparing for baptism, and was rechristened Lazzaro after the dead son of his godfather, the Venetian aristocrat Renier Zen. The Zen family coat of arms decorates Lazzaro's sumptuous hat, which he has removed as he kneels in prayer. Like my great-great-great-great-grandfather Addo Brathwaite, who was forcibly converted to Christianity during his enslavement in Barbados, Lazzaro had his most deeply held beliefs—and his very identity—suppressed by the church.

Dido Elizabeth Belle and Lady Elizabeth Murray

ca. 1778

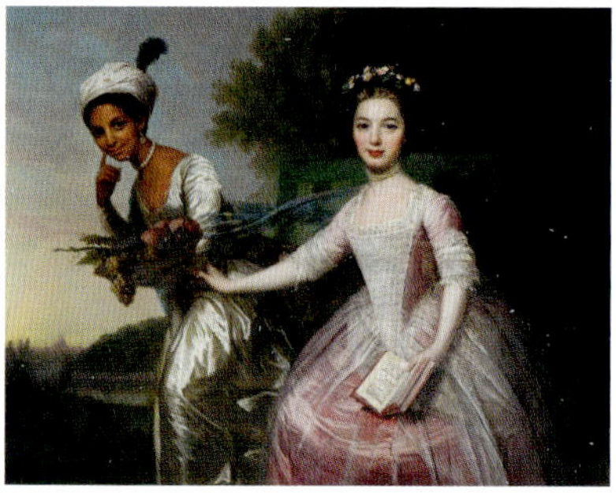

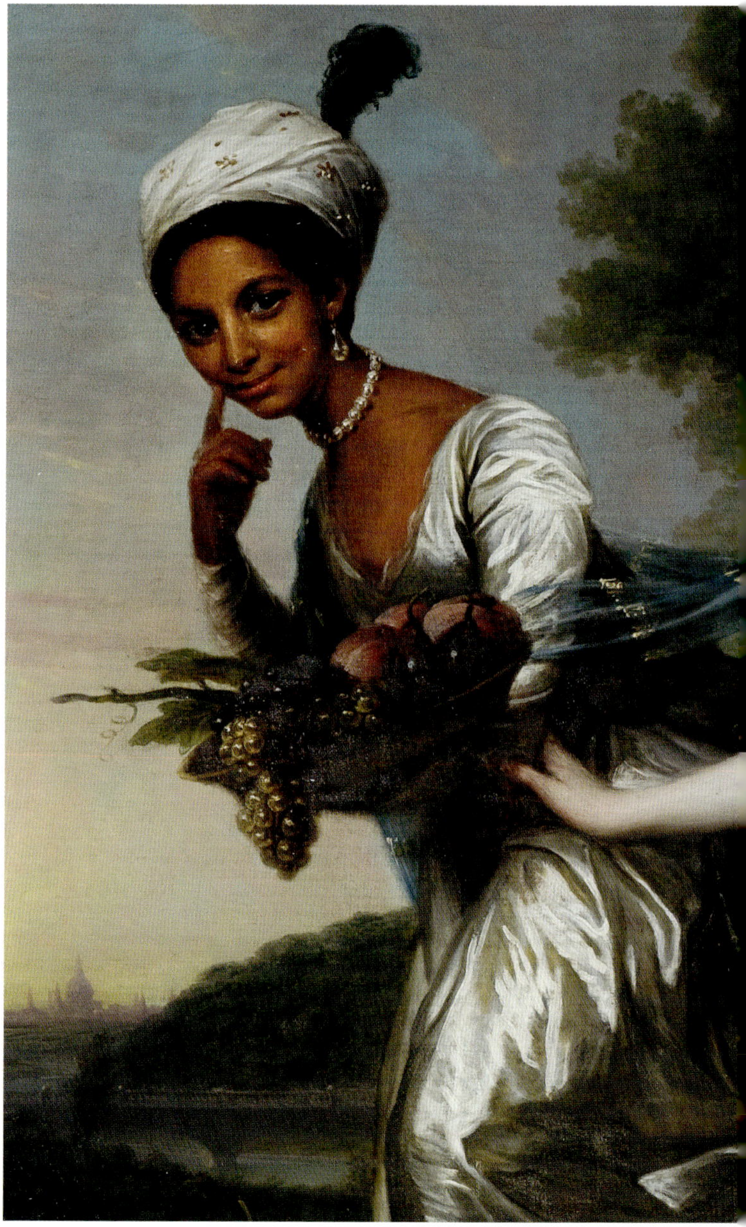

David Martin
Scottish, 1737–1798

Oil on canvas
119 × 139 cm
(46⅞ × 54¾ in.)
Perth, Scotland, Scone Palace

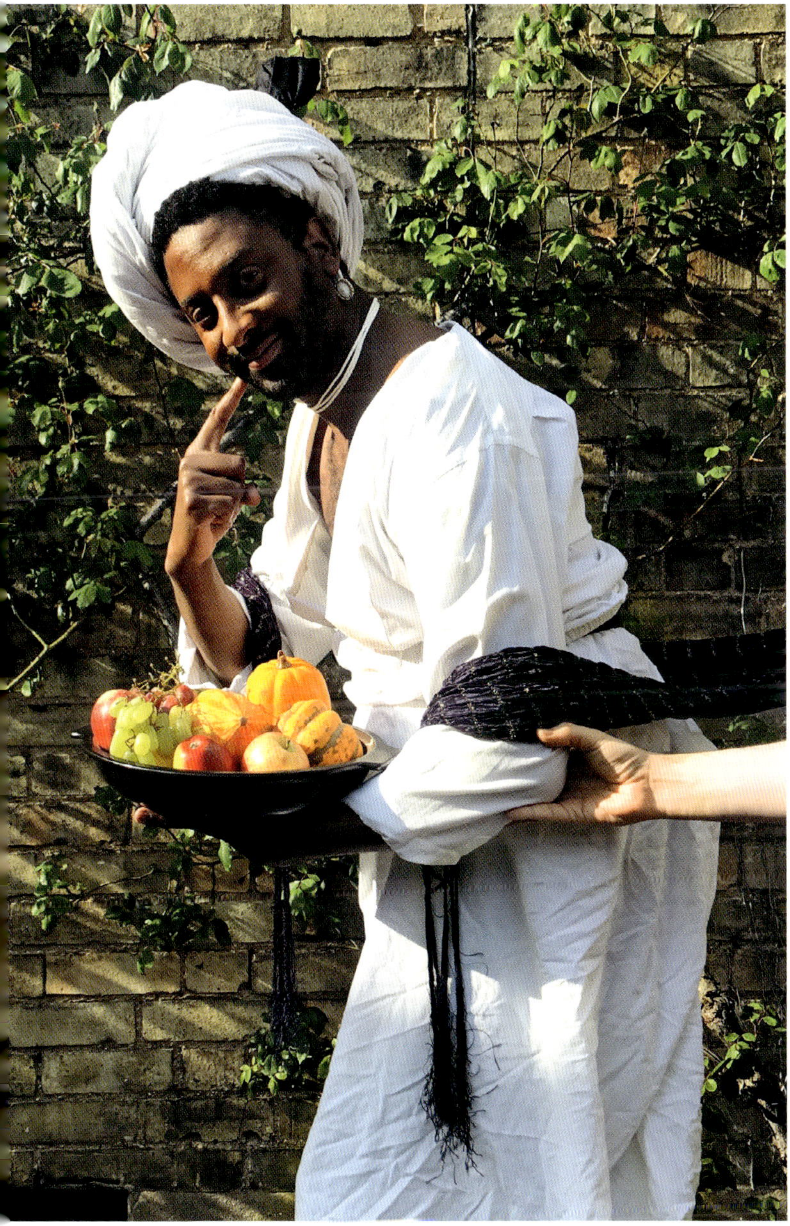

Act 2

Reworked with a bowl of fruit, bedsheets, and a hatpin. Until the 1990s, this painting was known simply as *The Lady Elizabeth Murray*, with the identity of Murray's Black companion—actually her cousin—unknown. Dido Elizabeth Belle was the illegitimate daughter of an enslaved Black African woman named Maria Bell and Royal Navy officer Sir John Lindsay. Dido spent much of her life at Kenwood House in North London, living with her great-uncle William Murray, Earl of Mansfield. In the 1772 Somerset case, as lord chief justice, the earl famously ruled that slavery had no precedent in common law within Britain. It is certainly possible that Belle influenced her uncle's views. Is her gesture in this portrait meant to challenge the racially based commodification underpinning the British aristocracy?

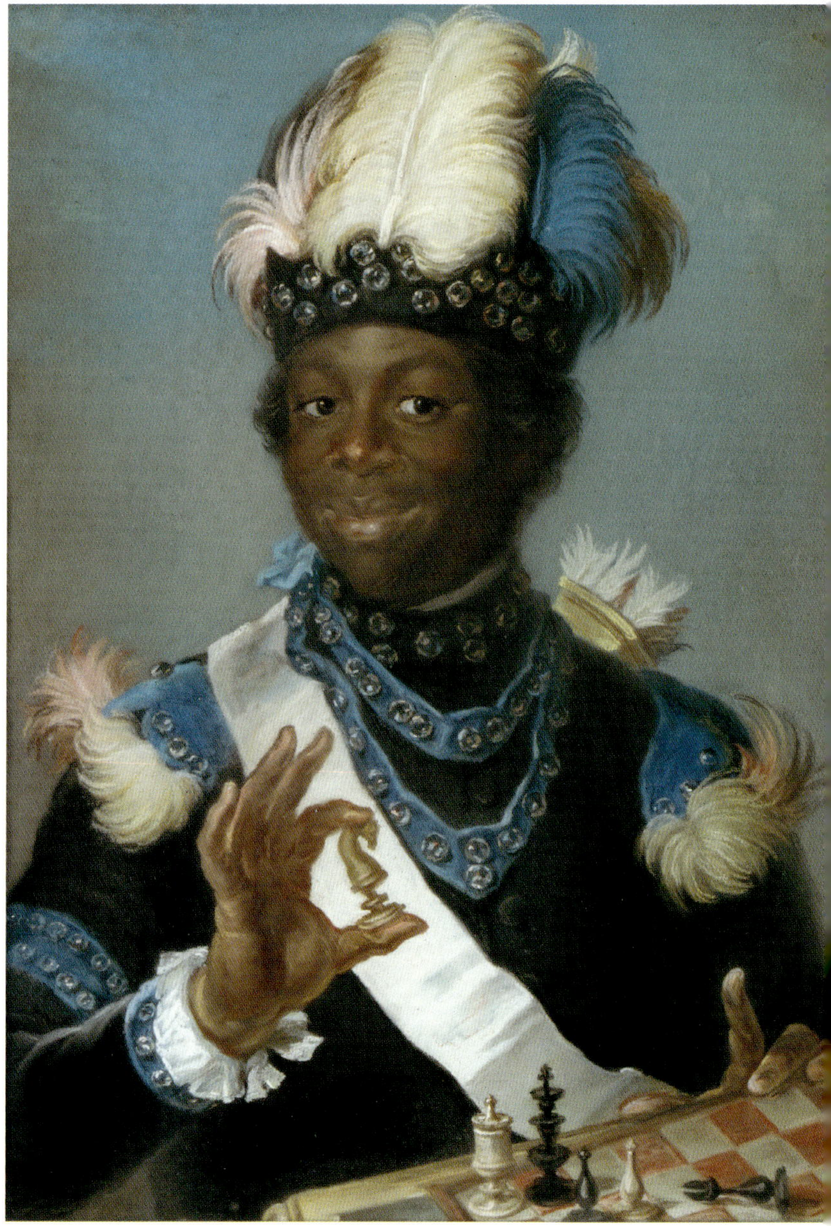

Adolf Ludvig Gustav Albert Couschi, Called Badin

1775

Gustaf Lundberg
Swedish, 1695–1786

Pastel on paper
74 × 57 cm
(29 × 22½ in.)
Stockholm,
Nationalmuseum

Reworked with sponges, a colander, neckties, handkerchiefs, and Jenga game blocks. The Afro-Swedish intellectual and diarist Couschi is depicted here as a cunning chess player. He was born enslaved on the Caribbean island of Saint Croix, then a Danish colony. At age seven, he was trafficked to Europe and presented as a gift to Louisa Ulrika of Prussia, queen of Sweden. Despite being categorized as a *Kammermohr*, an

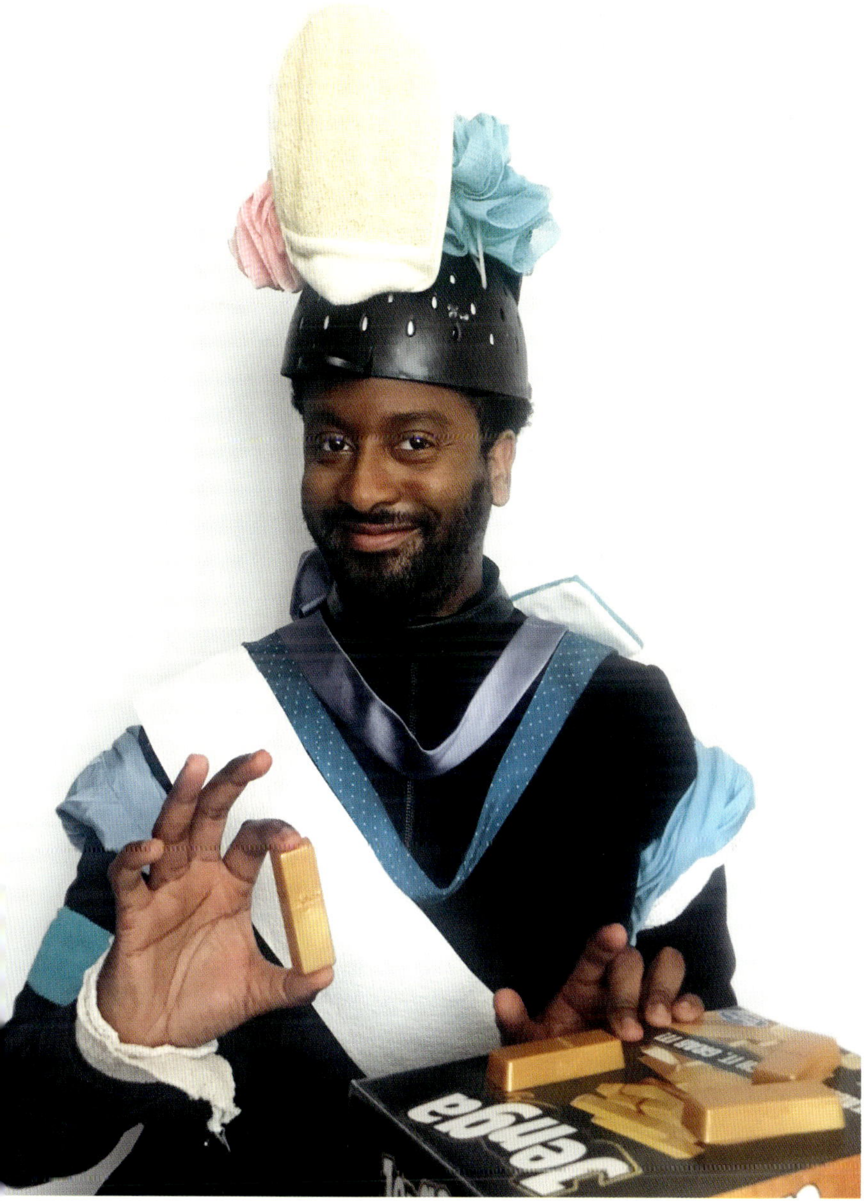

Act 2

eighteenth-century German term used to describe a Black court servant, Couschi was officially adopted by the queen and educated alongside his stepsiblings. Fluent in French, German, and Latin, as an adult he managed royal estates, collected books, and performed as a ballet dancer and an actor. Despite his accomplishments, we cannot ignore the tragedy of his forced migration to Stockholm. His involuntary exile from kin and community no doubt haunted him. Yet I see a glimmer of justice in his smile and confident gaze. He not only seems determined to win but also appears to revel in the knowledge that he is actively undermining racial stereotypes.

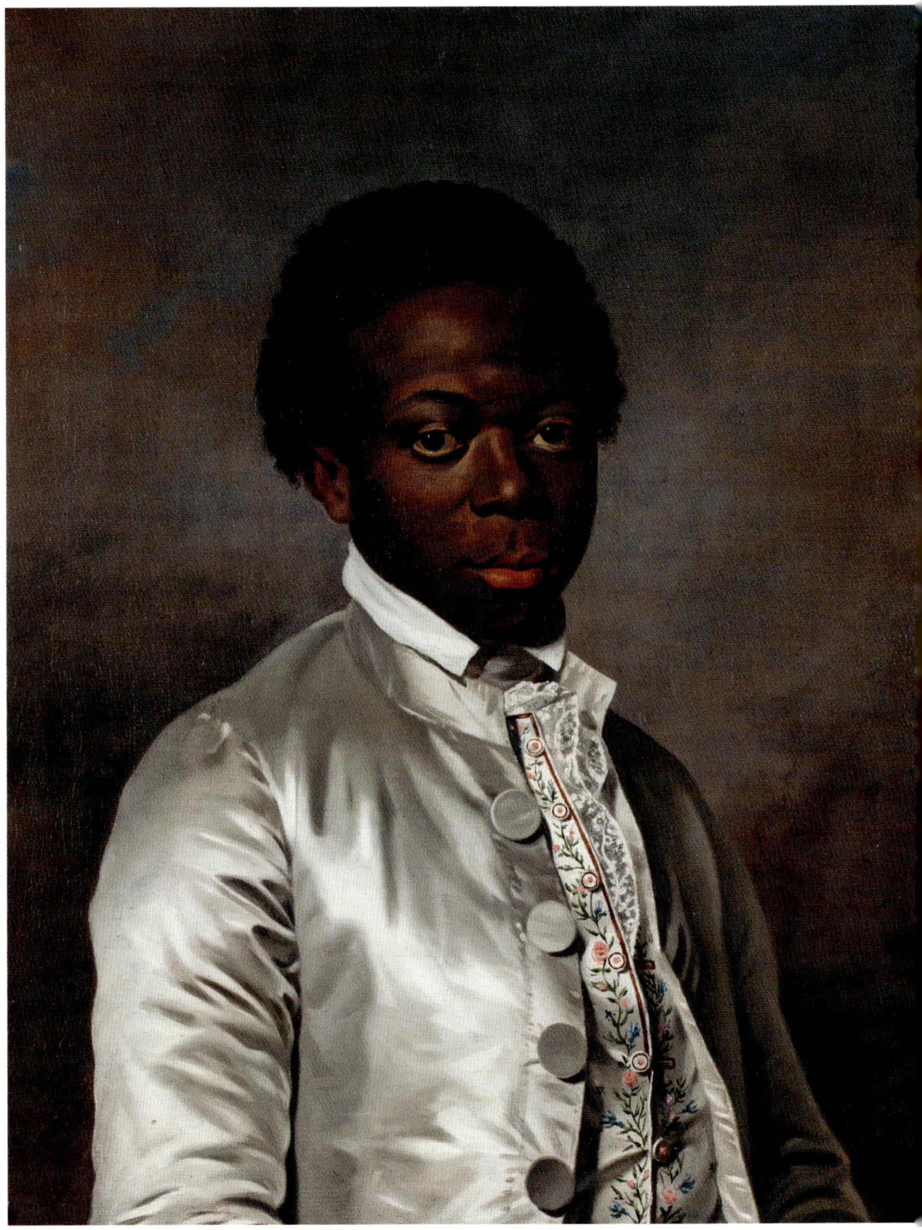

Portrait of a Youth in an Embroidered Vest

1785

Marie Victoire Lemoine
French, 1754–1820

Oil on canvas
65.1 × 54.6 cm
(25⅝ × 21½ in.)
Jacksonville, Florida,
Cummer Museum of Art
& Gardens, AP.1994.3.1

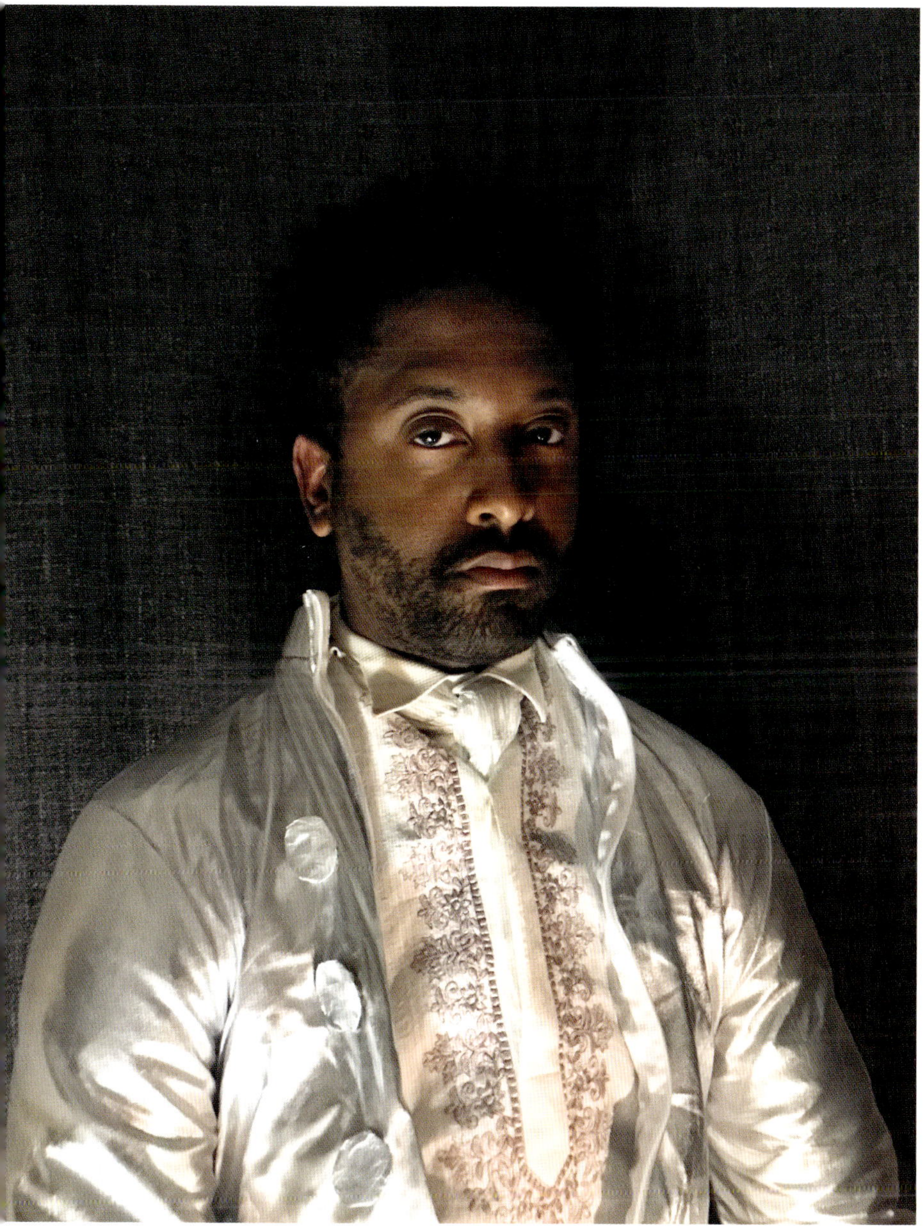

Act 2

Reworked with a space-suit costume. Born into a middle-class family in Paris, Lemoine was one of the few professional women artists of her time. The identity of her youthful subject is not yet known, but his exquisite clothing suggests that he might have been the son of a wealthy family or a favored domestic servant. One theory is that he may have worked for the Duchess of Orléans, who is known to have employed Lemoine. The artist has paid particular attention to the texture of the boy's Afro coils and the nuance of his skin tone, placing his Blackness in harmony with, rather than in opposition to, the dazzling satin he wears.

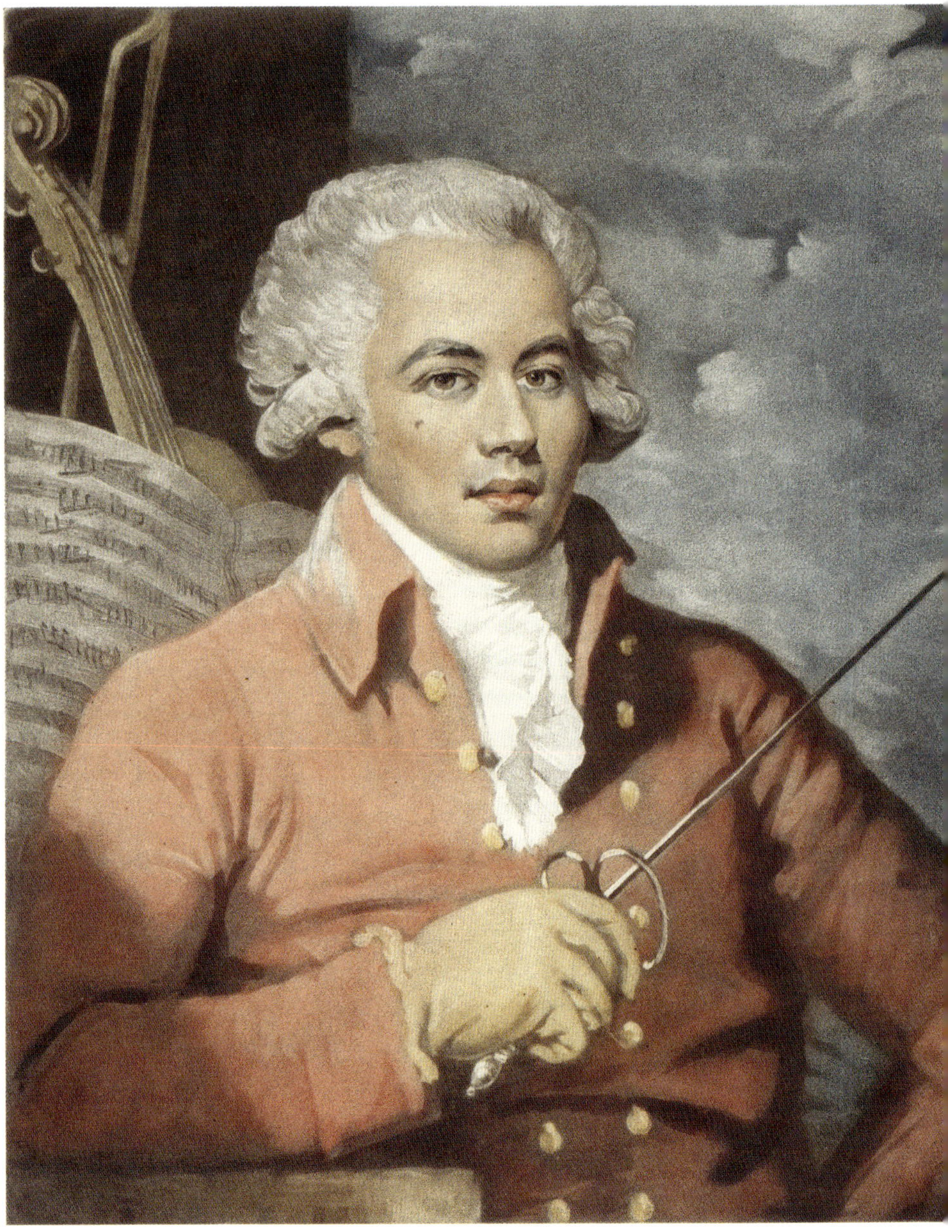

Monsieur de Saint-Georges

1788

William Ward
(after Mather Brown)
British, 1766–1826

Color mezzotint
with hand coloring
Sheet: 38 × 27.7 cm
(15 × 11 in.)
London, British
Museum, 1905,1110.75

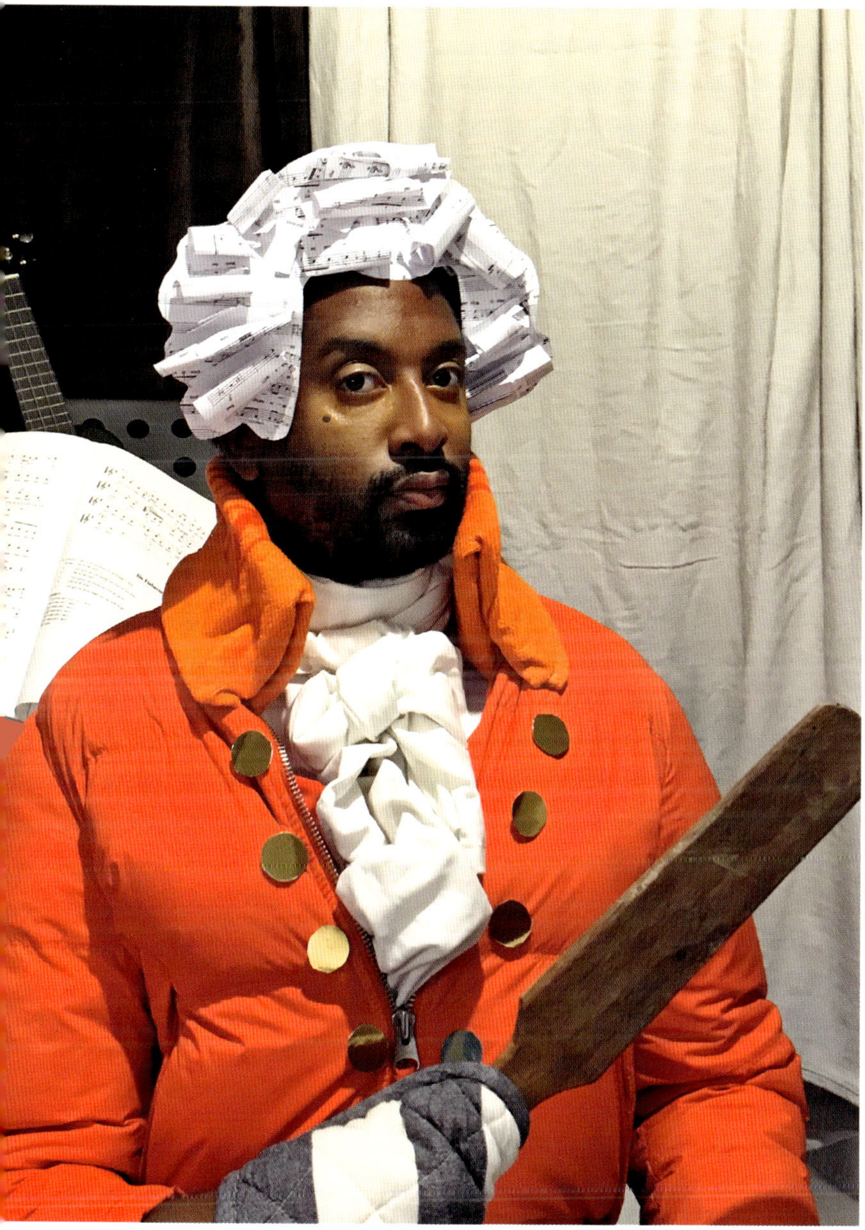

Act 2

Reworked with a book of Barbadian folk songs, a wig made from pages of an opera score, a puffer jacket, an oven mitt, and Grandpap's cou-cou stick. Joseph Bologne, Chevalier de Saint-Georges, was a celebrated swordsman, composer, violinist, and conductor, and a contemporary of Wolfgang Amadeus Mozart and Franz Joseph Haydn. He was born on a plantation on the Caribbean island of Guadeloupe, the son of a French enslaver and an enslaved Senegalese woman known as Nanon. His output as a composer includes numerous symphonies, sonatas, concertos, operas, and string quartets. He was a violin virtuoso who conducted one of Europe's best orchestras, the Concert des Amateurs, and even taught music to Marie Antoinette. Here we see him at the zenith of his fame. With a violin and sheet music behind his right shoulder, he cuts a dashing figure in his padded fencing jacket.

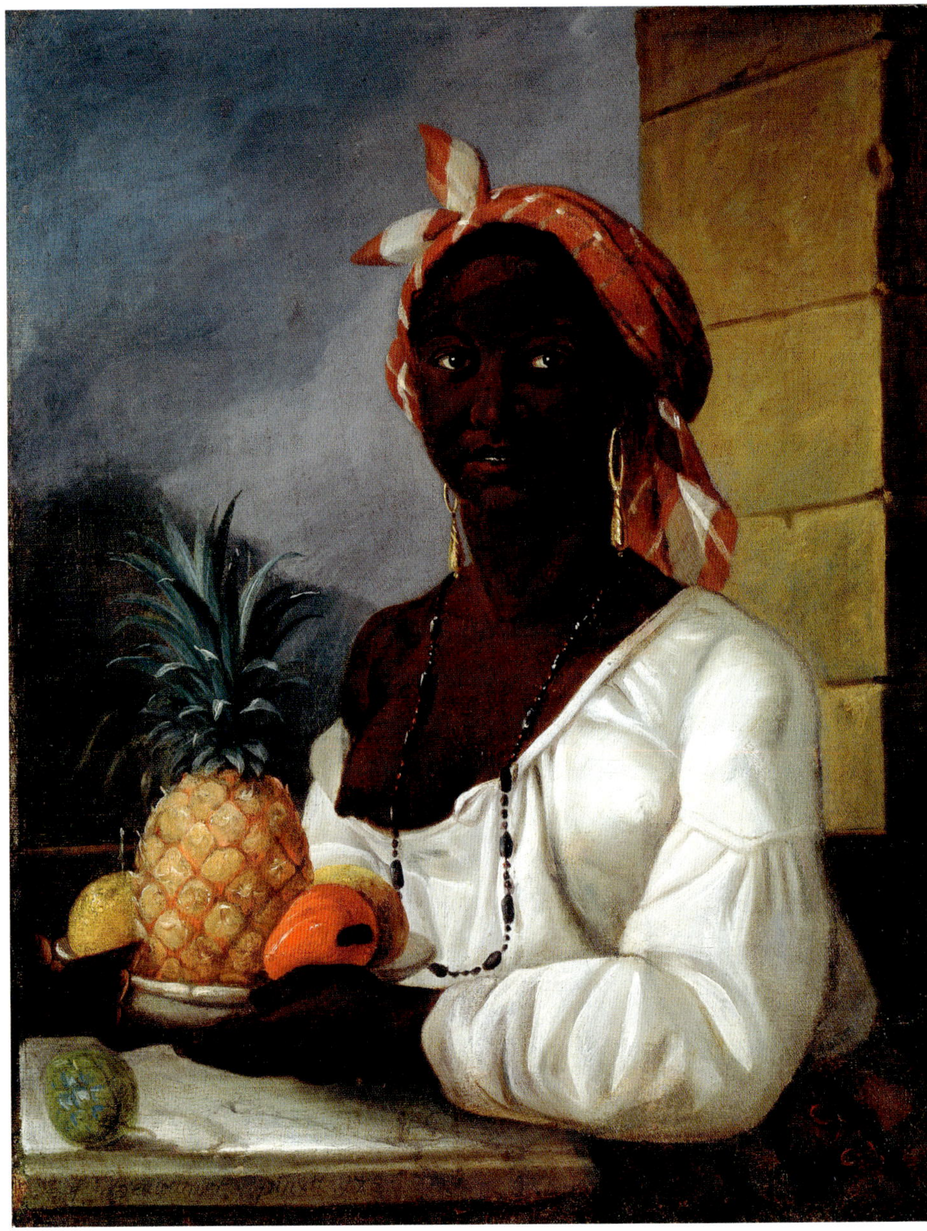

Portrait of a Haitian Woman

1786

François Beaucourt
Canadian, 1740–1794

Oil on canvas
69.1 × 55.6 cm
(27 × 22 in.)
Montreal, McCord Museum,
M12067

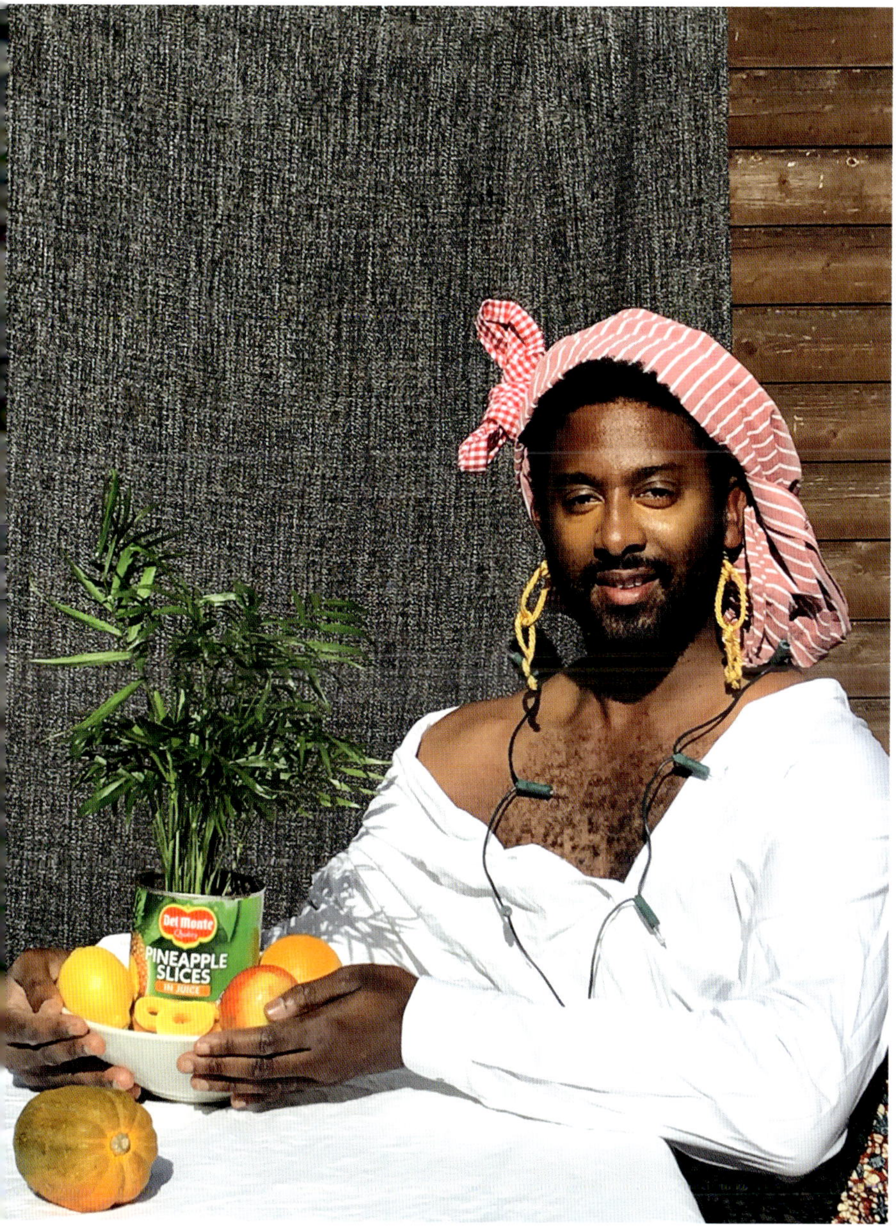

The subject is Marie-Thérèse-Zémire, documented as the property of the artist's wife. Reworked with tinned pineapple and Christmas lights. Marie was said to be twenty-nine at the time of her death in 1800, which means she was fifteen when this portrait was painted. Juxtaposing tropical fruit with her exposed breast, Beaucourt reinforces colonial stereotypes of enslaved Black women as sexually available, consumable, and fertile. To me, her expression speaks to the complex position of Black women in this system of domination. Beaucourt is thought to have painted the portrait when he and his wife were in the French colony of Saint-Domingue (now Haiti), before they took Marie to Quebec. Had she not been trafficked by the Beaucourts, she might have lived the rest of her life as a free woman, given that revolution was soon to emancipate Haiti's enslaved population.

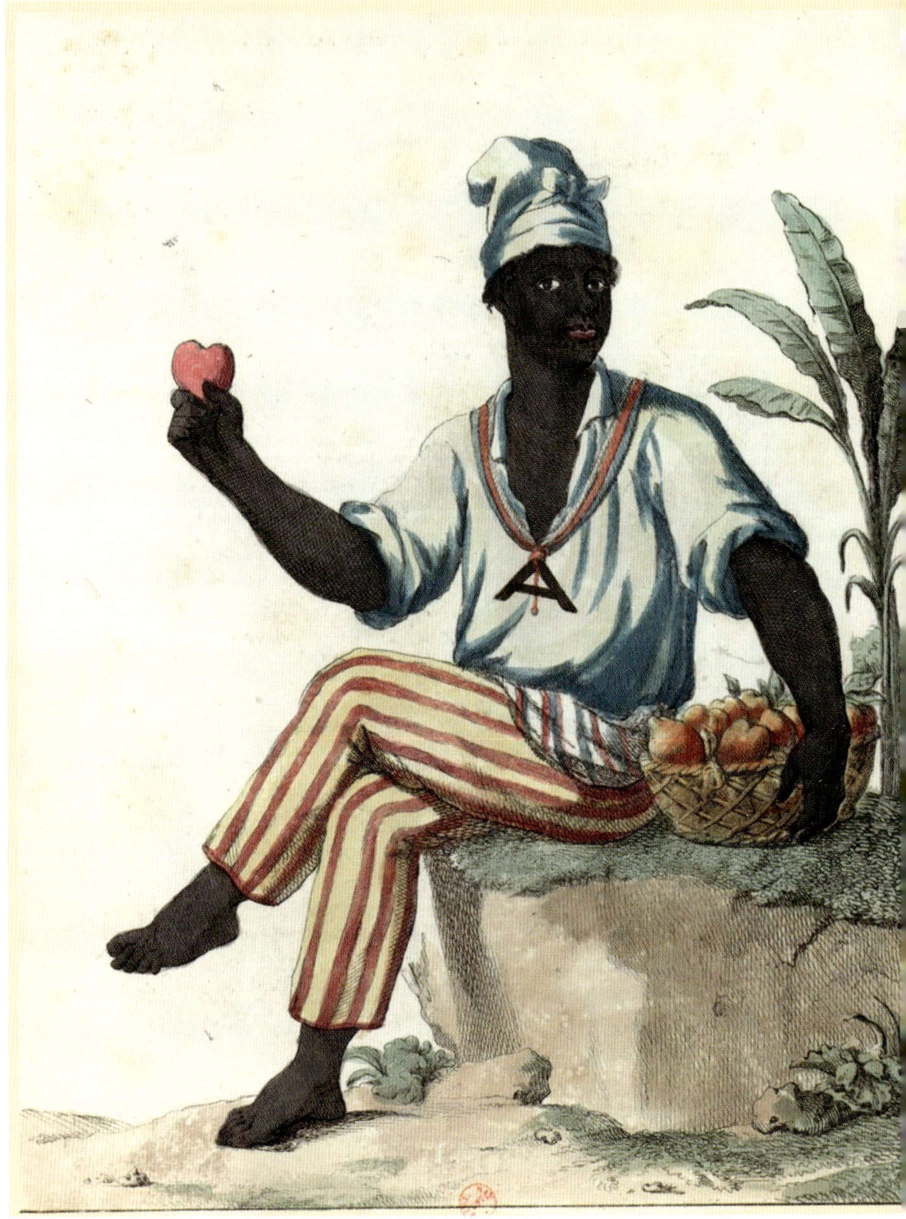

Moi Libre

1794

Unknown artist

Published by Chez Basset, Paris
Hand-colored etching
Sheet: 30 × 23 cm
(11¾ × 9 in.)
Paris, Bibliothèque nationale
de France (BnF), Rc-A-09806

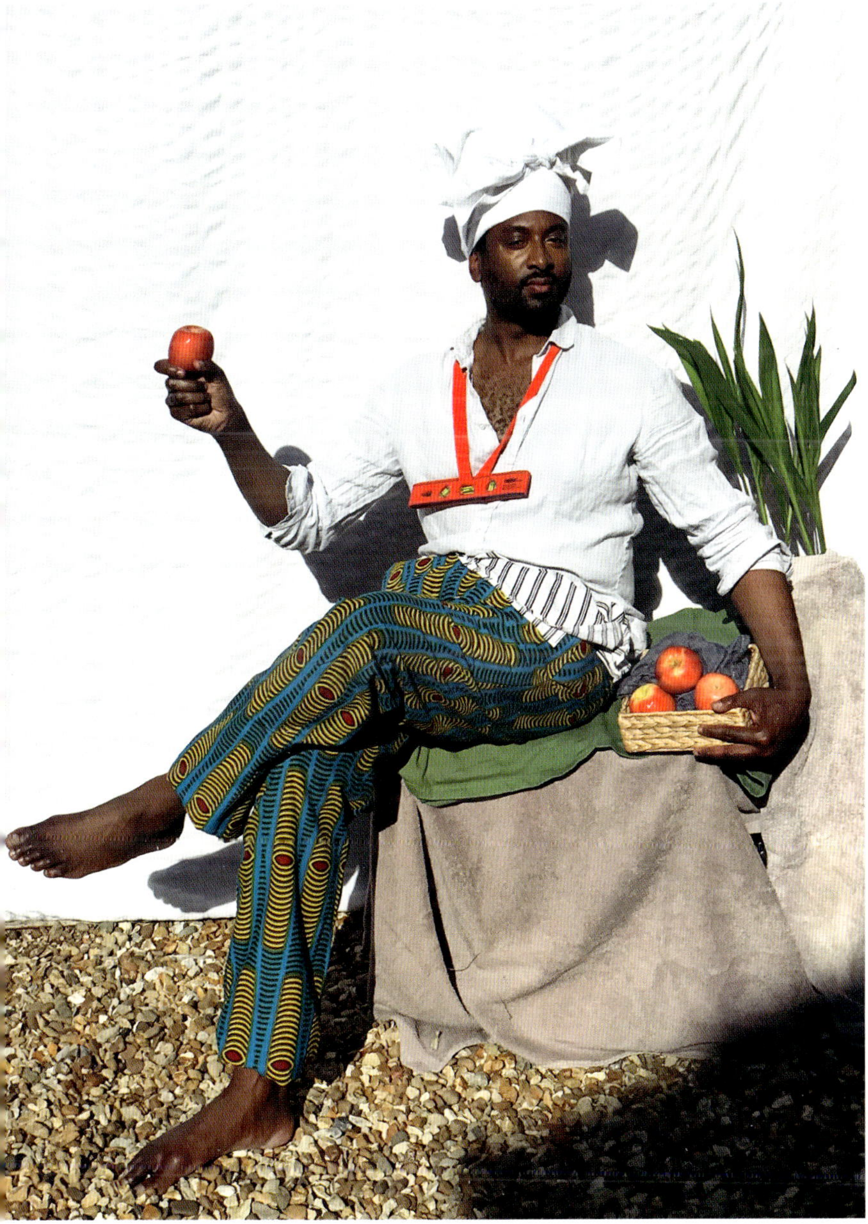

Act 2

A freeman holds a tropical fruit to signal his vocation in a French Caribbean colony. Reworked with Côte d'Ivoire print fabric, a spirit level, and an apple. Made after the abolition of slavery in 1794 by the Convention nationale, an assembly that governed France during the French Revolution, this engraving was likely a piece of pro-emancipation propaganda. The subject is depicted as a French citizen, dressed in clothing resembling that of a revolutionary sansculotte (radical and militant partisan). He is wearing a pendant in the form of a set square, which might be read as a symbol of equality, uprightness, honesty, and dependability. His head wrap resembles a liberty cap, signifying freedom.

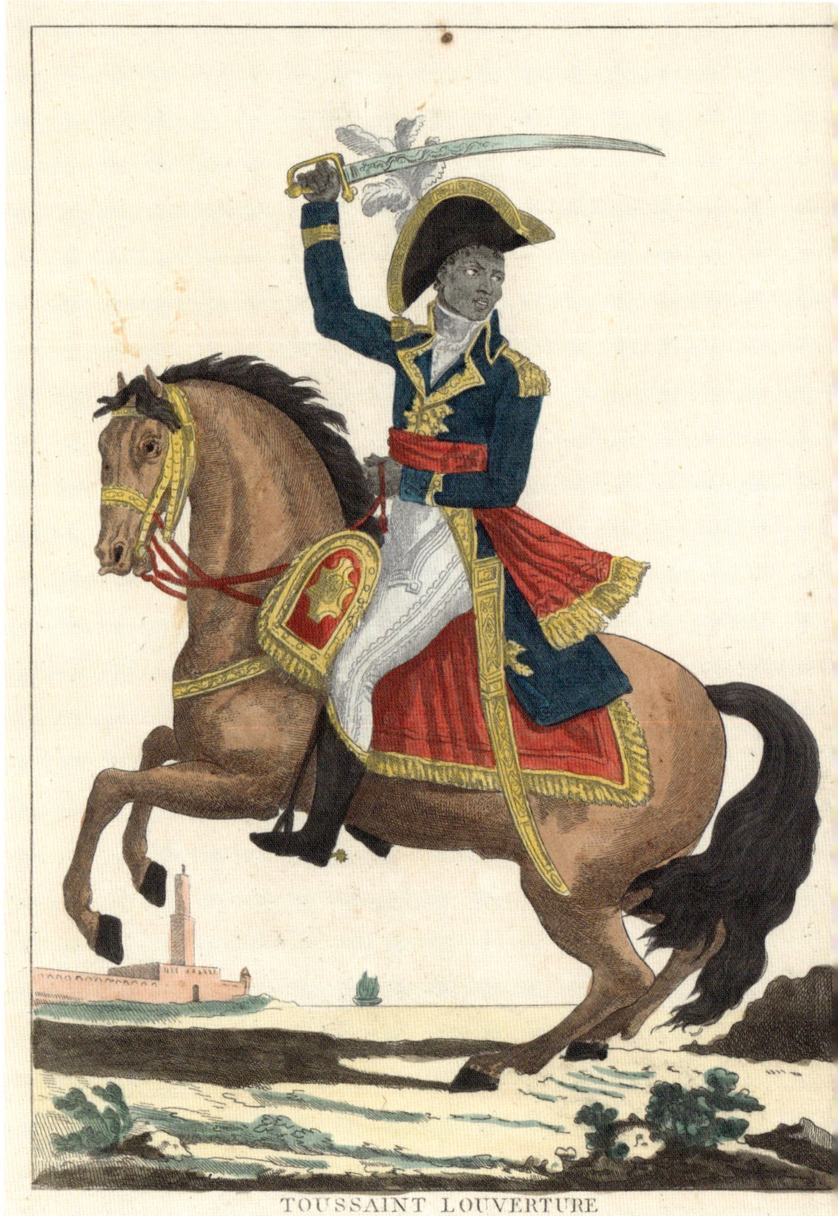

Toussaint Louverture on Horseback

1802

Unknown artist
French

Hand-colored etching
Sheet: 42.1 × 27.3 cm
(16⁹⁄₁₆ × 10¾ in.)
New York, Metropolitan Museum of Art, 83.2.936

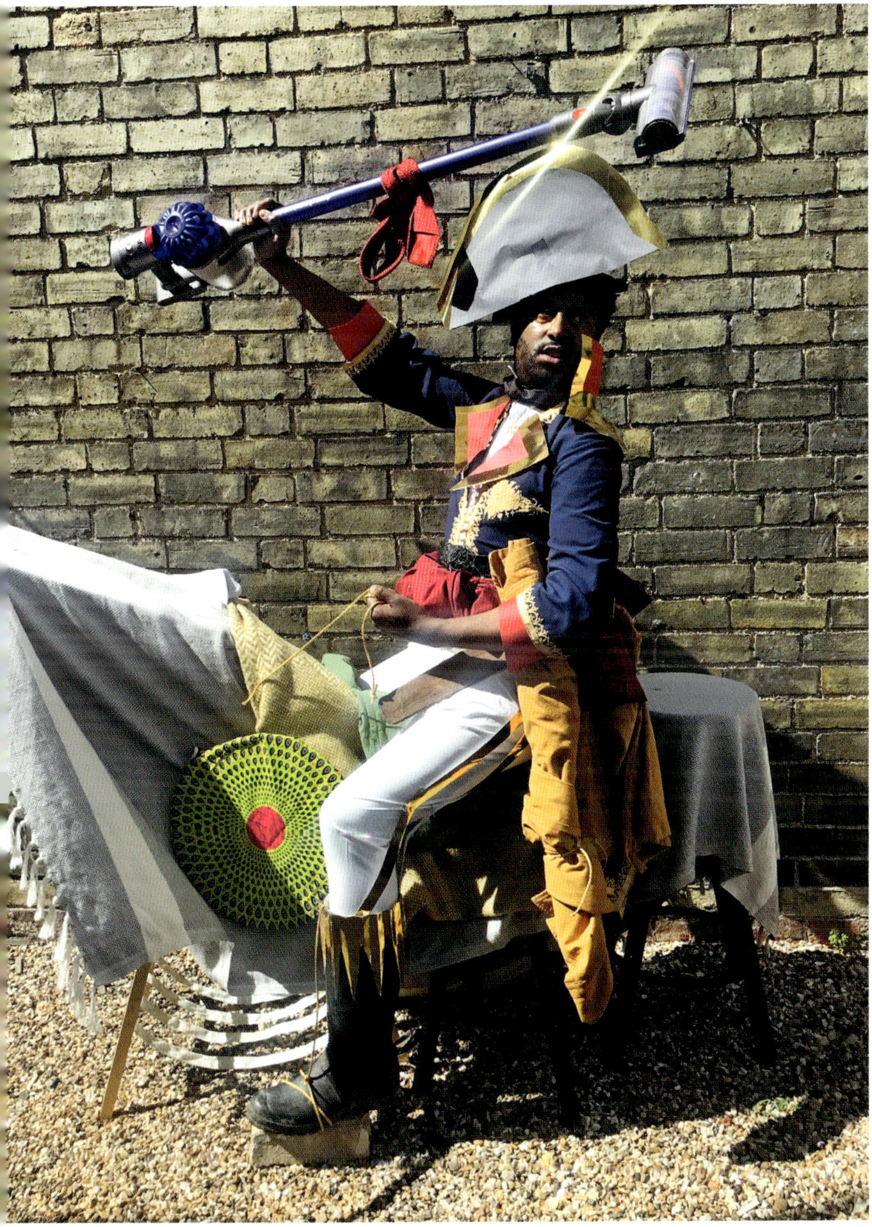

Act 2

Toussaint Louverture, "Bonaparte of the Antilles," was a general and leader of the Haitian Revolution. Reworked with a vacuum, a clotheshorse, and a West African print. Far from Paris but decked in formal Gallic regalia, Toussaint appears to embody the ideals of the French Revolution: liberty, equality, and fraternity. He is Black and Haitian, but ultimately French. Powerfully posed on a rearing horse, his sword held aloft, he is the picture of spirit, virtue, and fortitude, and was despised and feared by monarchs and enslavers. There is nothing here to suggest that the real Napoleon would retake Haiti and that Toussaint would die a prisoner one year later.

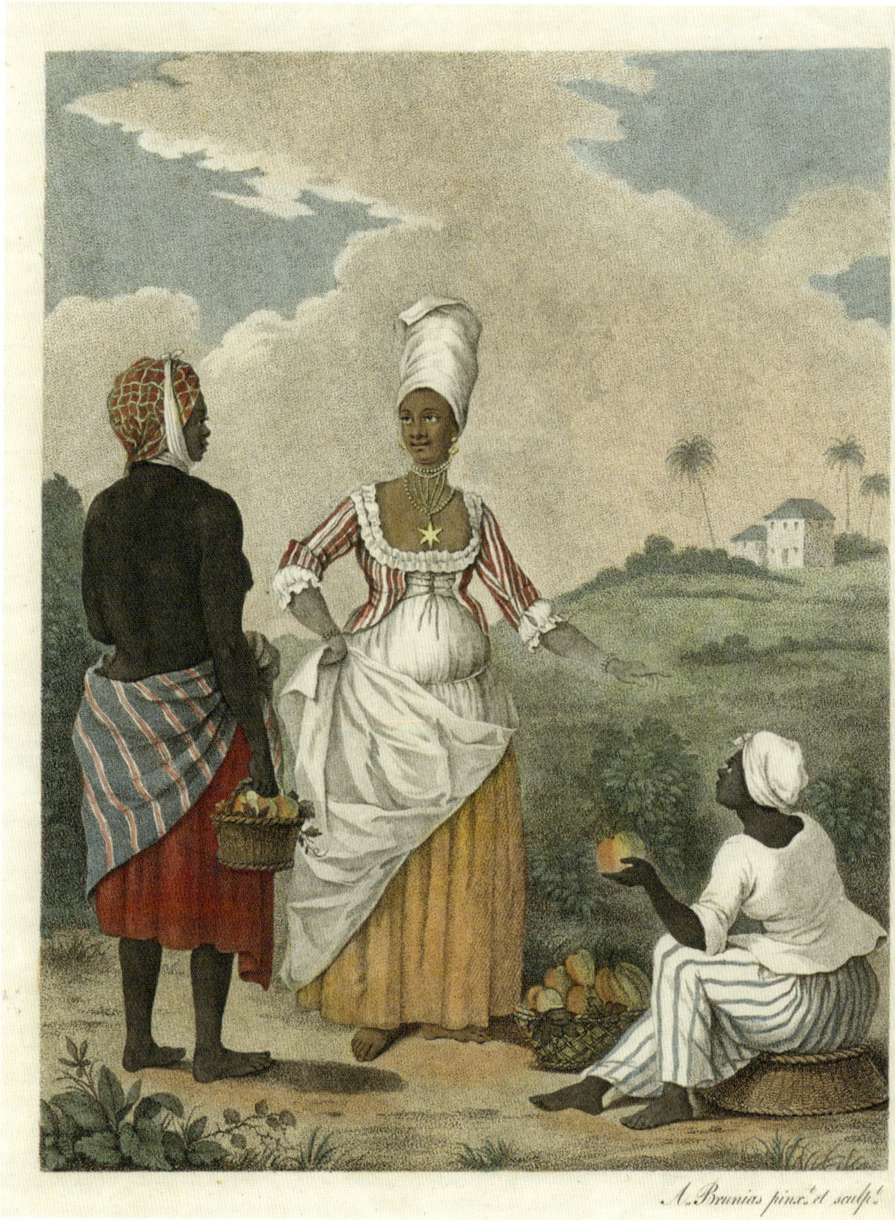

Women in Barbados

late 1770s, printed 1810

Agostino Brunias
Italian, 1730–1796, active in Britain

Stipple engraving and etching with hand coloring on wove paper
Sheet: 31.5 × 23.5 cm
(12³⁄₈ × 9¼ in.)
Schomburg Center for Research in Black Culture, New York Public Library, pre.x.225

Originally published under the title *The Barbadoes Mulatto Girl*, here reworked with Granny's patchwork quilt and a map of the Caribbean. The brutal iron collar around the neck of the woman at left was a typical instrument of punishment inflicted on enslaved people who tried to escape. She turns away from us, locking eyes with the central figure, a woman of mixed race who wears an elaborate star necklace and, in a distinctly creole twist, a head

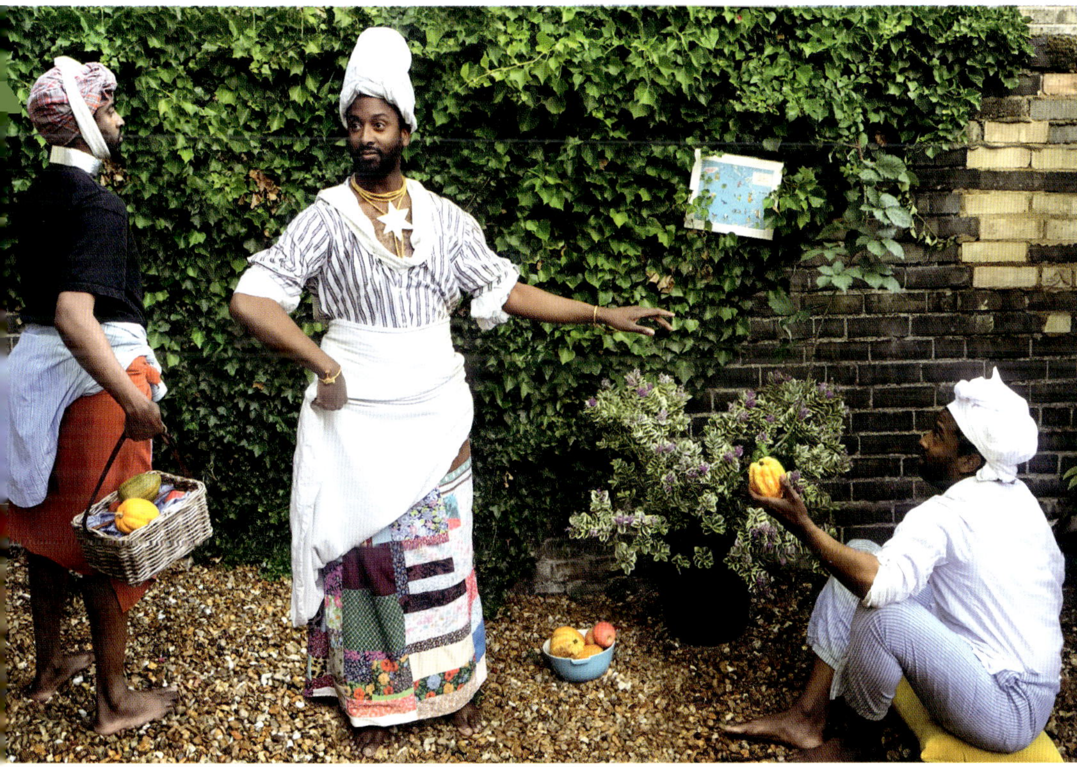

Act 2

wrap resembling the West African *gele*. Her pose and gesture imply that she bears some sort of power over the other two women. The seated figure holds up a large citrus fruit known as a pomelo. All three women wear striped fabrics, viewed at that time as a sign of imprisonment or enslavement. In the distance, on a hill, appears the plantation's great house. This image reminds us that the hierarchies established by Europeans in the Caribbean and the Americas were founded on painful stereotypes of colorism, misogyny, and sexual exploitation.

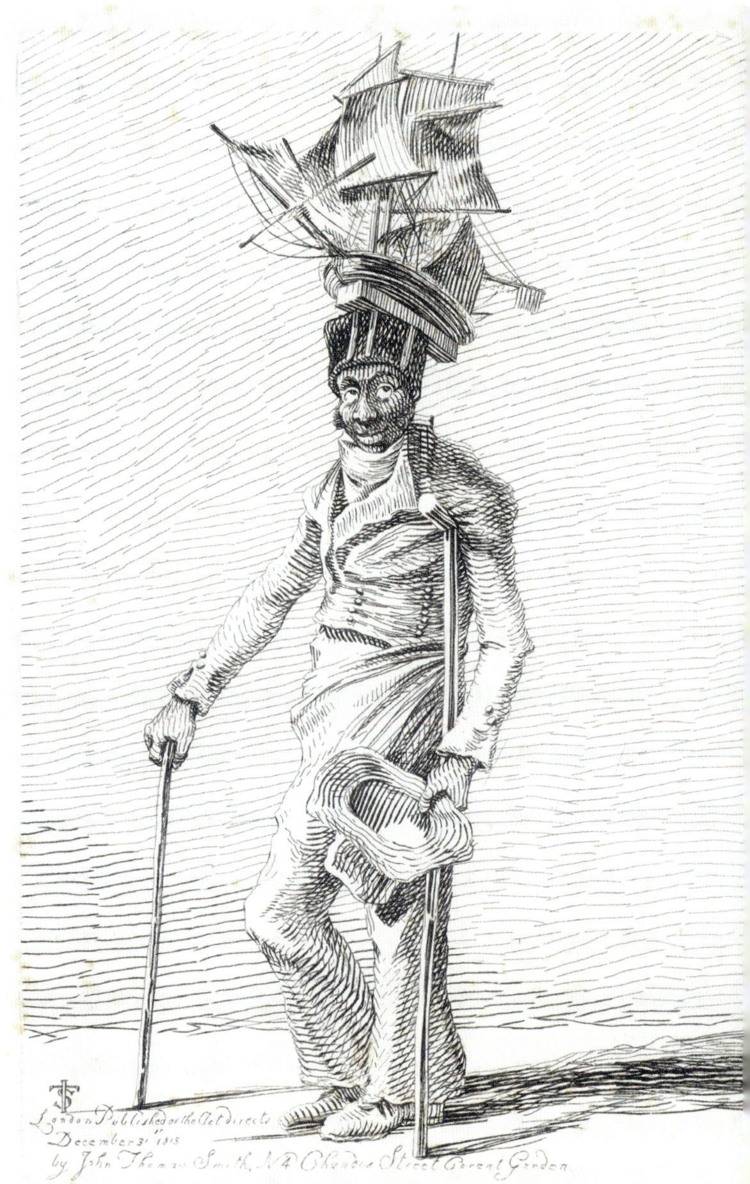

Joseph Johnson

1815

John Thomas Smith
British, 1766–1833

In *Vagabondiana*, 1817
Etching on paper
Sheet: 42.1 × 27.3 cm
(16 9/16 × 10 3/4 in.)
London, Victoria and
Albert Museum, E.3453-1902

Reworked with cardboard, a mop, and an Afro-print flag. A Black man stands crookedly, supporting his twisted body with a crutch under one arm and a stick in the other. He holds a shabby hat while an enormous model of a ship perches precariously on his head. Discharged from the British Merchant Navy after being wounded, Johnson was not entitled to a seaman's pension, nor could he claim an allowance from the parish because he was

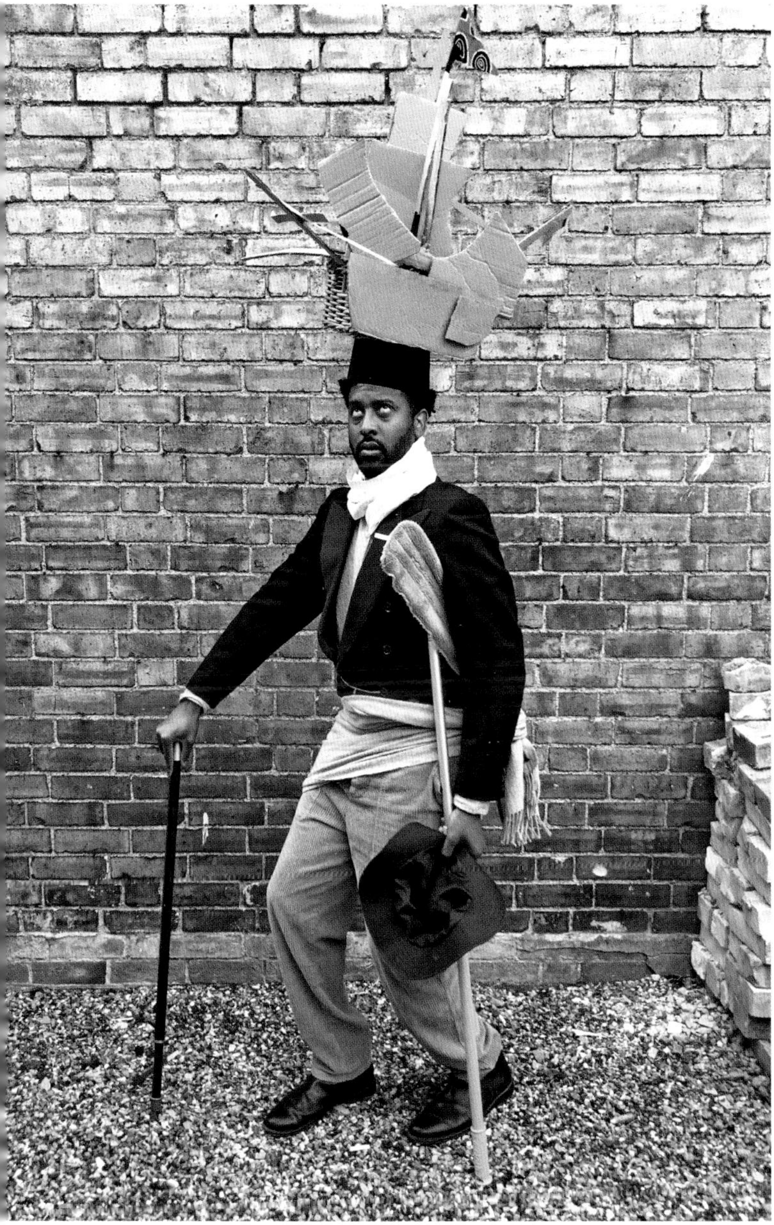

Act 2

born abroad. So he had little choice but to take to the streets. The ship on his head recalls the elaborate headwear worn to this day in Junkanoo festivals across the Caribbean. Contemporary accounts describe how Johnson sang nautical songs while giving "the appearance of sea-motion." But these carnivalesque performances were colored by the shadow of slavery. By the end of the eighteenth century, there were more than a million enslaved Africans in the British Caribbean colonies. Surely the symbolism of a Black man "belowdecks" was not lost on the Londoners who witnessed his act.

TOP

"Cotton," Norwich

ca. 1823

BOTTOM

Black Charley, Norwich

1823

John Dempsey
British, 1802/3–1877

In *A Folio of British Street Portraits*, 1824–44
Watercolor
32 × 23 cm ($12\frac{5}{8}$ × 9 in.);
31.5 × 22.7 cm ($12\frac{3}{8}$ × $8\frac{15}{16}$ in.)
Hobart, Tasmanian Museum and Art Gallery

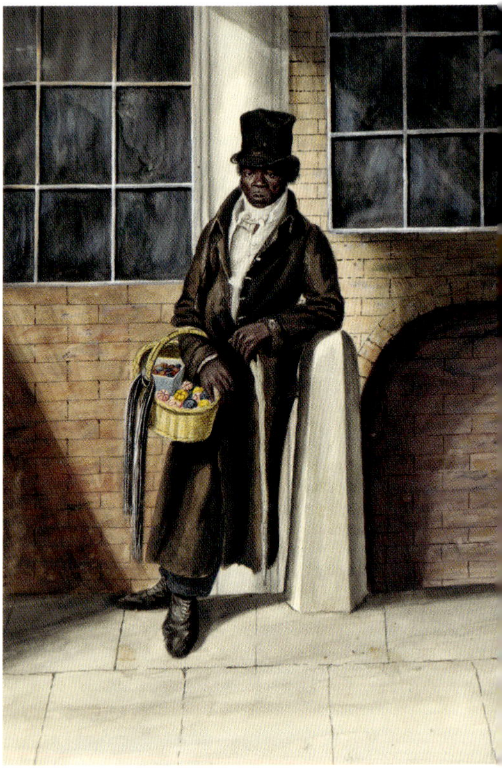

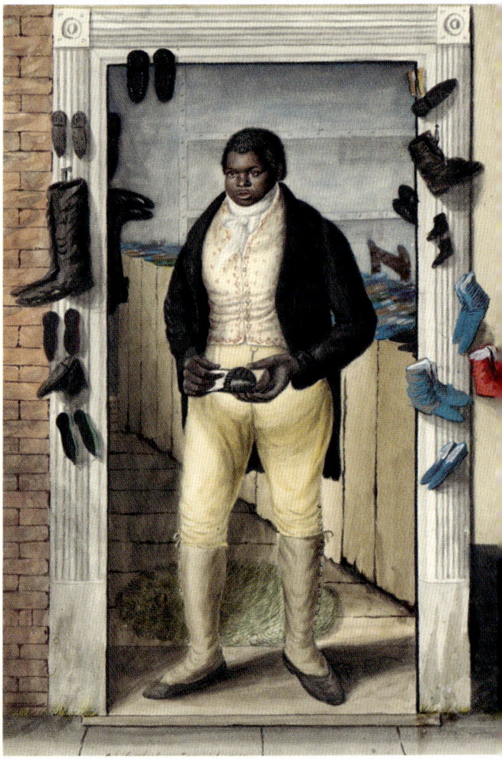

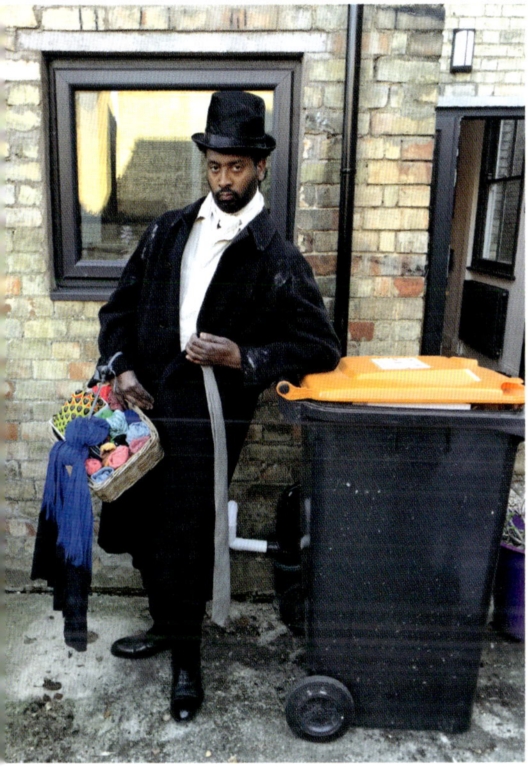

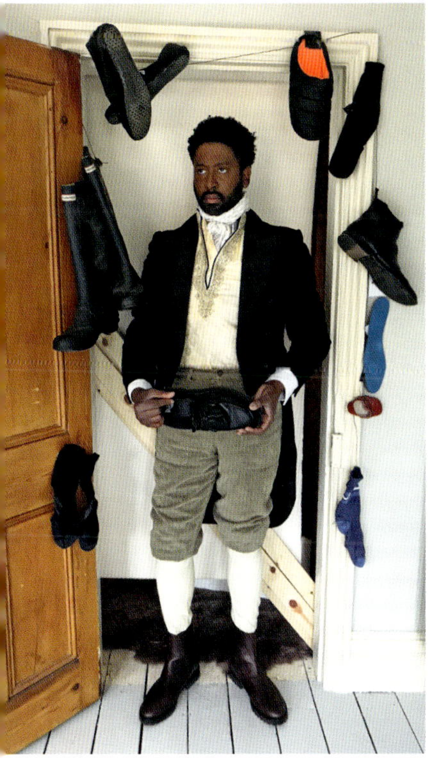

The original artworks come from Dempsey's extensive folio of the British working class. The itinerant tradesman known as Cotton sold haberdashery on the streets of Norwich, England, during the 1820s; his likeness is reworked with a recycling bin and swatches of West African prints in a basket. The other portrait, reworked with an array of footwear that includes my red baby shoe, is thought to depict Charles Willis Yearly, who sold secondhand shoes in Norwich. Neither servants nor enslaved, Cotton and Charley effectively puncture the myth of Georgian England's homogeneity. Captured in the doorway of his shop, Charley wears an embroidered waistcoat, a double-breasted coat, and a starched cravat tied with a flourish that lends an air of superiority. Breeches were somewhat old-fashioned by the 1820s, which suggests that either Dempsey painted Charley at an earlier date or, like the shoes hanging from the door frame, his outfit was secondhand. I wonder whether Charley's disproportionately large hands might be Dempsey's not-so-subtle way of illustrating that Charley not only sold shoes but perhaps also made and mended them.

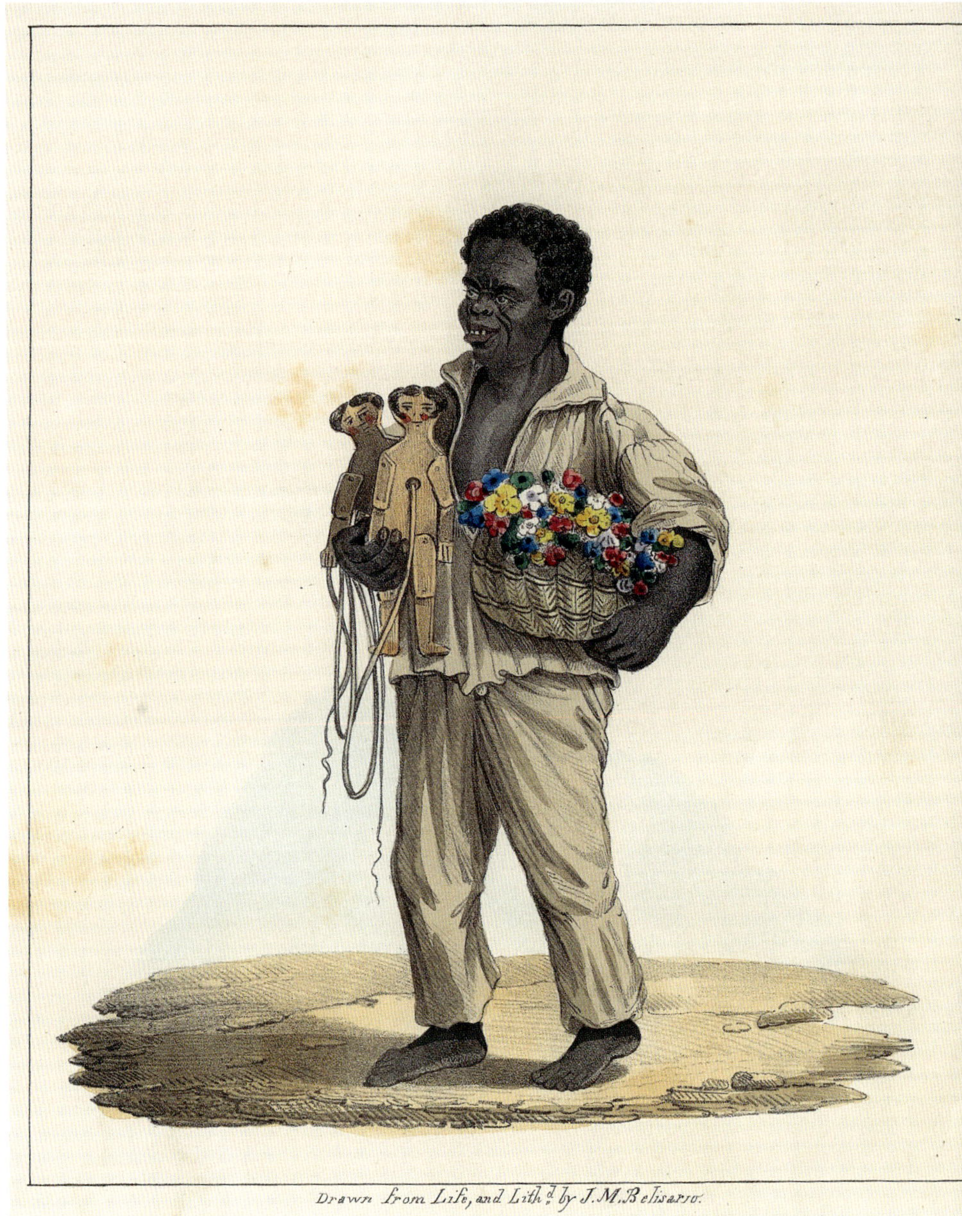

Lovey

1837

Isaac Mendes Belisario
Jamaican, 1795–1849

In *Sketches of Character in Illustration of the Habits, Occupation, and Costume of the Negro Population in the Island of Jamaica, Drawn from Nature, and in Lithography*
Hand-colored lithograph
Sheet: 37.5 × 27.3 cm (14¾ × 10¾ in.)
New Haven, Connecticut,
Yale Center for British Art,
Folio A 2011 24

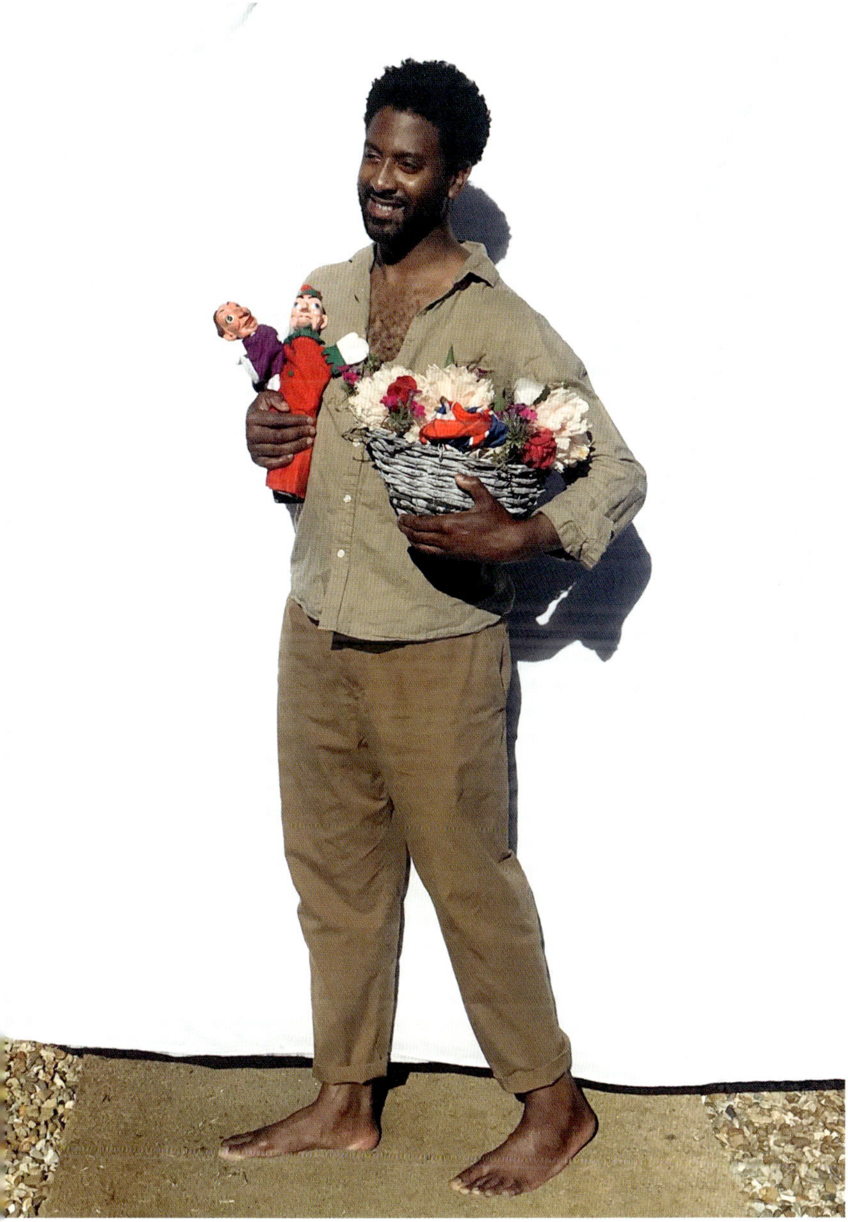

Act 2

A barefoot street performer carries wooden puppets and a basket of flowers. Reworked with Punch and Judy puppets. In a description accompanying this lithograph, Belisario, a white, Jamaica-born artist, writes that his subject was born in Kongo, where he was called Kangga. In 1803, Kangga was baptized and given the name Louis. “For reasons only known to himself,” says Belisario, this man “assumed the appellation of Lovey.” Perhaps by choosing a new name, Lovey was exerting his limited agency in a society ruled by the commodification of Black bodies. When Belisario drew Lovey, slavery had been abolished in Jamaica. Under the so-called apprenticeship system, however, formerly enslaved people aged six and up on August 1, 1834, the date abolition took effect, were bound in service to their former oppressors for at least four more years. Belisario’s *Sketches* contributed to the enduring myth that the Black population was happy in their enslavement.

Peter Brathwaite's interventions offer a passport back and into art history. They help us navigate, interrogate, isolate, pause, and slow down the moments in time and in place where the Black subject has been made visible. Brathwaite invites us, through his restagings, to consider broader questions concerning Black presence in Western visual culture. His photographic constructions tease out the who, what, why, and when of Black portraiture, wherein lie many unresolved and nuanced questions. Whether Brathwaite is restaging a specific section or the full content of a painting, he is doing vital cultural work: he

The Imagined Museum

A Conversation about Erasure, Encounter, and Entanglement

Mark Sealy and Peter Brathwaite

embodies his Black subjects as centered, sentient people rather than objectified bodies locked out of the grand narratives of history. He resurrects these subjects and releases them into our now. When they are known or recognizable, as in paintings or etchings portraying the brilliant revolutionary Toussaint Louverture, they are elevated further in our consciousness. When their identity is unknown, Brathwaite infuses them with a new sense of agency, preventing them from being eclipsed by the presence of others. I spoke with the artist in the summer of 2021 to learn more about his motivations and practice. —Mark Sealy

MARK SEALY Peter, it's a pleasure to discuss the work you've been making. It's interesting that you start by picking through moments in history, all the way back to the Domesday Book, that seminal document in the formation of English identity. Here we have this incredible image of you "hanging" on a letter in the book (p. 102).

PETER BRATHWAITE I'm delighted to be speaking with you, Mark. I'd had no idea there was someone who looked like me in that book! The slightly haphazard way in which I encountered each image meant that I didn't find this one until about halfway through the project.

MS It's quite painful if you look at the detail of it. It's almost as if the letter of the Domesday Book is lynching the Black subject.

PB I was a bit taken aback by the clenched teeth. He really seems to be hanging on for his life.

Someone asked me recently, "What have you learned by embodying these characters?" One big thing is the inherent trauma attached to so many of these images. Stepping into them means that I inevitably end up living aspects of the pain. So I deliberately search for joy and humor too. That's my coping mechanism for approaching this art.

MS So much of Western art is about standing in front of something and reviewing it rather than feeling it. But if you spend more time with some of these images, you begin to feel a sense of embodiment in different times and places. What I love about photography and painting is the silence of the moment that happens in that space.

PB With my interpretations, I think generally people read the humor first and then unravel what's bubbling underneath, observing the steps and moments of stillness that go into the making of these re-creations. I like to imagine that the signposts I provide help people relate to my own work of decoding the original artworks. For me, this process is a bit like reading a score. I'm looking for the subtext, and reading what the composer has given me, and mapping out how to interpret it.

MS Our ideas of who we are can't be separated from the erasure that happens through culture. Black individuals in history—Black lives matter, but they've also been erased. What I like about this project is that these bite-size moments are sort of like jazz. When you look at them, they go off, Coltrane-like, in all sorts of directions, and each one has the capacity to open up different systems of knowledge that connect the dots of the picture in new ways. In that respect, one of the most successful reconstructions, I think, is Diego Velázquez's *Kitchen Maid with the Supper at Emmaus* (ca. 1617–18, pp. 34–35).

PB That was quite challenging to put together. When I was looking at the original painting,

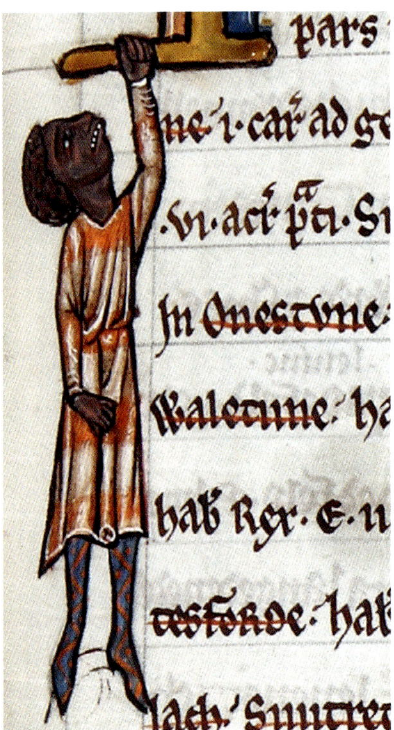

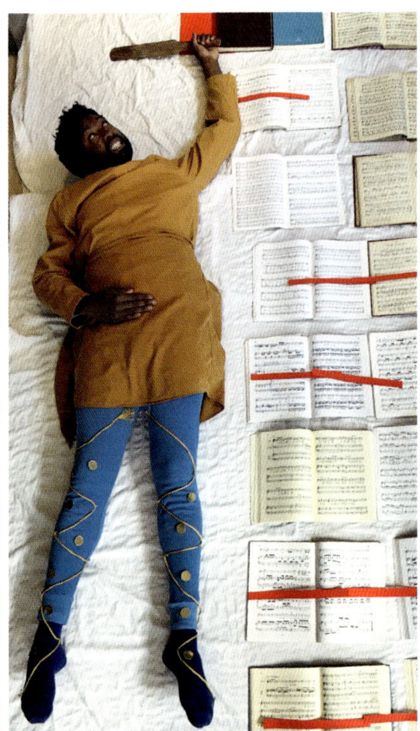

◄◄
Initial I, in *Abbreviatio of Domesday*, ca. 1241. Illumination and gilding on parchment, folio: 34.7 × 24.5 cm (13¾ × 9¾ in.). Kew, England, National Archives, E 36/284 f.196

◄
Re-creation by Peter Brathwaite

I was drawn to the darkness. I was trying to decipher the woman's emotional state—whether she knew what was going on behind her and who those people were. It was incredibly difficult to shrink myself into her pose, and all the time I was trying to understand her relationship to what was happening over her shoulder. Which meant I had to find something to stand in for what I was "seeing" through the back of my head. I chose Johann Sebastian Bach's *Saint John Passion*, which, to me, is perfection in music. It is also an articulation of faith and my relationship with faith. Then in front of me are domestic, *earthly* things. The pot is a gift from my mum. I couldn't stop it from gleaming as much as it does. It's funny how the dynamics of an image are altered by what's available.

MS What pulls you into this moment is that it's seemingly so quiet. Here's a Black maid in the kitchen (welcome to our world!). But then you've got this incredible aspect behind: Christ appears to the disciples. The radical theatricality of that is brilliant. Then there's this pot, which almost becomes Christ's presence, made manifest through this present from your mother, which is, in a sense, life itself.

PB When I look back at these images, sometimes it's hard to distinguish what was improvised and what was intentional.

MS We know that some artists, like William Hogarth, used Black subjects in their paintings to refer to some kind of transgression. But the way that you've made this, instead of being a sideshow, she's center stage.

PB Yes, and specifically someone of mixed heritage. The work's traditional Spanish title describes her using the derogatory term "mulatto." It is a label that scars my heritage, and something I must unpick whenever I'm looking into the archive at family names. I was very much wanting to give her presence and agency, and shed these terms of classification and stratification. There's a lot about hierarchy here, especially hierarchy in the face of the divine.

MS It does feel as if this person in the kitchen is about to sing, as people often do. Aretha Franklin singing "Amazing Grace." People often say that images speak to us. This one, you could argue, is a metaphor for racism: Why do I have to deal with what you put on the table? It's got nothing to do with me, really. This isn't mine. Why am I having to speak to your problem all the time? The great philosopher Emmanuel Levinas basically says: If I look into a face and don't take responsibility, if I refuse to see the other, then that's when violence happens. I have to make you my equal. Then it becomes impossible for me to harm you. I have to take care of you. I think by restaging these portraits and offering up these subjects, whether named or unnamed, you are inviting us to take care. Jasper Becx's *Don Miguel de Castro: Emissary of Kongo* (ca. 1643, pp. 40–41), for instance. When was the last time you conjured up in your mind an image of Belgium's reign in the Congo and saw someone like Don Miguel?

PB I love that portrait so much, and his attendants as well (p. 104). They illustrate how

Blackness and Black identity refuse to be shoved into one single category. These images, assembled, burst out of the series like a jack-in-the-box. They help to deconstruct imperial narratives.

MS It's like you're dropping a hot molecule into this cool European world of understanding who's worthy of being seen and who's not. This portrait sets things bubbling around a little bit. It unpicks in one smart move the legacy of those violent and debasing images that have been propagated from day one of the colonial encounter. Here is this global person who travels, speaks different languages, is cultured, is doing important diplomatic and trade work.

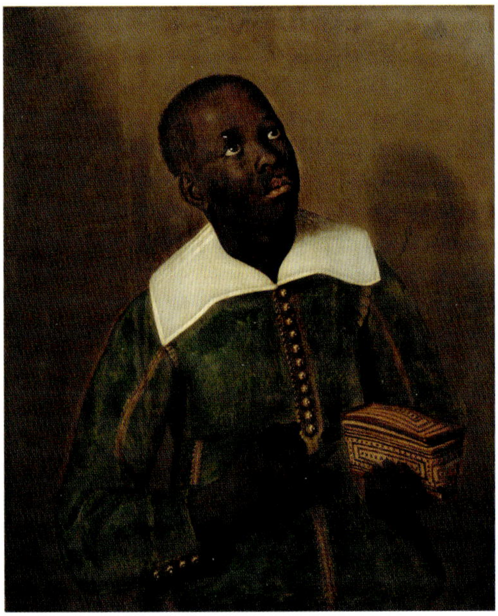

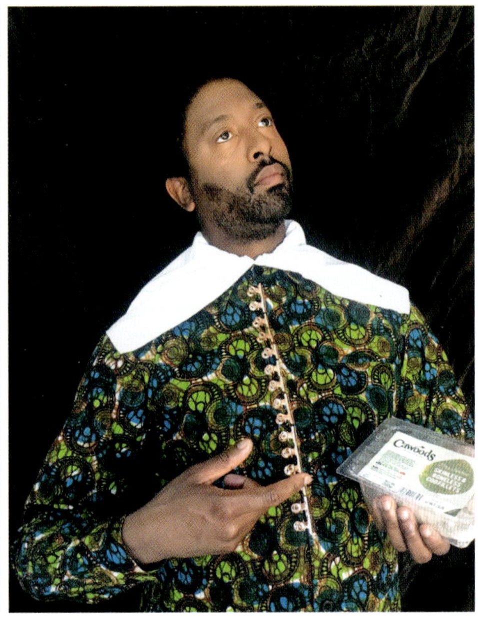

◄◄

Attributed to Jasper Becx or Albert Eckhout, *Diego Bemba, a Servant of Don Miguel de Castro*, 1641–45. Oil on panel, 75 × 62 cm (29½ × 24½ in.). Copenhagen, Statens Museum for Kunst, KMS9

◄

Re-creation by Peter Brathwaite

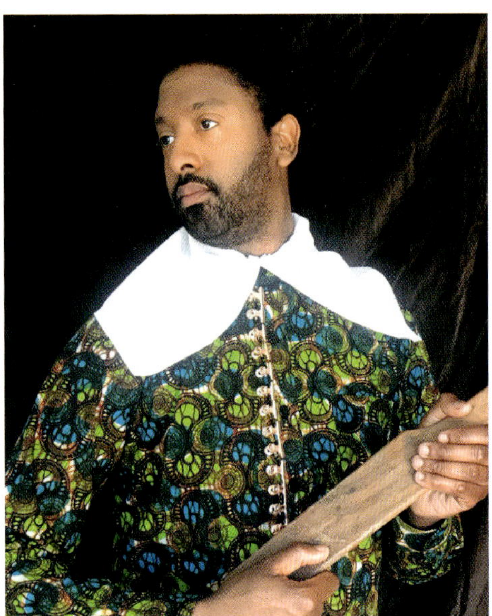

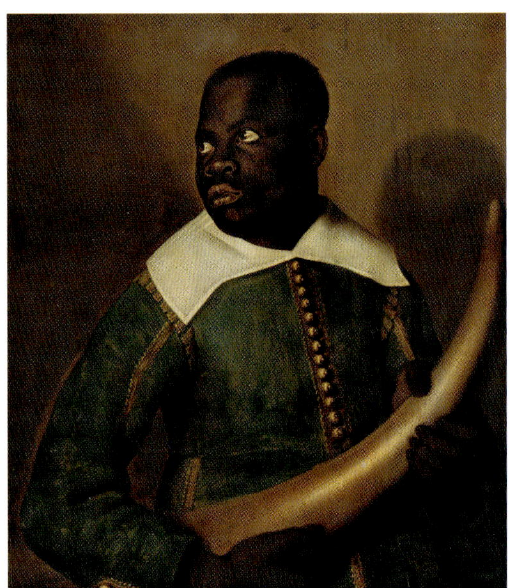

◄◄

Re-creation by Peter Brathwaite

◄

Attributed to Jasper Becx or Albert Eckhout, *Pedro Sunda, a Servant of Don Miguel de Castro*, 1641–45. Oil on panel, 75 × 62 cm (29½ × 24½ in.). Copenhagen, Statens Museum for Kunst, KMS8

It contradicts images of "savages" circulated by missionaries, and it amplifies the genocidal violence of the 1884–85 Berlin Conference, where the scramble for Africa began. There are triggers at work here. Each one of these images is like a loaded gun.

PB It's funny: when I got to fifty re-creations, I wasn't sure whether I was going to carry on.

MS You hit fifty during lockdown?

PB Probably around June or July of 2020.

MS There was a lot of anxiety around that time, wasn't there? I was deeply worried in the spring. Friends were becoming ill and we were starting to get a bit claustrophobic. That's when you did the early seventeenth-century *Allegory of the Sense of Smell* (pp. 42–43).

PB I found it fascinating that a Black subject was chosen to represent the sense of smell.

MS There's an uncomfortable correlation between something that should smell nice, the flowers, and this Black character, whose expression offers something menacing and grotesque.

PB This painting was made in the early seventeenth century, around the time Barbados became a British colony. I'm reminded that in Barbados's capital, Bridgetown, enslaved people who tried to escape were confined to an outdoor public holding cell known as The Cage. Their presence there, once they'd been caught, was announced in the newspapers so their enslavers could come and collect them. The Cage ended up being moved from the city center because the smell was so overpowering—the runaways were left there in their own filth.

MS On the surface, these flowers should be beautifully uplifting. But underneath the seeming pleasantness of this moment lies a history of violence. There's an anguish in the faces. All the things you have that are pleasant—all your tobacco, your sugar, these flowers—if I could only have the luxury of being able to enjoy the smell. That is an incredibly transgressive positioning of the Black subject, helping us understand that he feels very uncomfortable.

PB It's an impossible image in many ways. There is no way to imagine a smell that is good or beautiful.

MS Yes, almost the antithesis of the maid. I do like the ones where there's a high chiaroscuro. You have to forgive me because I'm drawn to the things that unhinge us a bit—dark and violent things. One of my mantras is to ask. What's the work this artwork is doing? I think this one is offering an unsavory wager. What's savory to you is unsavory to me, because what's savory to you is painful for me.

Let's talk about the big still life with the servant and the parrot (pp. 46–47). What a mad construction, right? There's so much to unpack in terms of what is going on here: reworked clip-on birds, West African print, salt fish, hot pepper sauce.

PB You'll notice Richard Ligon's book *A True and Exact History of the Island of Barbadoes* (1657) near the bottom in the restaging. In Ligon's travelogue are scenes describing a lavish lunch on the plantation of the enslaver James Drax, who "lived like a king." The party have eaten so much, they can barely move from the table. A punch is brought out at the end of the meal, and it's full of sugar and has boiled eggs floating in it. All the while, the enslaved people are laboring in the fields and sugar works. These seventeenth-century "banquet pieces" provide an opportunity to bring all of this historic imagery to the table now. It's the past, it's the present, it's where I'm going and where I come from.

MS This is why I would push back hard on people thinking your work is simply playful. On the surface you're smiling, but this is very dark historical stuff. What I also think is crucial is that when people say you're from the Caribbean, the experience of being on Jamaica, Barbados, Haiti, Martinique, et cetera, from the tip of Florida to the tip of Venezuela, is in fact a huge arc of histories and colonies. They were all in there—the Dutch, the French, the Spanish, the Brits.

PB In Barbados, the English built a society predicated on violence and the economy of violence. That's something I still grapple with: how this economy of violence became the norm and was maintained for centuries. It was normal to walk past someone who had been tortured.

MS Or held in a cage. In Barbados, the Church of England branded its slaves.

PB Unfortunately, my family has a very close relationship to that specific history—my white enslaver ancestor John Brathwaite was the lessee of the Codrington Plantations, owned by the Church of England's Society for the Propagation of the Gospel in Foreign Parts. On these plantations, enslaved people were branded with hot irons with the word "Society"—and at the same time the Church preached sermons saying that Black people and white people were equal.

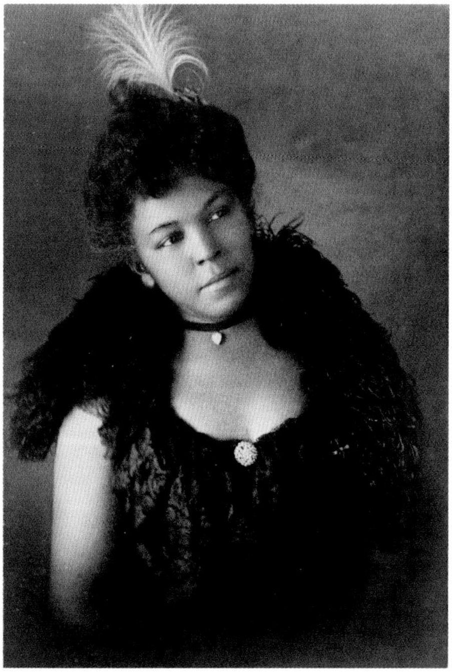

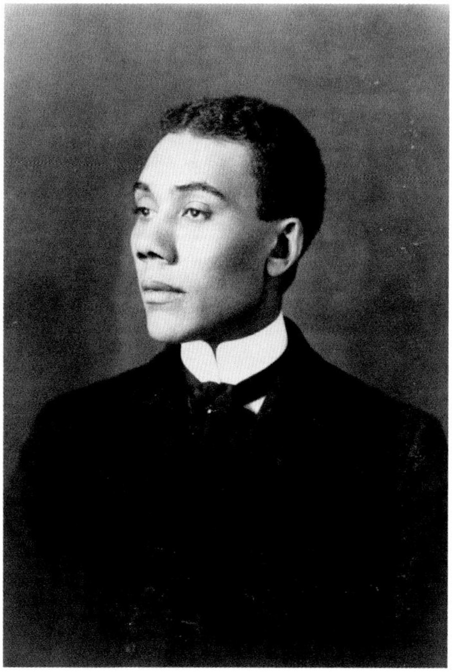

◄ Portraits in W. E. B. Du Bois's *Types of American Negroes*, vol. 1, 1900. Gelatin silver prints, each 9.8 × 4.1 cm (3⅞ × 1⅝ in.). Washington, DC, Library of Congress, Division of Prints and Photographs, LOT 11930 nos. 73, 58

MS We need to be very careful about bringing back the ghosts. I was thinking recently about W. E. B. Du Bois at the 1900 Paris Exposition, where he exhibited portraits of African Americans to give greater understanding of what Black subjects look like (p. 106). I often cite him as one of the first Black photography curators. All he was trying to say is: Look, Black lives matter. We have wealth, we have strength, we have complexity, we're not just one shade, not just one subject. We are fully civilized and equal to you. The tragedy is, we're still doing that work. We're still producing portraiture that tries to tell people we matter, we have a history, we have love, we have pleasure and pain, we have creativity.

PB In a sense, I'm trying to expose this exceptionally long history of suppression. In my musical practice, I'm constantly looking for works that have been previously suppressed or banned. It's about restorative justice. This is me shaking and rattling all those things that were gotten rid of or silenced.

MS That's an important point. You have a voice, obviously, but what's happened over the course of this project is that it's become a visual thing. This need to speak to the past has become a reinterpretation of its images. We can only read the past through the lens of our time. One important thing about objects from the past, whether they're paintings or something else, is that if we reanimate them today, we're in dialogue with them still, rather than fixing them in the time of their making. They become tools we can work with. European history wants to bury these characters, but if you bring them forward, we can have a conversation now about who we are.

PB We need allyship.

MS As Stuart Hall said, "We're only here because you were there." That's the trade-off. When the "us" and "them" becomes "we." Because everything we're talking about here has to do with encounter and entanglement. The work shouts very clearly and loudly that you can't deny this entanglement.

PB I think that's how I made the leap from my own ancestry to this larger narrative of entanglement. There are things in my history that I cannot walk away from.

MS Other artists are puncturing and punctuating these histories in a similar way. Yinka

▼
Yinka Shonibare CBE (British, b. 1962), *Untitled (Effnik)*, 1996. Chromogenic print, 112 × 91.5 cm (44 × 36 in.). Private collection

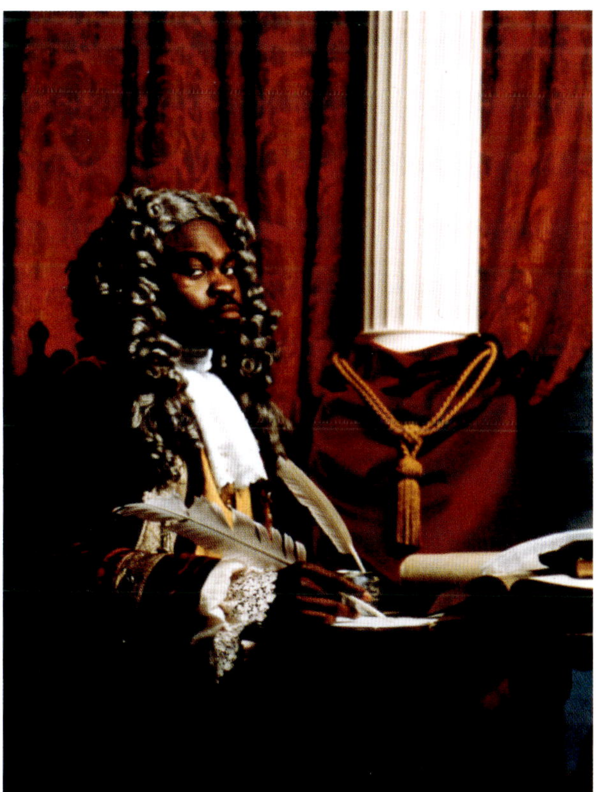

Shonibare has made pieces where he dresses up as a Black character in full fifteenth- or sixteenth-century regalia (p. 107). Omar Victor Diop as well (p. 150). Many artists are still working through the past. Imagine a museum where the majority of faces look like this. Imagine if we were to go around the hallowed neoclassical architecture of a National Portrait Gallery and they had accumulated all these works and exhibited them as a simple, everyday experience—a permanent show. Maybe that's what this project is: an imagined museum made real, where you can enjoy the complexities of Black life as an everyday thing. This is what's so radical about your work in the digital realm. You've curated a space to play out the transformative theater of Black narratives in the everyday.

PB Yes, by just presenting what is there.

MS Let's talk about Toussaint Louverture (pp. 90–91, 109). I think we do ourselves a disservice by not focusing on Haiti as the revolutionary epicenter of Black resistance. It's a brilliant reconstruction. The sense of anticipation in your face, in his face.

PB I was connecting with the shock waves that were broadcast through the Caribbean by the Haitian Revolution (1791–1804). The news traveled far and wide about how the enslaved population of Haiti drove out the British and the French and set up the first Black republic. Enslaved people were never passive; they were actively challenging their status as chattel, as property, and driving the abolitionist movement. That is something that's important to clarify and recognize in our shared history. Black people in the Caribbean were resisting in various ways: secretly speaking their Indigenous languages, performing previously banned African rituals like leaving sacred offerings of food at burial sites, dancing and drumming, or on the surface appearing to accept Christianity while covertly practicing their own religions.

In Barbados, Bussa's Rebellion (1816), named after the enslaved man who is acknowledged as the leader of the uprising, showed the actions enslaved Africans were willing to take to secure their freedom. Beginning in my ancestral parish of Saint Philip, it was Barbados's largest insurrection. Sugarcane fields were set alight on about half of the island. The uprising was brutally quashed and declared unsuccessful by the enslaver class, but when you interrogate imperial sources, it is clear to see just how much it destabilized Barbados's plantation society. It's also a history that shatters the commonly held myth that enslaved people in Barbados were especially "docile." The rebellions of enslaved individuals in colonies across the Caribbean are potent reminders of the very long history of Black resistance to white supremacy.

MS Whenever I think of Toussaint and Haiti, I always come to the idea that freedom will have to be fought for; it's not going to be given.

PB It's interesting you should say that, because the papers I'm holding in my hand are my great-great-great-great-grandfather's manumission papers. Addo Brathwaite was granted his freedom in the wake of the revolt in Barbados in reward for good conduct. We don't know exactly what this good conduct entailed, but quite possibly it involved protecting his white enslavers during the uprising. Which is a complicated history. There are different levels of resistance as well as different aspects of resistance.

MS Different aspects of survival. Survival is complicated. You might not always be at home with the things you have to do or say.

PB I suppose that's what influenced my decision to use certain props—it's relocating that resistance, that survival, that quest for freedom into the domestic sphere. The vacuum cleaner signals the fact that my great-times-four-grandfather is referred to in family records as a "favorite house slave." He was seventy-three at the point when he acquired his freedom, having endured the Middle Passage and lived most of his life enslaved. There are so many unanswered questions. We can only hypothesize about the

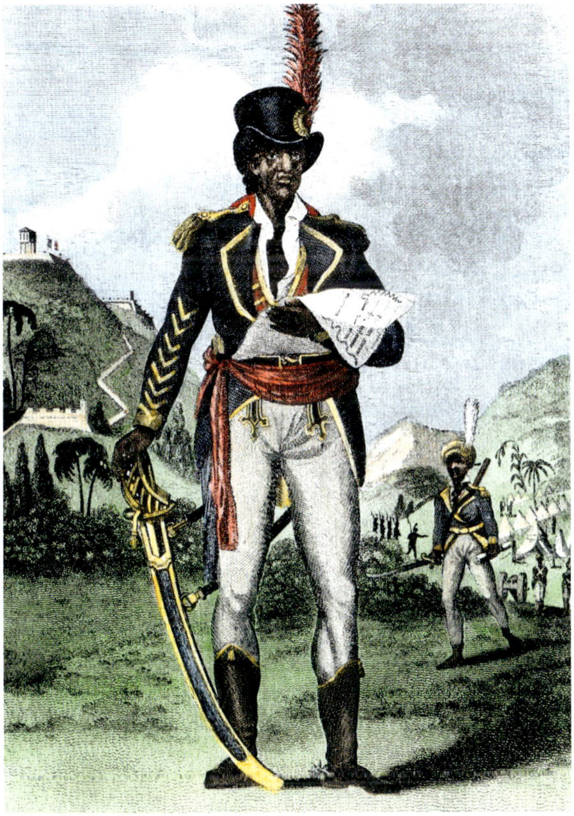

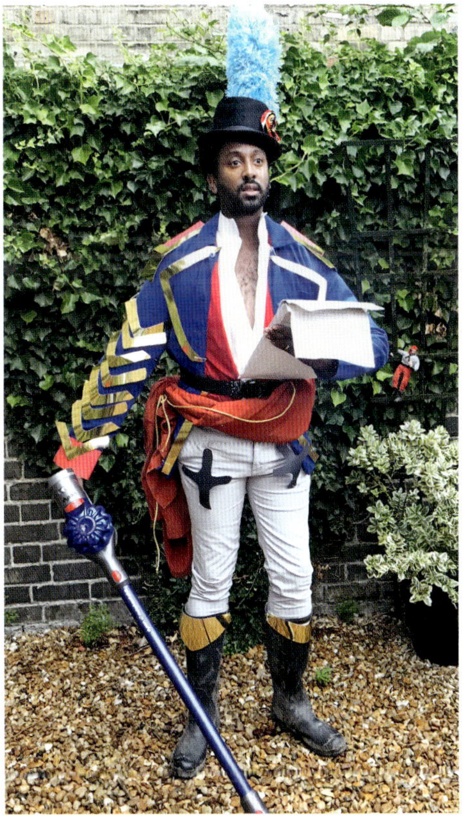

▸ Toussaint Louverture, in Marcus Rainsford, *An Historical Account of the Black Empire of Hayti* (London: Albion Press, 1805). Hand-colored engraving, sheet: 23 × 16.9 cm (9 × 6¾ in.). North Wind Picture Archives

▸▸ Re-creation by Peter Brathwaite

reasons my ancestor was granted his freedom and whether he supported the insurrection.

MS This is what we mean by allowing the Black imagination to run free throughout this history. At seventy-three, he's pretty resilient. He's survived. He's done the hard time. What do you do in this position? Do you join the revolution or do you play the long game? Are you selling out or are you surviving? Which brings me to your version of Alice Neel's *Black Man* (1966, pp. 136–37). It's almost as if this person is about to speak.

PB He's obviously very comfortable in his own skin—the slight lean to one side, his left hand positioned as if to reinforce something he's about to say.

MS A calm response is about to come to someone who needs correction. You think you know who I am through this title, *Black Man*? You think you've heard me? The gesture alone is very political.

PB I find that a lot with these images. It's playing with the idea of being present but not. What are we really seeing?

MS It almost begins to collapse time. This could be now, obviously, but it's the height of the civil rights movement. Well, we've been fighting for a long time. Fifty years on, we're still having this dialogue around the Black subject having a voice. That Black man is the Black person we want in the room, right?

PB Of course.

MS That leads us nicely to Sonia Boyce's *Rice n Peas* (1982, pp. 142–43). We can't talk about Caribbean or African food without rice and peas! I've heard people argue over rice and peas—the right way, the wrong way.

▼ (left)
Kehinde Wiley (American, b. 1977), *Le Roi a la Chasse*, 2006. Oil on canvas, 243.8 × 182.9 cm (96 × 72 in.). Courtesy Sean Kelly, New York

▼ (right)
Re-creation by Peter Brathwaite

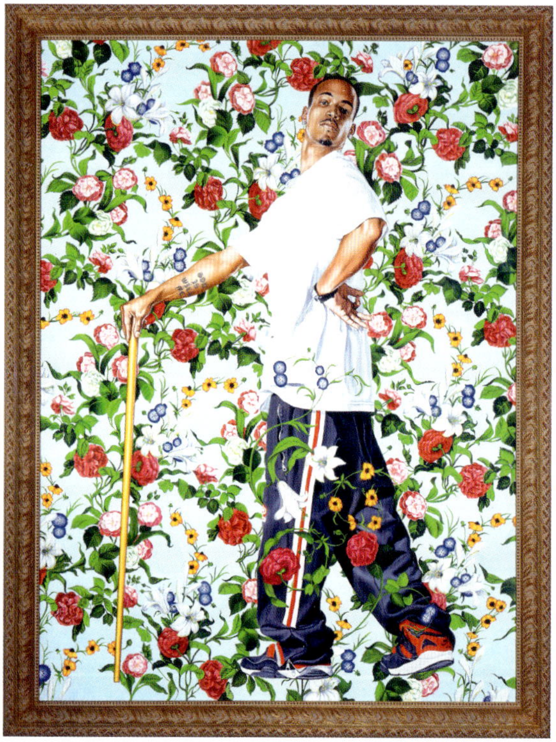

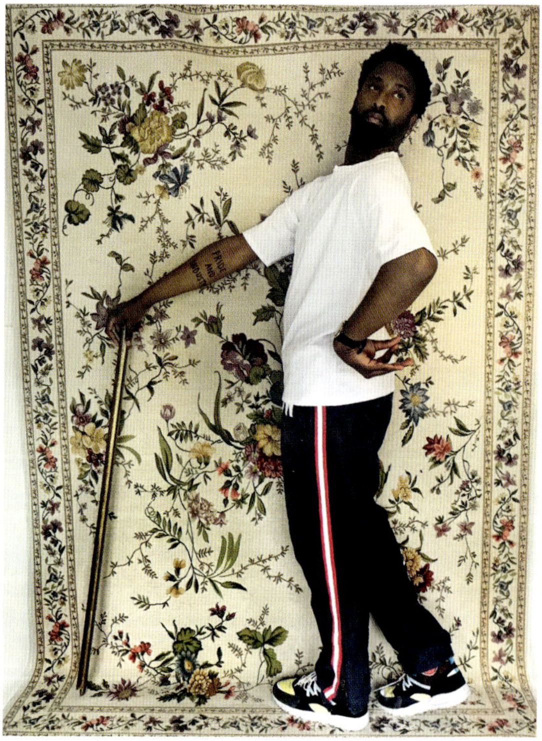

PB Which peas—*gungo* or black-eyed?

MS Yes! I understand it's a self-portrait, but it comes with an inquiry. Do you get me? Do you understand what I'm trying to share with you here? There's an intensity you mirror quite well—that offstage, I-can-see-you-coming look. You're a stranger and you're welcome, but I'm not sure how close I'll let you get. This is like the antithesis of *Black Man*.

PB There's a wariness and a weariness in this piece. I wanted to re-create it because I immediately identified with this idea of keeping a certain part of yourself private. It's a common thread in the Black British experience—keeping certain bits of yourself for yourself and your kin. The recipes and the names of foodstuffs, whether they be Caribbean or British, are deeply personal but also a protective shield.

MS I feel the anxiety of parenting in the work's text: "My mother used to shout at me every mealtime because I ate so little, and so slowly." You and I have both spent time in Newcastle. Wallsend, where I grew up, has a lot of children living in poverty. To feed your children well is still a challenge for many people. The power of matriarchy is just oozing out of that Boyce artwork. It's interesting that you don't emphasize that in your reworking of it.

PB Actually, this re-creation was a tribute to my mum handing centuries-old Bajan recipes over to me. I've been frantically trying to learn how to make them. There is an urgency to preserve the recipes and memories, while also wanting to be shielded by them. These recipes have made the journey with us.

MS Underpinning this project are the economies of lives—how we remember them, how we celebrate them. We're trying to go back through time and present the value of the subjects' histories, from the everyday to the momentous. I think here of Kehinde Wiley's painting *Le Roi a la Chasse* (2006, p. 110), elevating the everyday subject in this glorious reconstruction of an old painting, now re-reconstructed by you.

PB There's something delightful about the idea of a re-re-creation. I got to know the Wiley before I saw the original Anthony van Dyck (left). Wiley uses models he encounters on the streets and invites into his studio. They choose the poses, the gestures. I've had some really dynamic conversations with young people about Wiley's work; they're inspired by the way he gives agency to all his sitters. Approaching Wiley's work is like coming full circle. It's so

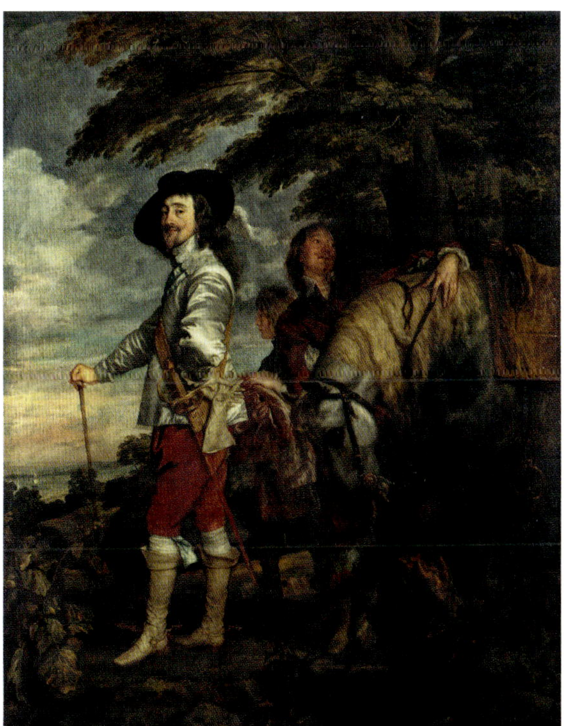

▼
Anthony van Dyck (Flemish, 1599–1641, active in England), *Charles I at the Hunt*, ca. 1635. Oil on canvas, 266 × 207 cm (104¾ × 81½ in.). Paris, Musée du Louvre, INV 1236

far away from some of the earlier artworks I've re-created. It seems to break out of itself, in a way.

MS Guess what can happen if you give Black people control and agency? We'll load ourselves onto the canvas. We won't be in the corner, we won't be at the margins, and we won't be some reimagined historical figure you fear. We'll take your history and flip it on its head. We'll take our everyday Black person and give them all the grace and grandeur of royalty. You don't just celebrate that; you amplify it as well. What this collection of portraits does is take audiences on an incredible political, cultural, historical, visual journey that helps people understand the importance of representational politics.

PB I'm looking right now at Kerry James Marshall's *A Portrait of the Artist as a Shadow of His Former Self* (1980, pp. 140–41). Both the re-creation and the original make me uneasy, but this is one of the most important pieces in the series. I watched as people engaged with it on social media, and it was obviously challenging for them. This is a full-on mask. It makes you grit your teeth. I wanted to put this in because it so clearly sums up this idea of being there but not. It's a study in black as a shade. We think of black as an absence of color, an absence of light, and that absence underpins the whole series, really.

MS Marshall's piece is incredibly complex and ties in to many of the things we've been talking about: having a voice, being seen, being heard, having a presence.

PB There's a white noise to it, ironically—a vibration that is unavoidable. For me, this work holds my own fears of reinforcing the colonial violence emitted by many of the images I choose to restage.

MS The politics of the project have uncomfortable undertones because of the work we have to do to push back, or push against, those histories.

PB There's a hollowness to this one that for me as a musician relates to the concept of "sonic Blackness"—the idea that a voice can sound Black. I'm really interested in this in terms of how, historically, the concept has been used to "other" or marginalize Black classical singers. I sense in the sitter's expression a comment about being reduced to a lack of whiteness.

MS It's like a play on Du Bois's double consciousness: this is the Black person that I know you are going to see, no matter what I present, because this is where I reside in your consciousness.

PB Yes, it's very exposing. And like all difficult history, it's not easy to digest. When people ask me what my favorite artworks in this project have been, I've become accustomed to saying *The Paston Treasure* (ca. 1665, pp. 48–49) or *Joseph Johnson* (1815, pp. 94–95). Those works resonate with me in a specific way, especially because there is music in both. But there's a different type of music at play in the Marshall that resonates deeply. Marshall has done all the work in his portrait; a lot of my re-creation is about stepping back to show that. I want you to be led by him and what his work is saying when you're viewing my work and this project.

MS I think we've got a long way to go before we can think of Ralph Ellison's *Invisible Man* (1952) as something from the past. Imagine reading that as a historical novel rather than one that feels relevant now. If we don't talk about individual images but rather about a body of representational fields—if you start to look at the images collectively—the restaging of the Black figure ties into a lineage of shouting, "I am here!" Part of your process is creating this affirmation, isn't it? Whether we like it or not, that's part of the work. Whether it's you performing onstage or replicating an old painting, we must constantly be hypervigilant about the impact of our person, whether real or restaged, on other people.

PB Because I'm a musician, I've got a special fondness for the portrait of Emmanuel Rio (p. 114), which was described as the portrait of "a gardener and horn player" when I originally found it. A few months later, in the wake of George Floyd's murder, the Art Institute of Chicago changed the title to include Emmanuel's name. We know that around age ten, this young man was sent to the court of Emperor Francis I in Vienna. He trained as a musician but experienced roadblocks: he went to a conservatory but was dismissed for lack of progress, then tried to make it as a musician in various ensembles but was sacked for being "disruptive." Embodying Emmanuel is traumatic because we're still having these conversations about representation in the arts, especially in classical music. But, that said, his name is now out there and his story is being told. He's no longer just an anonymous figure. Digging into these portraits and histories, I'm starting to see ripple effects and repercussions.

MS In terms of audience and reception of the work, I'm mindful that we also have a duty to think about pleasure. I think that does come through in your work.

PB Yes, there are many re-creations where I've suddenly stumbled across some aspect of pleasure and joy. In *The Paston Treasure*, for instance, I gave the young man a cou-cou stick carved by my grandfather Charles Richard Brathwaite. It's a small wooden cricket-bat–shaped cooking implement used to stir the national dish of Barbados, cou-cou, which is cornmeal cooked with okra and water. I celebrate this as preenslavement food—it made the voyage with us and was a regular meal for enslaved Africans in Barbados. It's a direct link with West Africa and the types of food the unnamed man in *The Paston Treasure* would have been familiar with. The original portrait is heavily curated to display the exotic items that the Paston family accumulated during their travels—including him, the young man, a commodity. Rather than him being there but not there, hidden in plain sight, I reimagine him tasting and savoring preenslavement freedoms.

MS There's a lot of food in this project, isn't there? And lots of gardens and flowers. That makes complete sense, in that many of these

▼ (left)
Albert Schindler (Austrian,1805–1861), *Portrait of Emmanuel Rio*, 1836. Oil on panel, 39 × 31.7 cm ($15\frac{3}{8} \times 12\frac{1}{2}$ in.). Art Institute of Chicago, 2005.153

▼ (right)
Re-creation by Peter Brathwaite

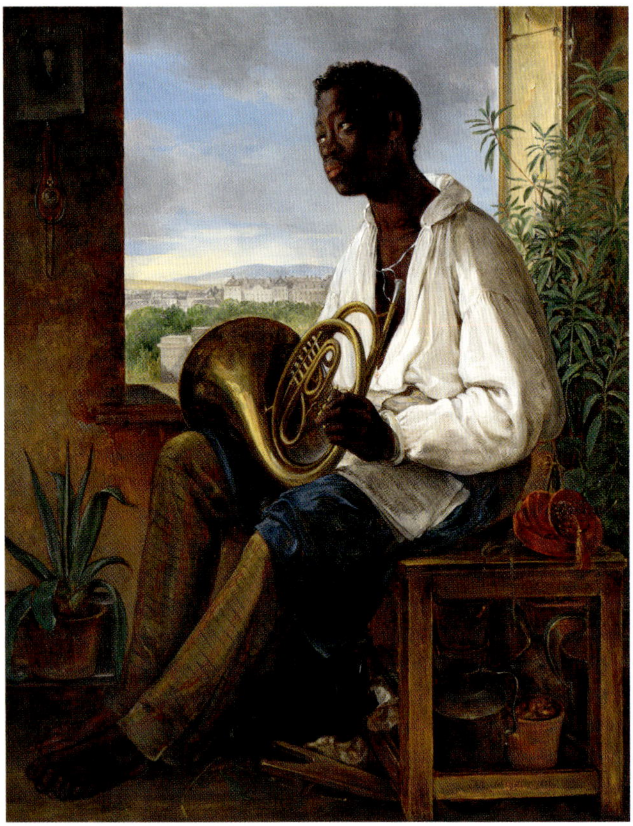

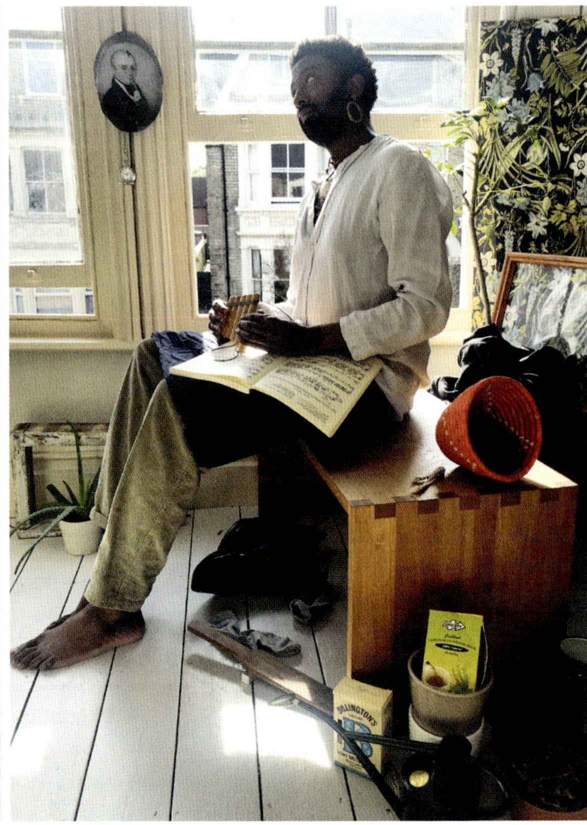

Black subjects are there for consumption, from extraction—this strange fruit, that exotic moment.

PB Yes, they're often portrayed as flora and fauna, but I refuse to let this limit them. In restaging these lives, each portrait becomes a fertile garden of possibilities. Like the kitchen garden plots that provided nourishment for Black laboring classes in Barbados both during and after enslavement, each of my re-creations is a plot with the potential to yield fortifying root crops, fragrant herbs, even floral tributes. In a word, sustenance. Maybe this method of "gardening" can help us heal?

MS I keep coming back to this idea that the project is a body of evidence. The case against the European cause of "enlightenment" is laid out here. When you begin to unpick the threads, the real story is one of criminality and injustice.

PB Think about Emmanuel Rio—he was in Vienna at a time when human zoos were being toured across Europe. His predecessors at the court were stuffed and displayed in a cabinet of curiosities.

MS We're not that far away from the human zoo—1830, 1930, it's not that far away. One could argue that apartheid is still in place in South Africa, it's just evolved into something else. African Americans are still fighting for their civil rights. And it's still quite precarious, isn't it, to be an Afro-European person?

PB Yes, definitely. I often think with respect to some of these works that there must have been some really interesting conversations between the artists and the sitters. What was being said while Emmanuel's image was being painted? And how would his words, his lived experience, resonate with me?

MS This is where the performance aspect comes in. When we're backstage, we're ourselves, we're private. Then the curtain opens, and we have to decide which of our multiple selves we are allowed to be. We are not mono subjects. We're a part of this story. Unshackle us from your imagination and let us into the conversation. The lack of generosity wrought by colonial violence and cultural erasure sits on top of so much. A lot of institutions—academic, creative—don't know how to be generous. This is why it's so important that there are different people in the room. It's not an act of generosity. There's a big difference between generosity and inclusion.

PB It's so important that people have access to this work. It's generally difficult to find, and you have to spend a lot of money on expensive, difficult-to-read books or subscribe to various academic platforms to be able to access the backstory. Part of my project is trying to disrupt that and provide more agency to viewers.

MS You've posed a question about what this form of art history looks like. You've done it through a visual mosaic of restaging and performance. You come out the other end with a very different sensibility about the work that paintings can do in understanding imperial forces.

PB And raising, I think, other difficult questions about how the work lives on and what we do next in terms of rehabilitation and change.

MS But what does change look like? This work is not just about art history, it's about what's going on outside the frame. I can only look at these images in terms of what's gone on outside the frame in time and in space. Where does Black joy live within visual culture? What does it look like?

PB I struggle with that a lot doing my family research. I'm always having to take it from the perspective of the white colonial traveler or missionary writing a report that mentions one of my ancestors. I just want to know what my ancestors really thought. I imagine myself listening through the closed door and hearing their muffled voices, speaking their own truths—joyfully!

MS History, for me, is alive. It needs to be constantly reworked in conversation with our present. If you can't invite the ghosts to sit down for dinner, they will always scare you. Even if we get it wrong sometimes, we have to do the difficult work.

Act 3

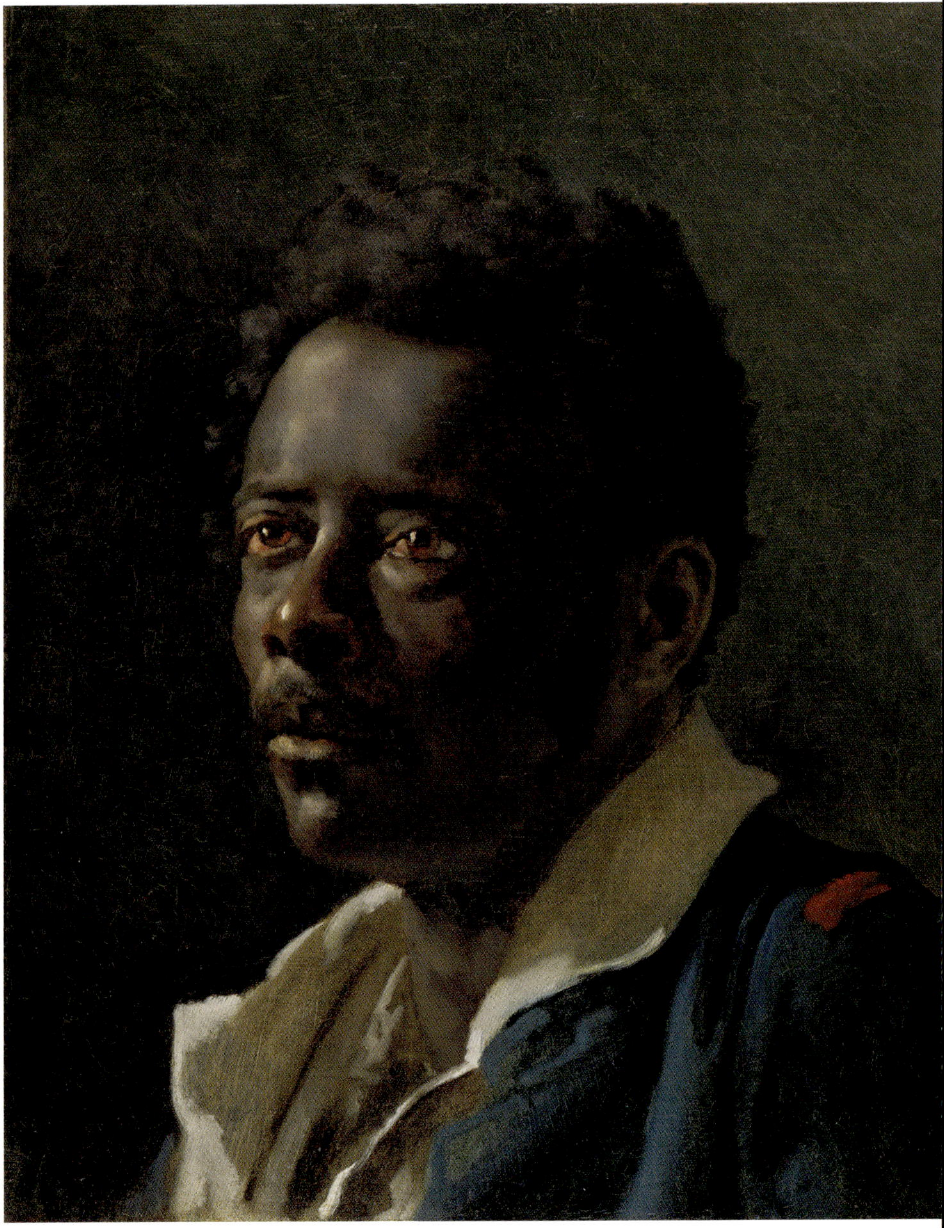

Study of the Model Joseph

ca. 1818–19

Théodore Géricault
French, 1791–1824

Oil on canvas
47 × 38.7 cm
(18½ × 15¼ in.)
Los Angeles, J. Paul
Getty Museum, 85.PA.407

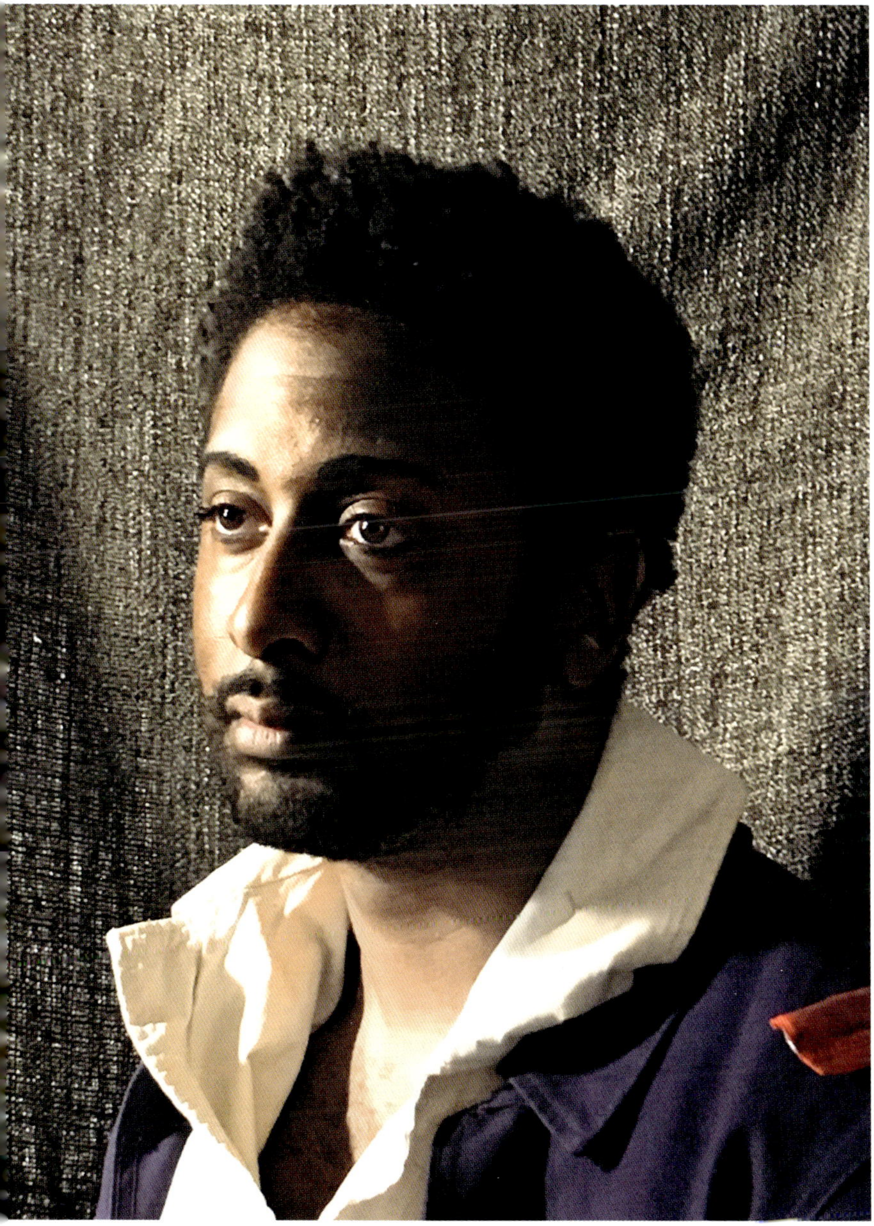

Act 3

Reworked with a French utility jacket. Joseph's full name was not recorded, but nineteenth-century accounts indicate that he was born in Saint-Domingue (now Haiti) around 1793. As a young man, he emigrated to France and worked as an acrobat in Paris, where he caught the attention of Géricault. Joseph was a principal model in Géricault's *The Raft of the Medusa*, a colossal painting that depicts a shipwreck off the coast of northwest Africa. By the 1830s, Joseph had been recruited to model at Paris's prestigious École des Beaux-Arts. Géricault's study is one of the most developed renderings of Black flesh tones and Afro hair that I have encountered. His attention to the balance of warm and cool tones in Joseph's skin makes this portrait luminous, inviting us into the world of an actual, distinct person.

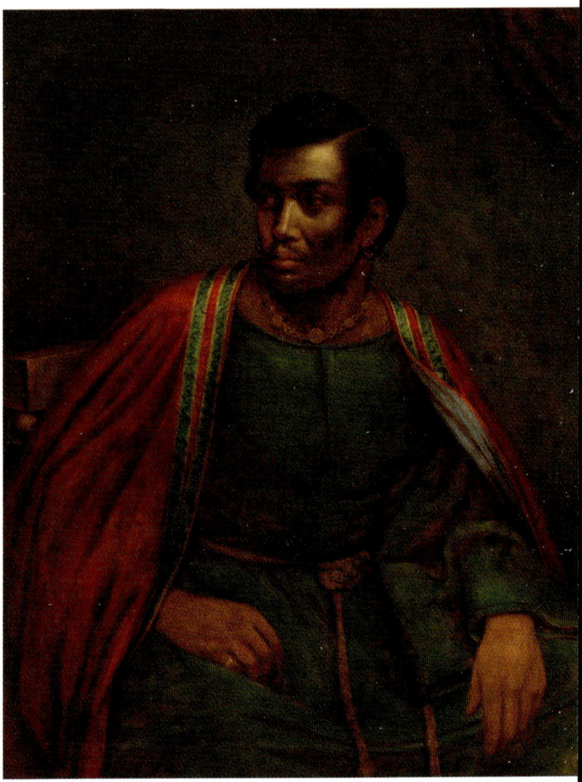

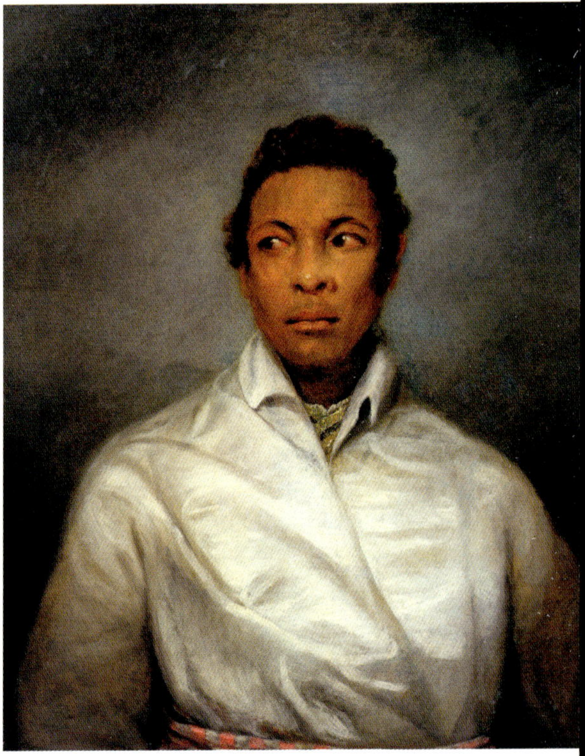

TOP

Ira Aldridge as Othello

ca. 1830

Henry Perronet Briggs
British, 1791/93–1844

Oil on canvas
128.3 × 103.5 cm
(50½ × 40¾ in.)
Washington, DC,
National Portrait Gallery,
NPG.72.73

BOTTOM

Ira Aldridge

ca. 1826

After James Northcote
British, 1746–1831

Oil on canvas
76.2 × 63.2 cm
(30 × 24⅞ in.)
Private collection, on loan
to the National Portrait
Gallery, London, NPG L251

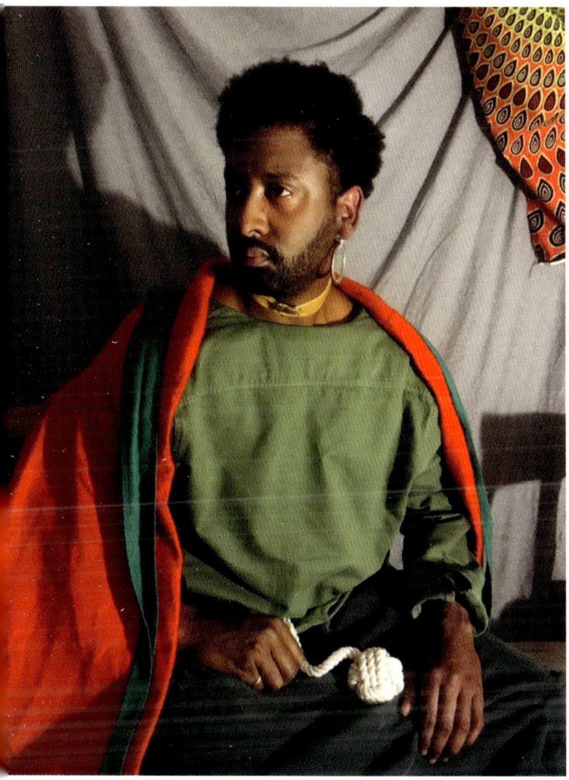

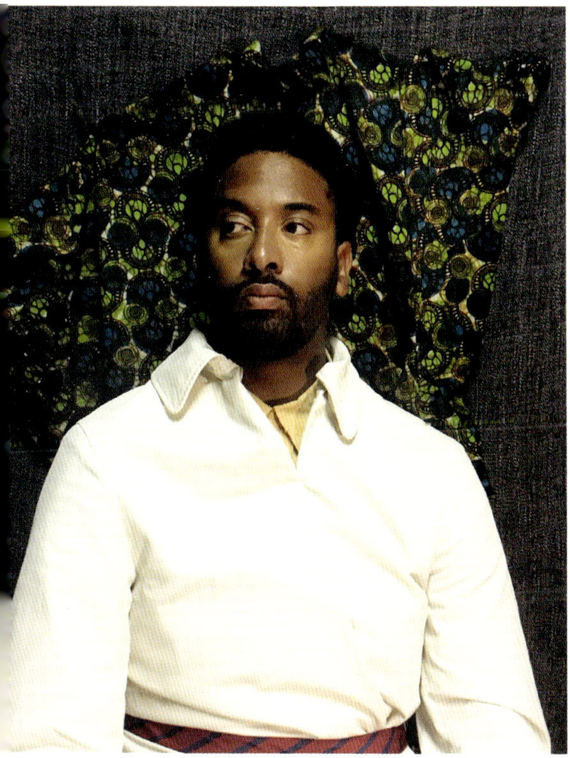

Born in New York City, Aldridge was one of the greatest Shakespearean actors of his age—but he was Black. Unable to work in the United States, he traveled to England in the 1820s and became the first Black actor to play the role of Othello in Britain. London was, at the time, England's cradle of proslavery lobbying, while Manchester opposed slavery. Perhaps in honor of this stance, the Royal Manchester Institution commissioned the Northcote portrait shortly after Aldridge's acclaimed performances at the city's Theatre Royal. The Briggs portrait is reworked with a Santa costume for a cloak, a curtain-pole ring for an earring, and a curtain holdback as a rope belt. The Northcote painting is reworked with West African wax-print fabric, a comment on the complexities of identity (I read that Aldridge fabricated a story that he descended from Senegalese royalty to aid his career). Aldridge's intelligent professional choices and acting talent gave him a platform to challenge his audiences' expectations. He was both a brilliant performer and an effective activist, and I feel proud, as a Manchester native, to know that this portrait was commissioned in my hometown.

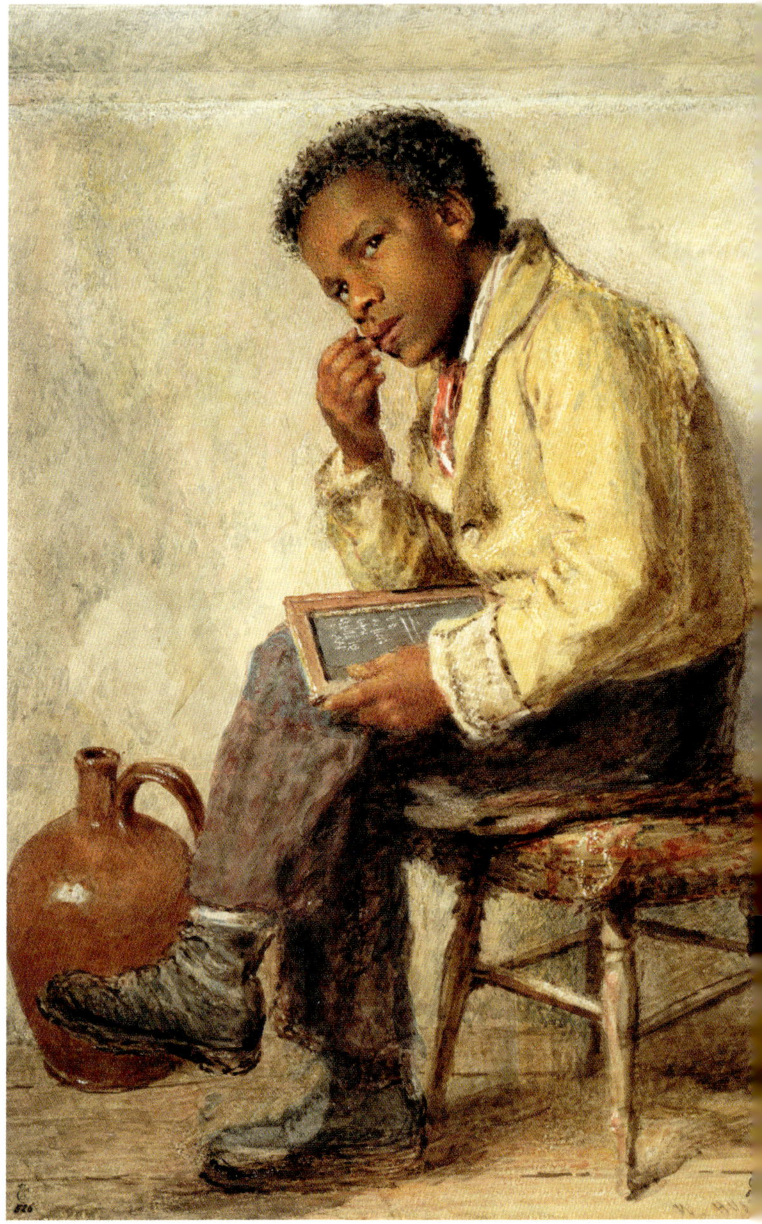

A Brown Study [Portrait of a Boy with a Slate]

ca. 1840

William Henry Hunt
British, 1790–1864

Watercolor
49.5 × 35.6 cm
(19½ × 14 in.)
London, Victoria and Albert Museum,
FA.526

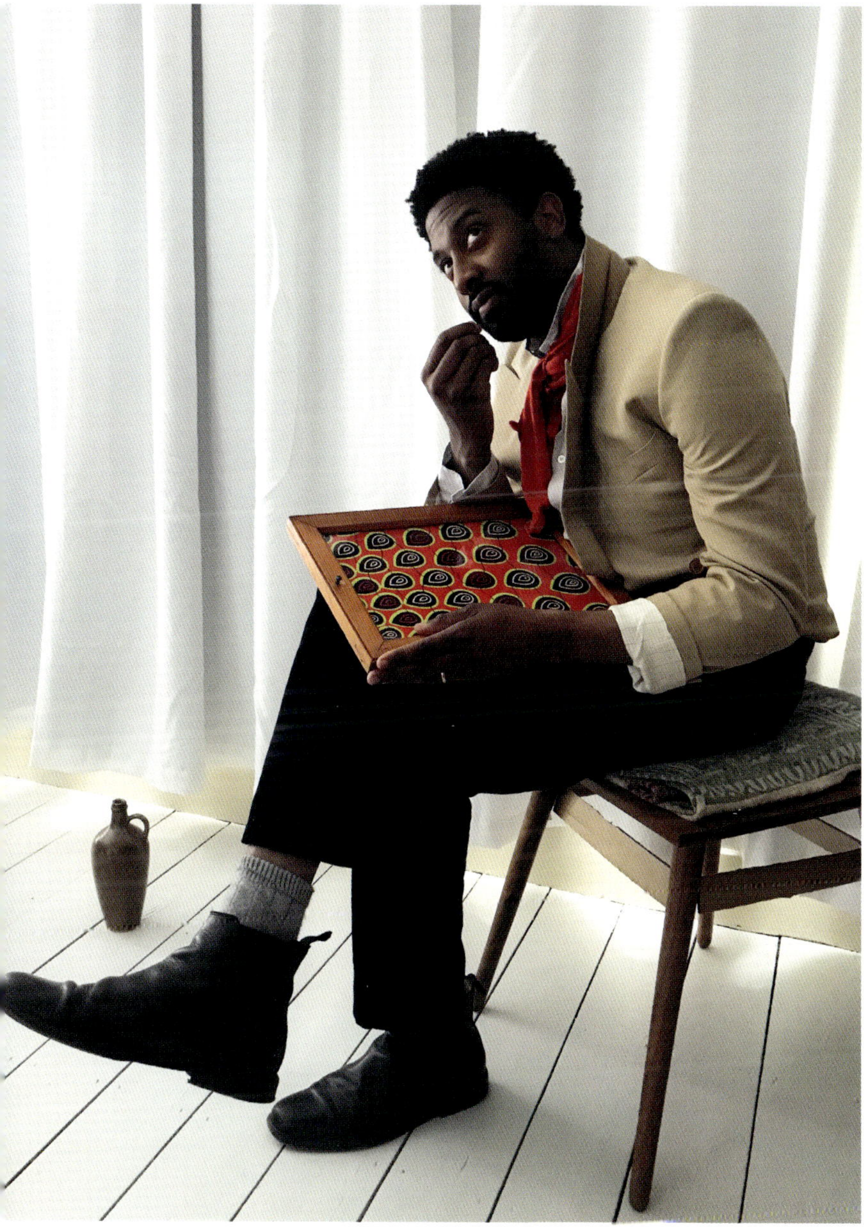

Act 3

Reworked with an African print and a small jug. Hunt was an influential watercolorist who specialized in still life and portraiture. Painted at a time when blackface minstrelsy was considered wholesome entertainment in England, this likeness stands in stark contrast to the caricatured representations of Black individuals that dominated Victorian visual culture. It is especially remarkable for showing a young Black male in Britain as a learner and a thinker. The boy's chalkboard and inquisitive expression undermine racial stereotypes and cultural signs that helped to assert nineteenth-century British identity as white.

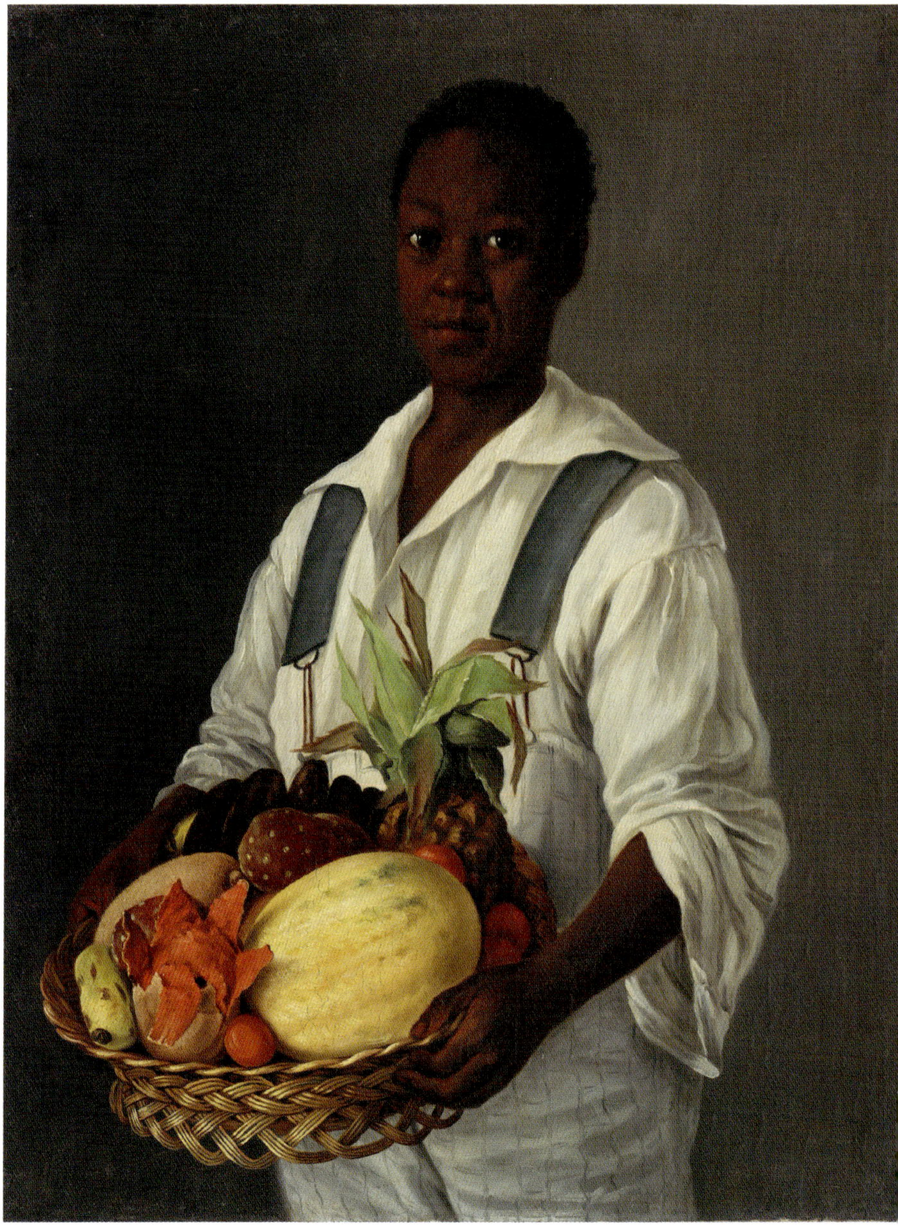

The Young Man from the Coast

after 1843

Agustín Arrieta
Mexican, 1802–1879

Oil on canvas
89 × 71 cm
(35 × 28 in.)
New York, The Hispanic Society Museum & Library, LA2391

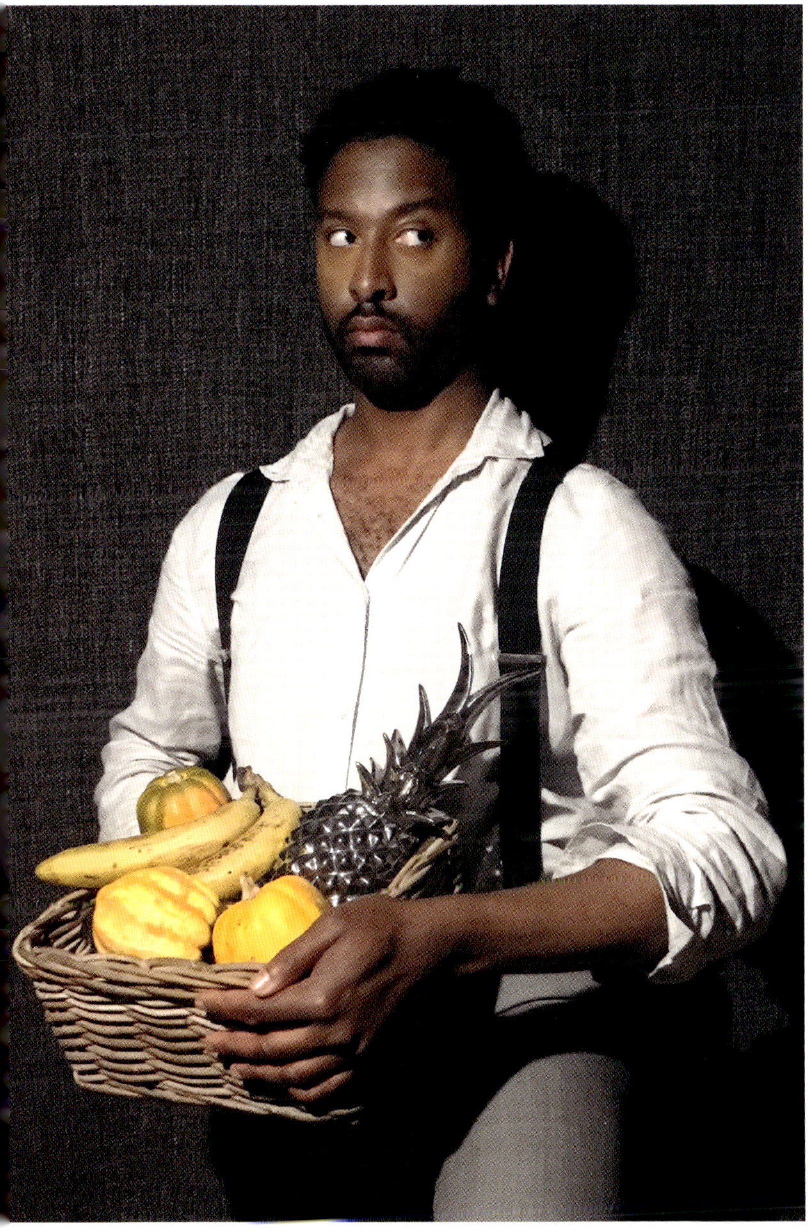

Act 3

Here we see a young man from one of the coastal states of Mexico, likely the Caribbean-facing state of Veracruz. Reworked in my attic space with a silver-colored ceramic pineapple. After Mexico abolished the trade in enslaved people from Africa, as well as enslavement itself, in 1824, formerly enslaved populations survived in close-knit groups throughout the country, especially in the coastal regions. The man's skin almost melds into the dimly lit space behind him, contrasting sharply with his white shirt and the whites of his eyes. This effect spotlights his Blackness, or otherness, and his lower socioeconomic status; he is both a servant and an outsider.

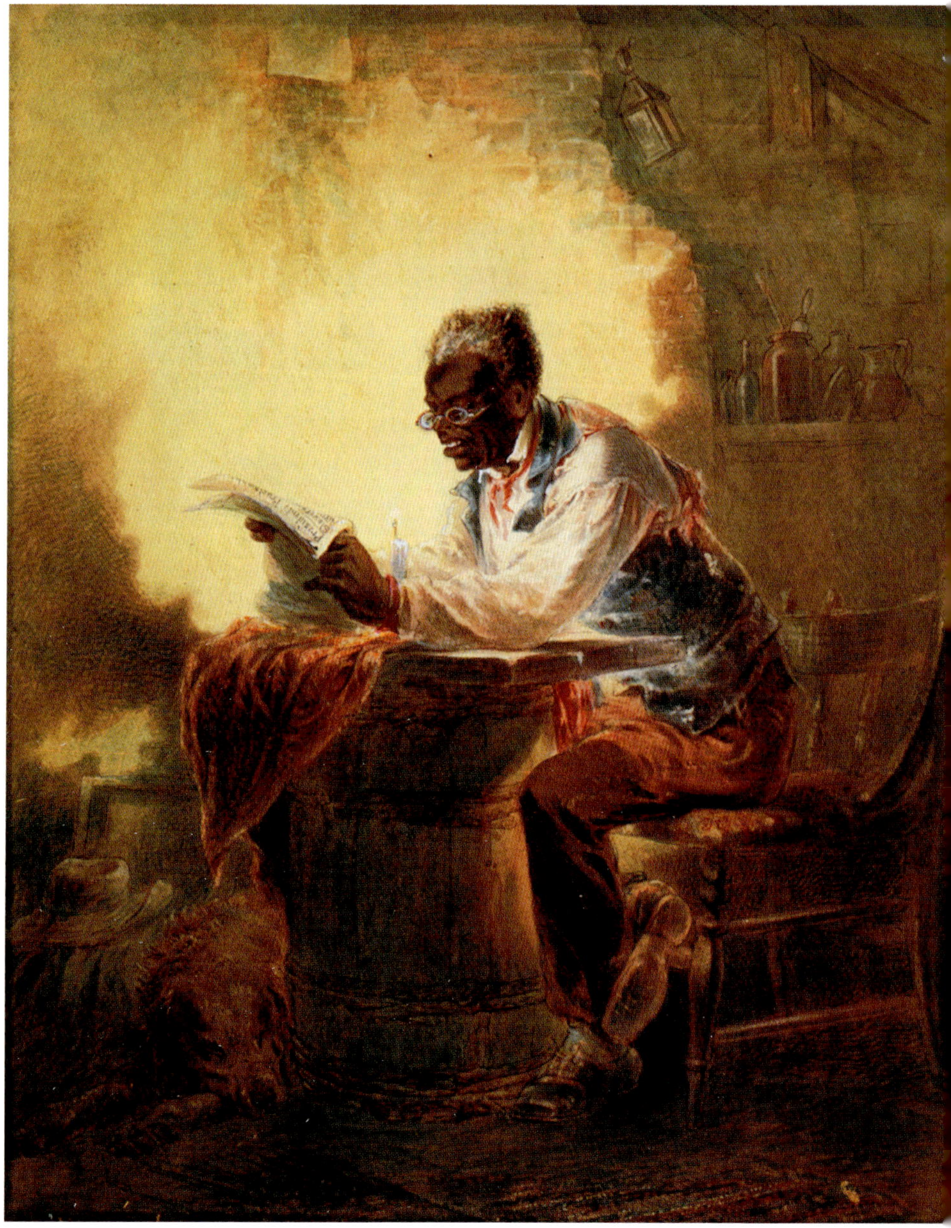

Untitled [Man Reading a Newspaper by Candlelight]

ca. 1863

Henry Louis Stephens
American, 1824–1882

Watercolor
30.5 × 25.4 cm
(12 × 10 in.)
Washington, DC,
Library of Congress,
2010718365

Reworked with copies of the documents that formalized my maternal great-great-great-great-grandmother Margaret's freedom from enslavement. This watercolor commemorates the day when Abraham Lincoln, president of the United States, issued the Emancipation Proclamation, declaring the enslaved "forever free." For this man, who is probably formerly enslaved, it is a joyful moment: a society based on the social, political,

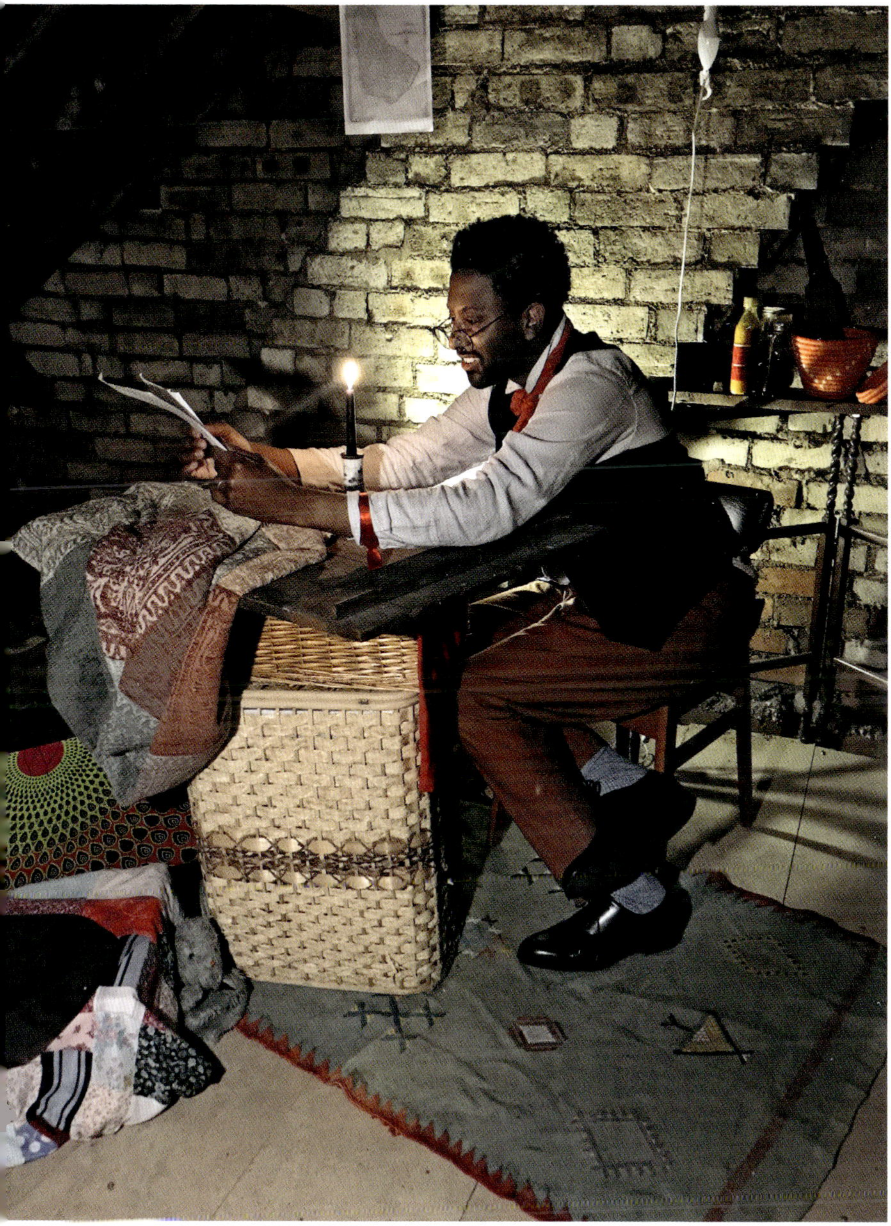

Act 3

and economic organization of white oppressors and enslaved Africans is no more. While restaging his portrait, I wondered how my own ancestor Margaret must have felt when she received her manumission papers in Barbados, more than fifty years before the scene shown here. What was her expression? Would she have digested the news alone? Margaret was the illegitimate daughter of Miles Brathwaite II, a prominent white enslaver, and an enslaved African mother who we assume was enslaved on the Brathwaite plantation. Margaret's mixed-race heritage gave her a marginal advantage in Barbados's racial hierarchy; she was granted freedom as a teenager and received an education. Although we do not have an image of her, we do have her manumission papers and a letter she wrote to her children and descendants. In many ways, these documents serve as a portrait of her.

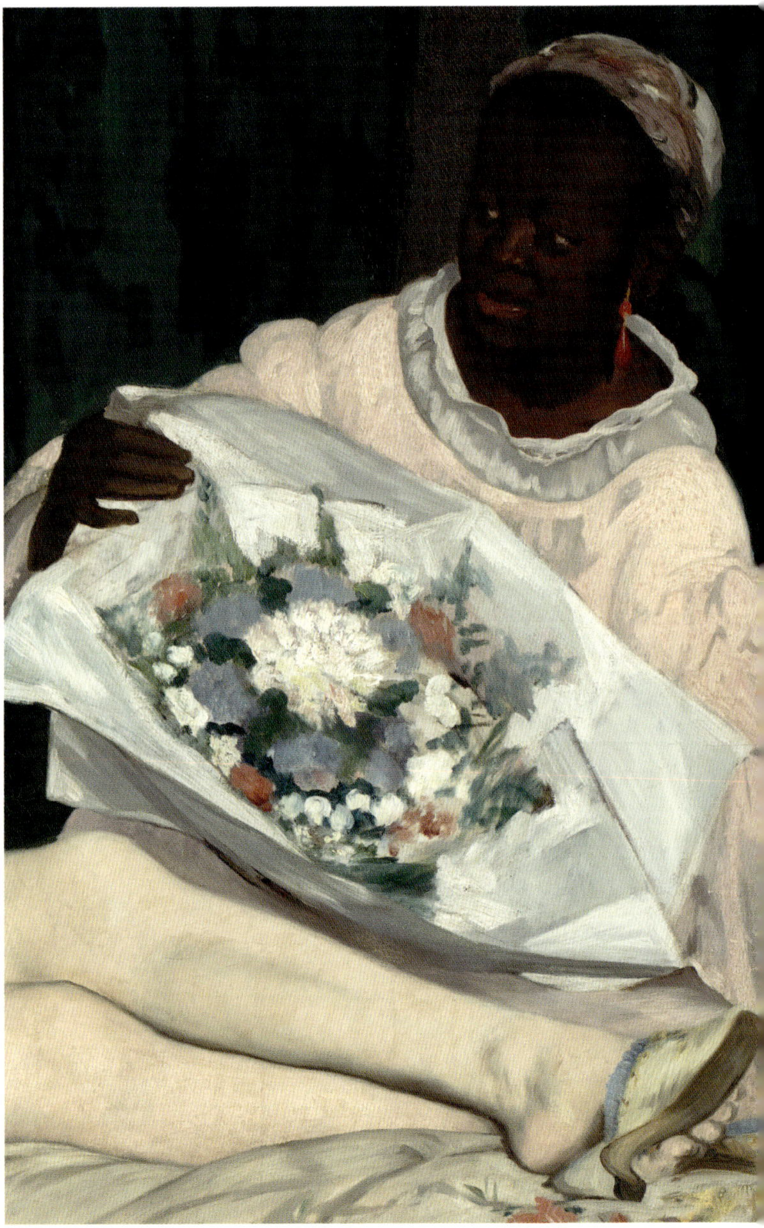

Laure [Olympia]

1863

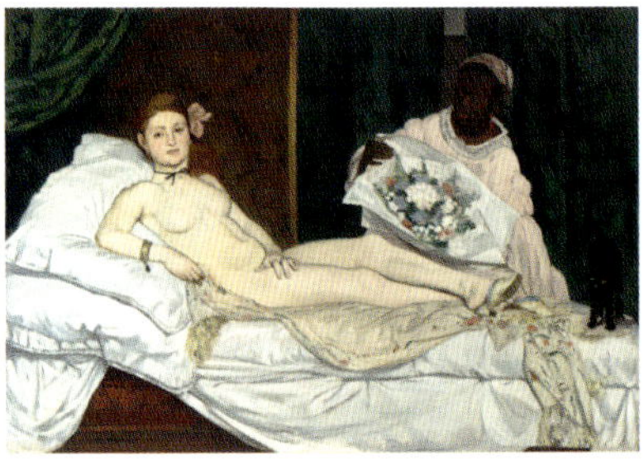

Edouard Manet
French, 1832–1883

Oil on canvas
130.5 × 191 cm
(51⅜ × 75¼ in.)
Paris, Musée d'Orsay,
RF 644

Reworked with lilies and roses wrapped in a selection of family historical documents. Manet's painting depicts a reclining nude woman, a sex worker, attended by a Black maid who brings a bouquet of flowers, presumably from a client. The work was considered shocking when it was first unveiled in Paris in 1865. It was only quite recently that the Black maid was identified as a model named Laure. Her age, country of origin, and full

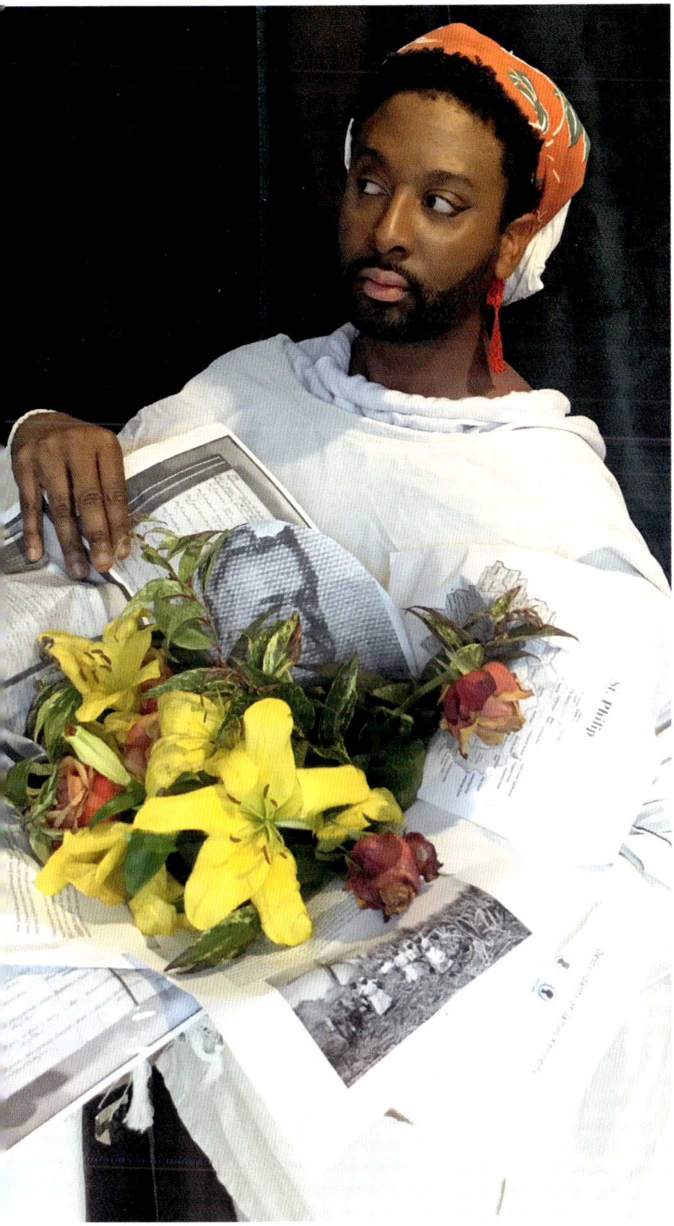

Act 3

name are not yet known, but Laure's presence alludes to the changing population of modern Paris. Laure is not exoticized in the same way as many other Black sitters in the European canon. She wears a style of dress typically associated with French working-class women of the time, and she appears to be of higher status than a housemaid. It was daring of Manet to make so many aspects of modern city life visible in his art, including an emerging Black working class. In 2019, two of Manet's portraits of this intriguing figure were retitled to identify Laure by name.

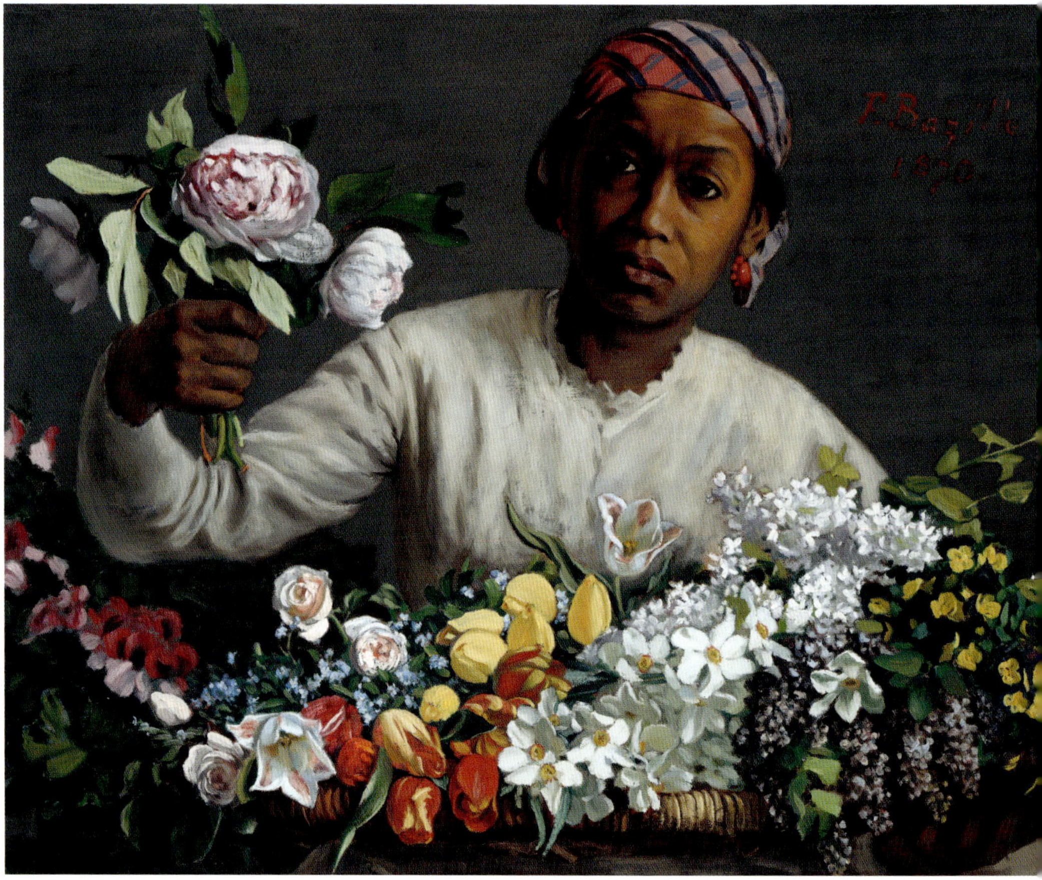

Young Woman with Peonies

1870

Frédéric Bazille
French, 1841–1870

Oil on canvas
60 × 75 cm
(23¾ × 29½ in.)
Washington, DC,
National Gallery of Art,
1983.1.6

A flower seller arranges a basket of seasonal blooms. Reworked with a madras handkerchief, homegrown peonies, an alstroemeria plant, and a Hawaiian shirt. Bazille painted this work at a time when his friendship with Edouard Manet had grown especially close. Peonies were Manet's favorite flower, and the Black subject in French proletarian attire recalls Manet's depiction of Laure in the painting known as *Olympia* (p. 128). Bazille's

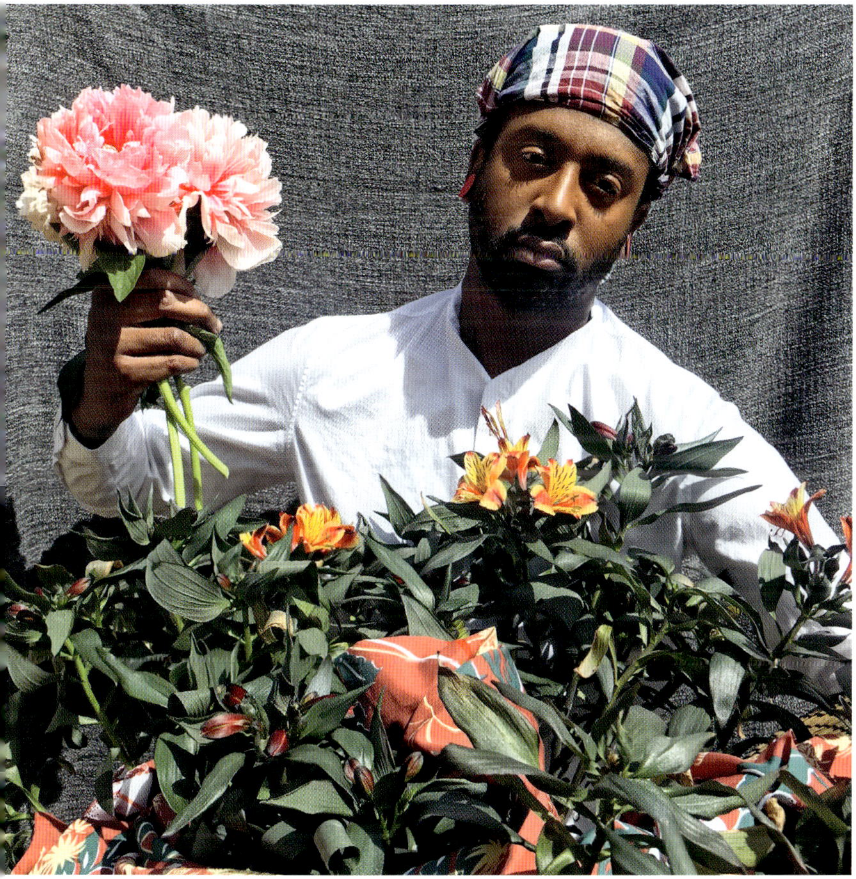

Act 3

model, like Laure, signals her Afro-Caribbean heritage with a madras head wrap, a typical component of dress in Dominica, Saint Lucia, and the French Caribbean. Rooted in laws that forced enslaved women to cover their hair, the madras head wrap was later reclaimed as a public declaration of Black femininity. Here the combination of the head wrap, modern Parisian attire, and Manet's favorite flowers suggests a blending of cultures imbued with symbolic power. Bazille painted this work just over twenty years after the French abolition of territorial slavery. To me, it reads as a plea for social equality and justice in a society that remained not only racialized but also extremely gendered.

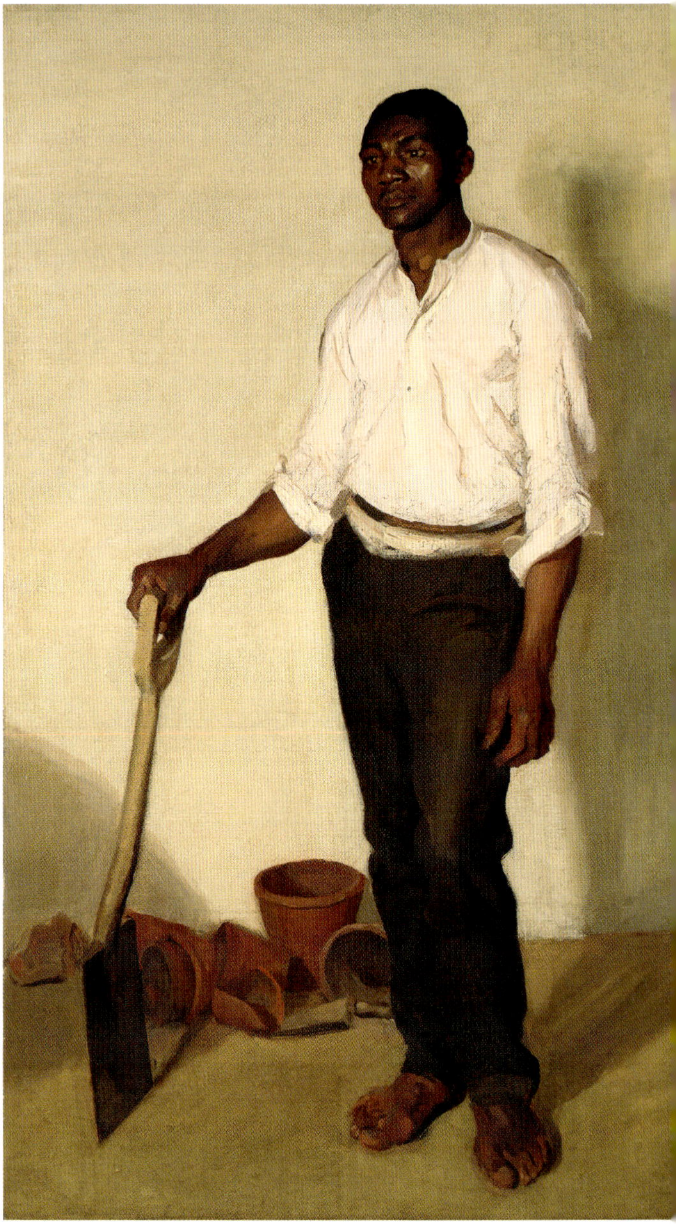

Portrait of a Gardener

ca. 1905

Harold Gilman
British, 1876–1919

Oil on canvas
131.5 × 77.5 cm
(51¾ × 30½ in.)
London, The
Garden Museum

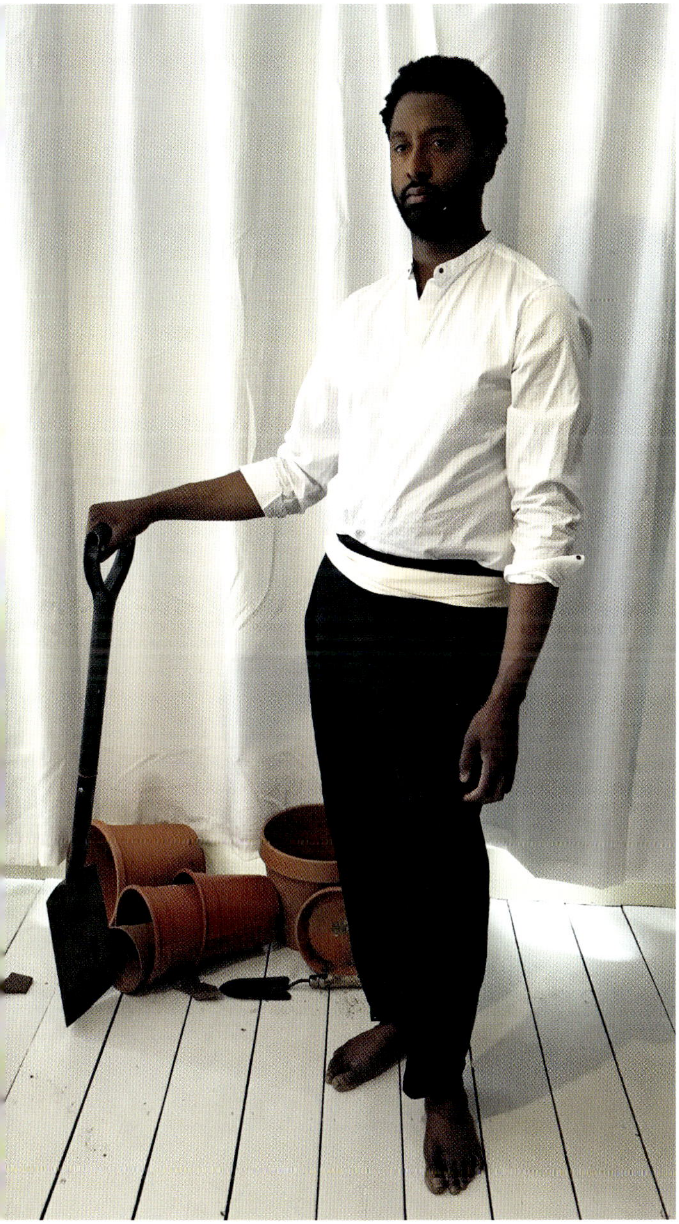

Act 3

A gardener stands bathed in light. Reworked with terra-cotta pots and a spade. Although the subject of Gilman's portrait has yet to be identified, he belongs to the rich lineage of Black individuals who contributed to the development of British horticulture. Perhaps the best known is Thomas Birch Freeman, who worked as head gardener at Orwell Park estate in Suffolk. Freeman later became a missionary on Africa's Gold Coast, where he collected and sent samples of tropical flora to Kew Gardens in London. This is one of the first full-length British portraits of a Black subject in everyday dress. The man stands alone as an individual, not relegated to a supporting role as in so many artworks that came before.

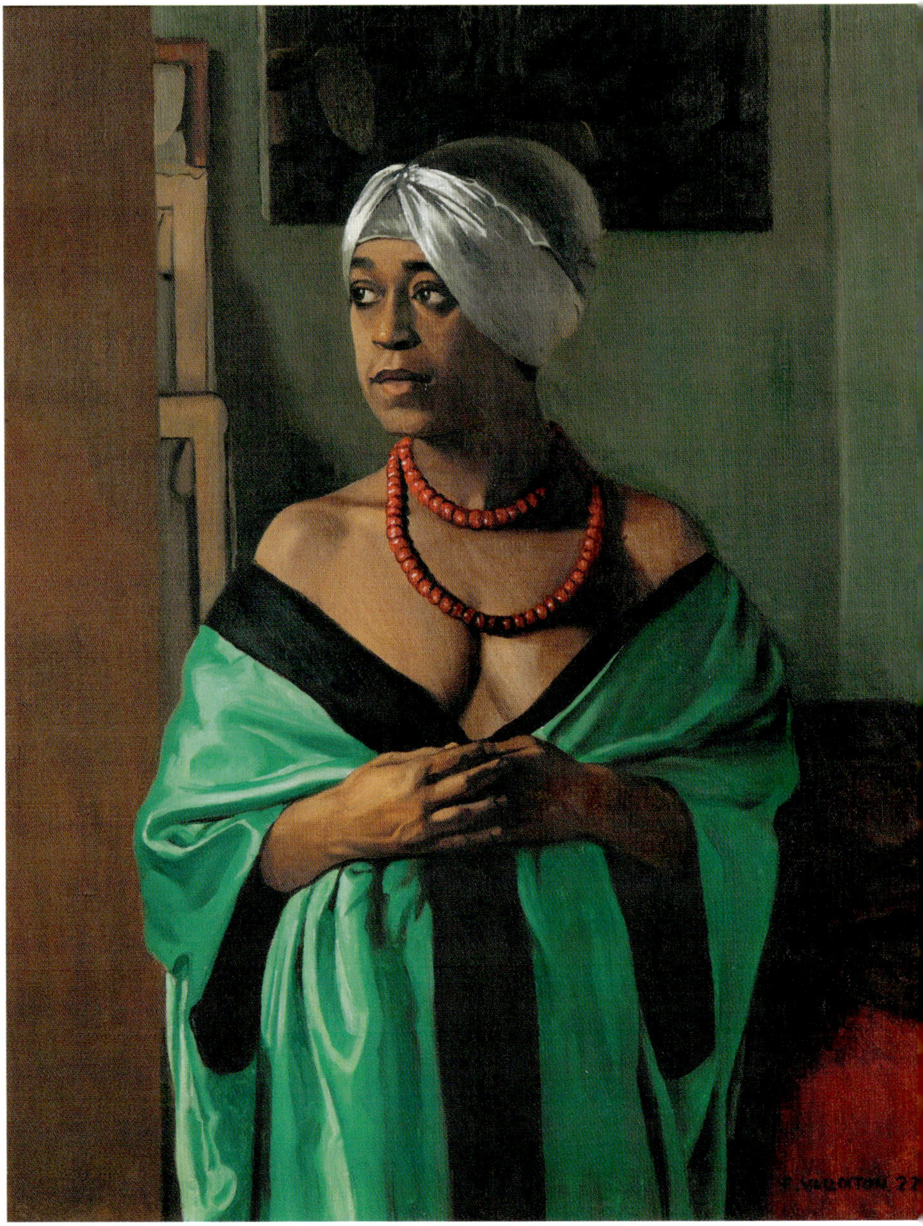

Aïcha

1922

Félix Vallotton
Swiss, 1865–1925

Oil on canvas
99.8 × 80.5 cm
(39¼ × 31¾ in.)
Private collection

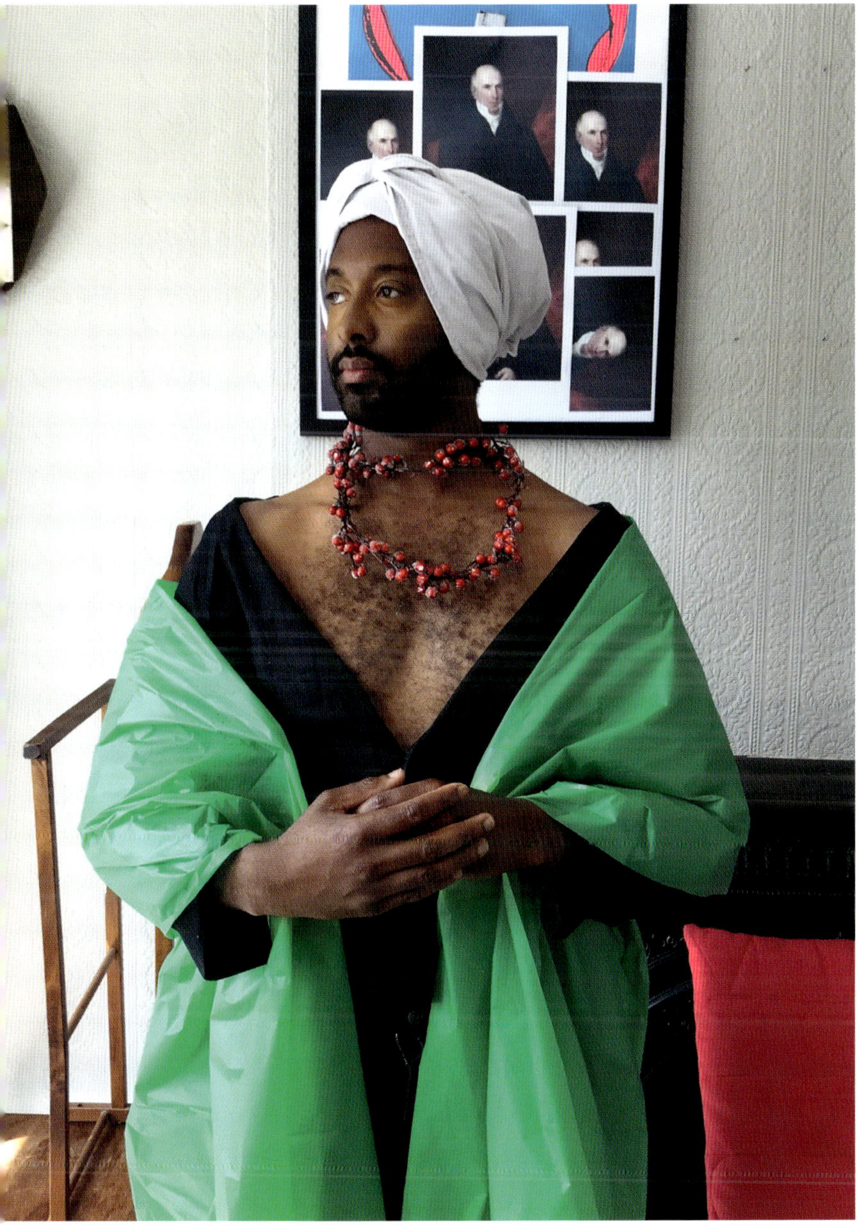

Act 3

Reworked with a green tablecloth, a black shirt, and Christmas winterberry decorations. Aïcha Goblet, the "Venus of Montparnasse," was born around 1898 in Hazebrouck, France. The daughter of a juggler from Martinique, she performed in the circus as a child and set her sights on Paris at age sixteen. There she rose to prominence as an artist's model, posing for the likes of Man Ray and Amedeo Modigliani. As a music hall dancer and an actor, she never became as famous as Josephine Baker but was esteemed by audiences and critics alike. In Vallotton's likeness, a pensive Goblet looks away from us, her signature head wrap shimmering in the dappled light. She is portrayed as an artist, not a racial type.

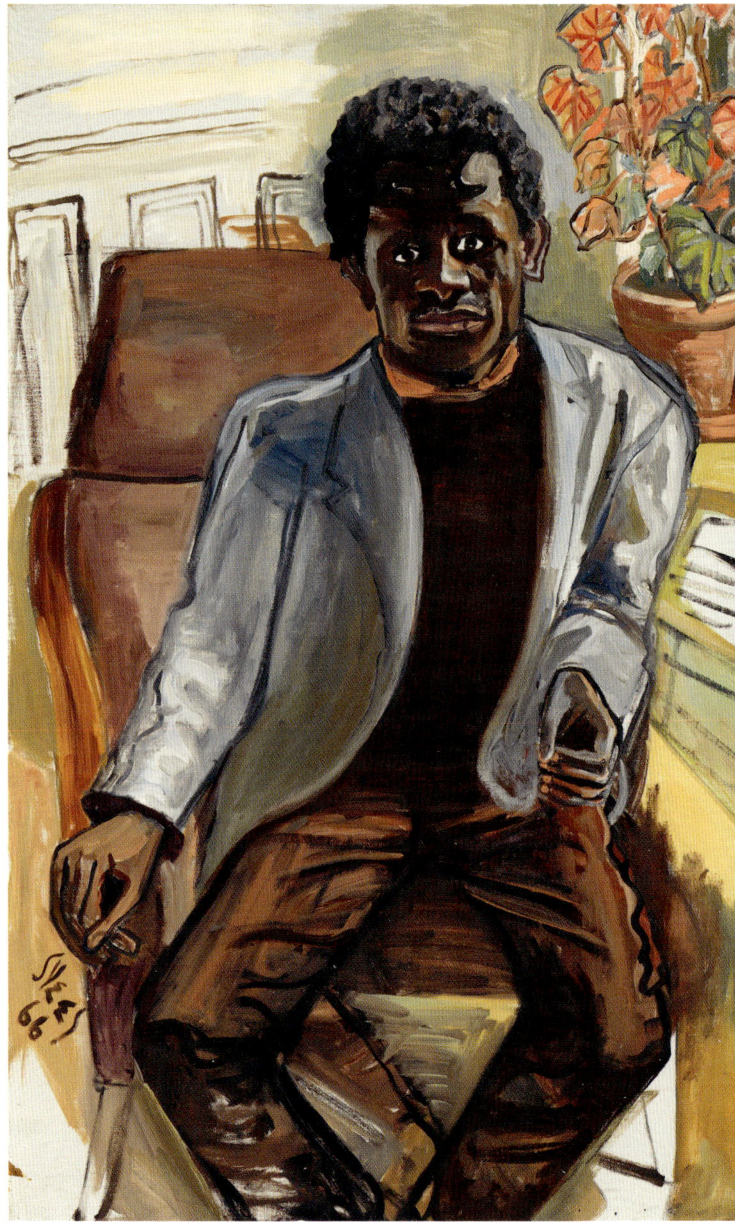

Black Man

1966

Alice Neel
American, 1900–1984

Oil on canvas
111.8 × 71.4 cm
(44 × 28⅛ in.)
Private collection

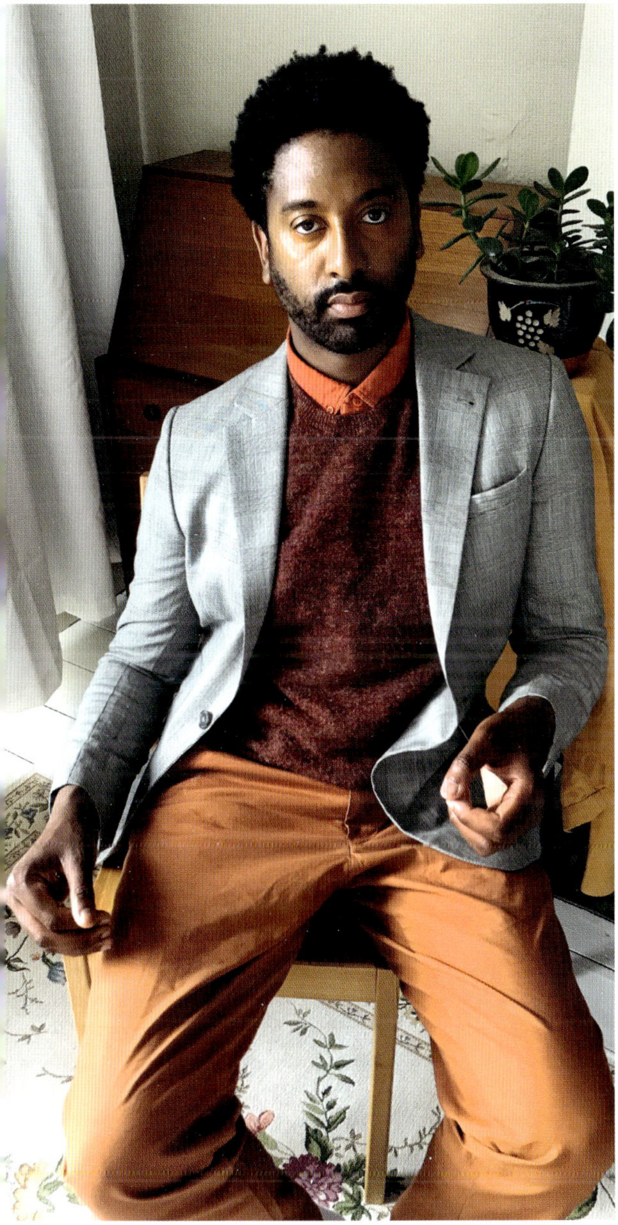

Act 3

Neel's original was painted in the midst of the civil rights movement. Reworked with a midcentury bureau and a jade plant given to me by my mother. In a warm, light room decorated with a houseplant (probably Neel's apartment on Manhattan's Upper West Side), an elegant man sits, leaning a bit to one side in his chair. The shape and slight stiffness of his right hand suggest focus or concentration. His body language tells us he has an opinion. What is he about to say? With his blazer, button-down shirt, sweater, and chinos, he is dressed in the Black Ivy League style adopted by civil rights activists such as Martin Luther King Jr. and Malcolm X—preppy armor as an intentional counterpoint to a revolutionary agenda.

Black Draftee (James Hunter)

1965

Alice Neel
American, 1900–1984

Oil on canvas
152.4 × 101.6 cm
(60 × 40 in.)
Antwerp, Belgium,
COMMA Foundation

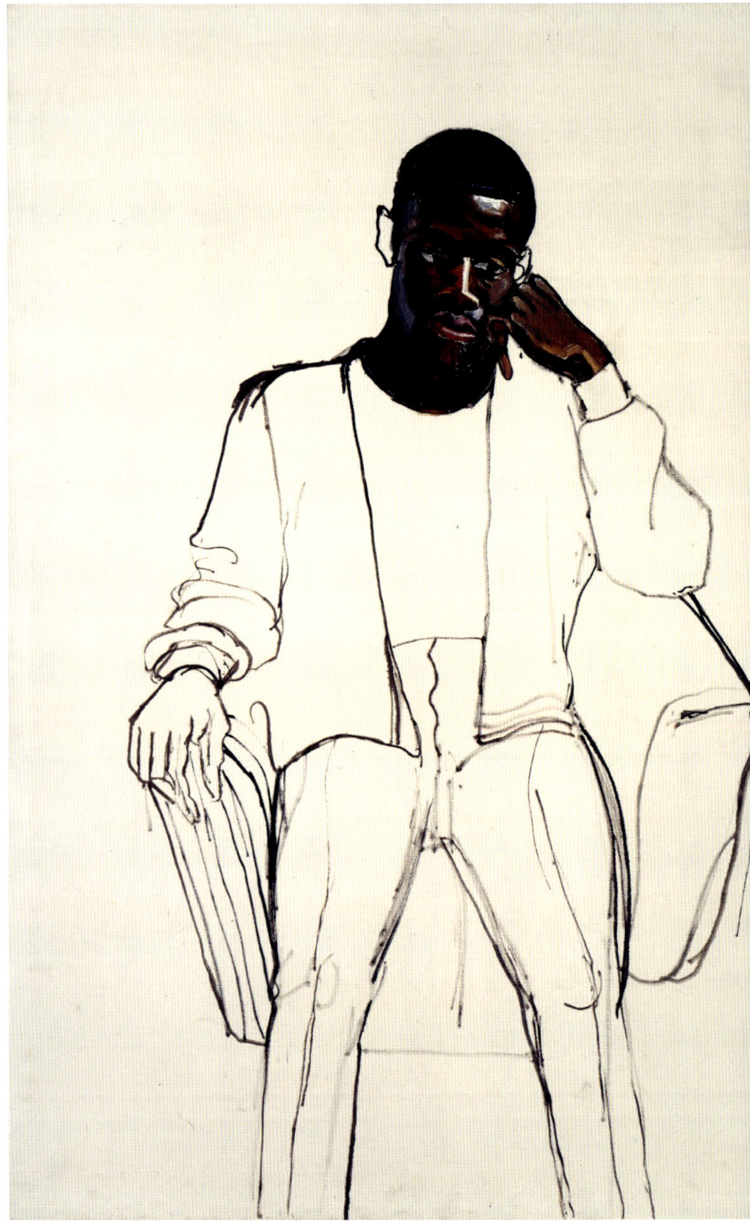

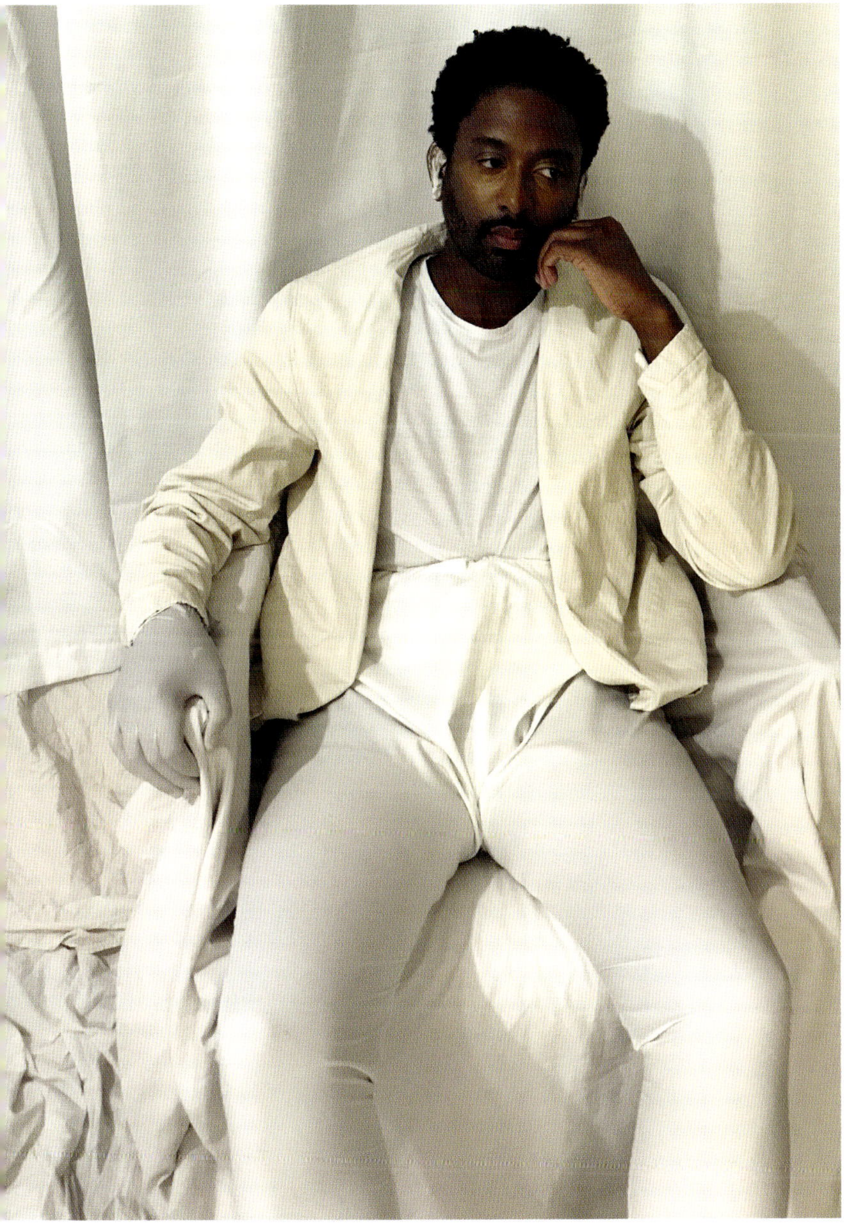

Act 3

Reworked with all-white clothing. Neel's portraits document the diverse tapestry of people she encountered daily while living and working in New York City. This example is particularly striking for having been left deliberately unfinished. Nobody knows what happened to its subject, James Hunter, whom Neel met by chance soon after he was drafted for service in the Vietnam War. Due to leave within a week, Hunter never returned for a second sitting. The stark, sketchy outline of his absent body contrasts with his fully realized face and the hand on which it rests. Neel seems to embed all of the unfulfilled potential of this life into her canvas. His expression is haunting.

A Portrait of the Artist as a Shadow of His Former Self

1980

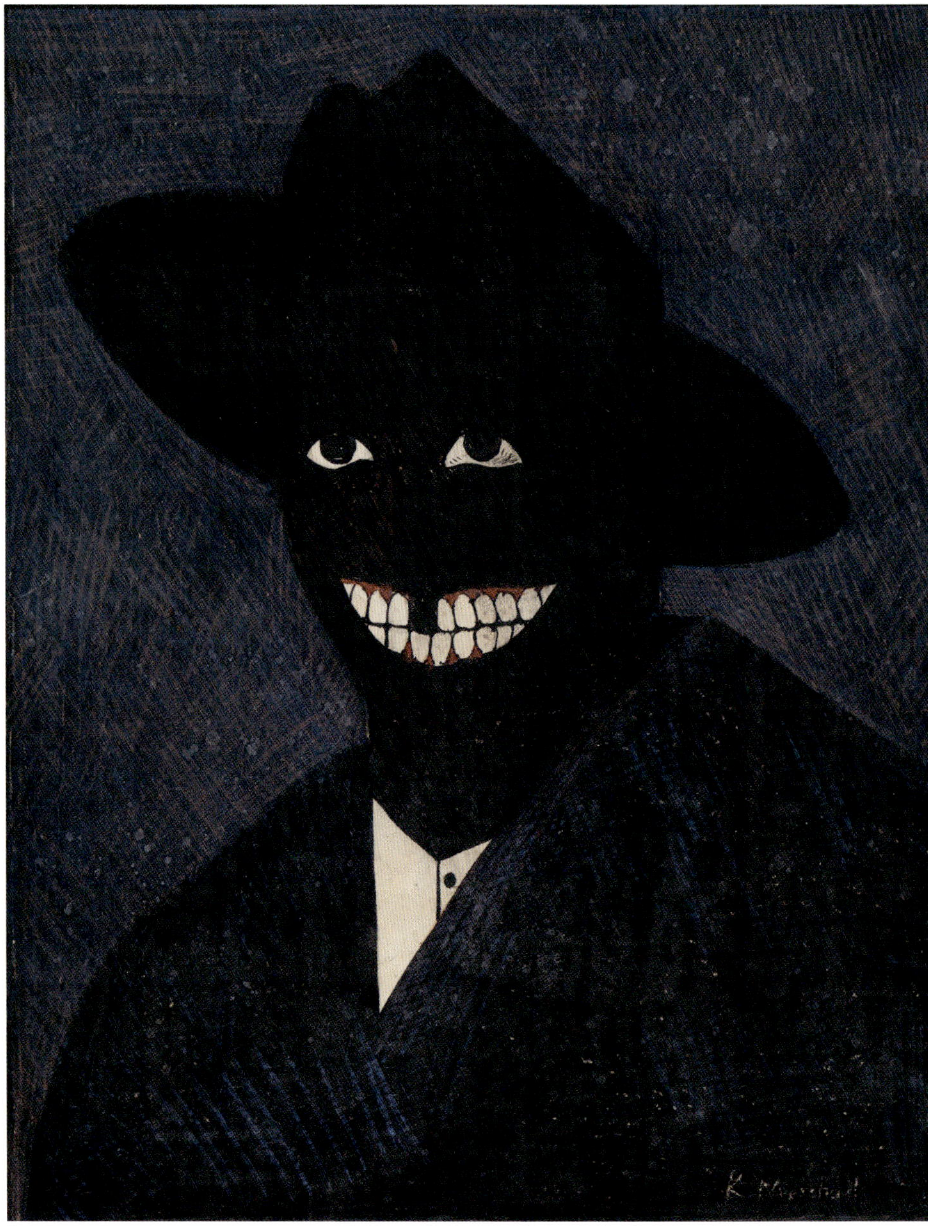

Kerry James Marshall
American, b. 1955

Egg tempera on paper
20.3 × 16.5 cm
(8 × 6½ in.)
Courtesy the artist and
David Zwirner, London

Reworked with a "Purpose" pin from the gift shop of the National Museum of African American History and Culture. Marshall's "self-portrait" uncomfortably takes in the pain and trauma of racist stereotypes in earlier representations of Black subjects. I see it as both a summing up and a subversion of the concept of race as exotic performance or commodity. Marshall's inspiration was Ralph Ellison's 1952 novel *Invisible Man*, whose

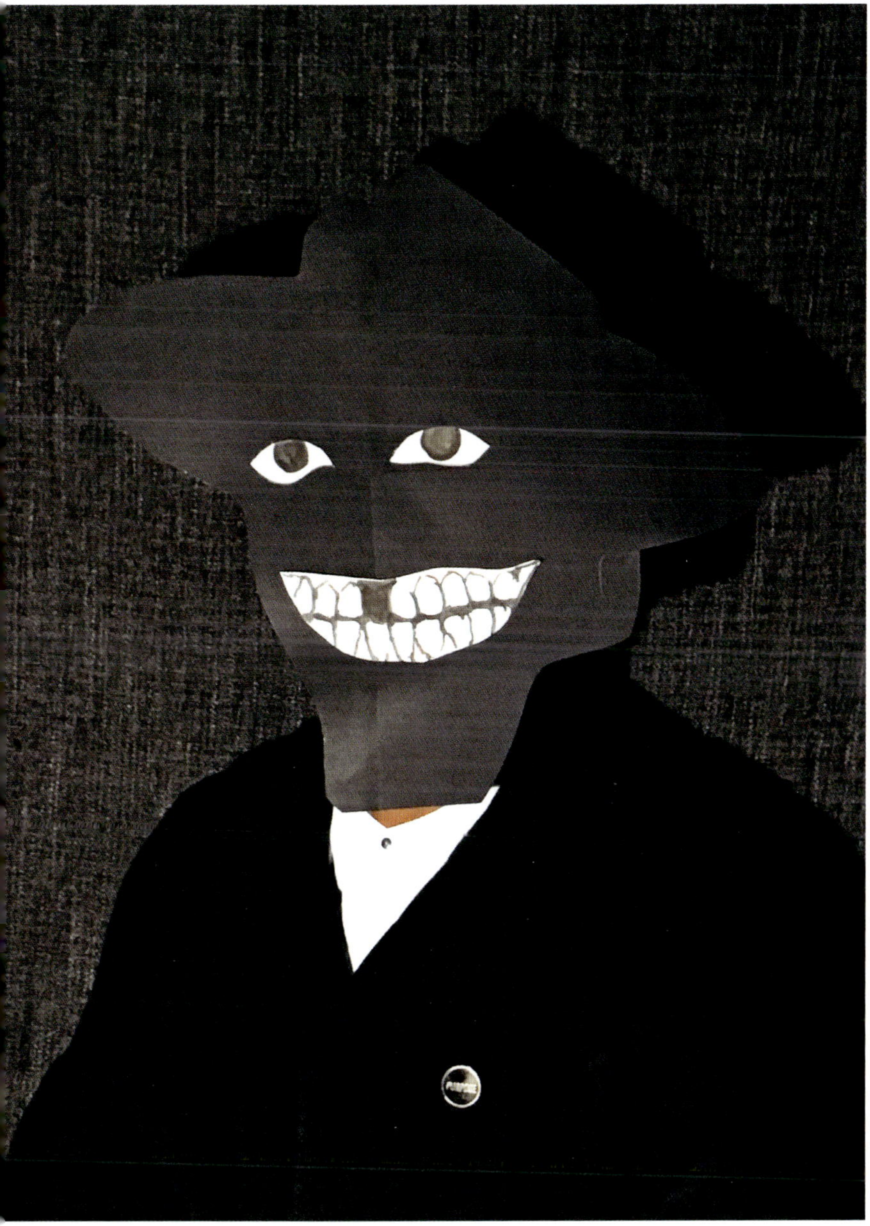

Act 3

protagonist knows that his Blackness makes him "less than" in white America. Marshall renders himself as a type, at once present and invisible. For me, as a second-generation Barbadian, re-creating this work offered an opportunity to recognize the irrepressible masking traditions of the African Caribbean. Through the subversive act of masquerade, my ancestors drew strength from performing their way through enslavement, emancipation, and beyond. Holding on to such traditions allowed—and still allows—them to remain visible, to be seen.

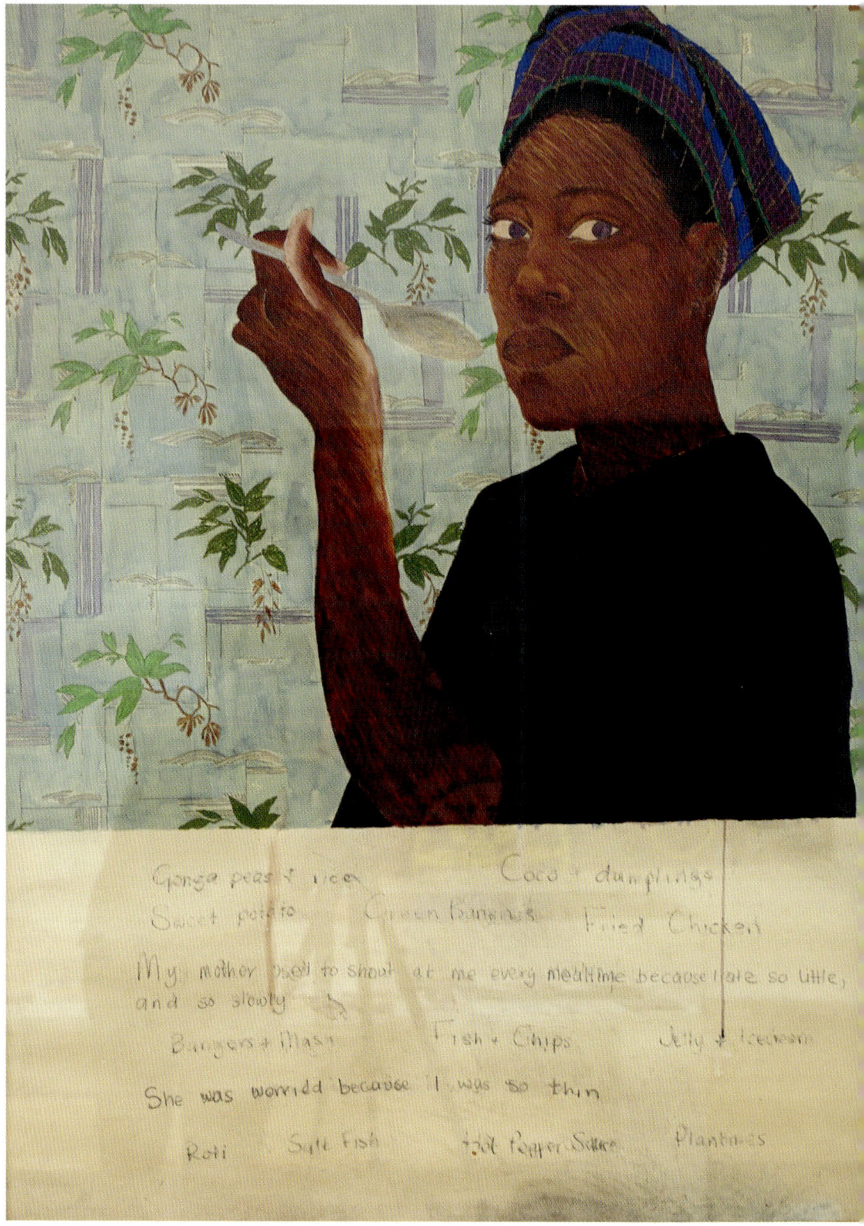

Rice n Peas

1982

Sonia Boyce
British, b. 1962

Pastel, watercolor,
and pencil on paper
137 × 104 cm
(54 × 50 in.)
Collection of Lubaina
Himid

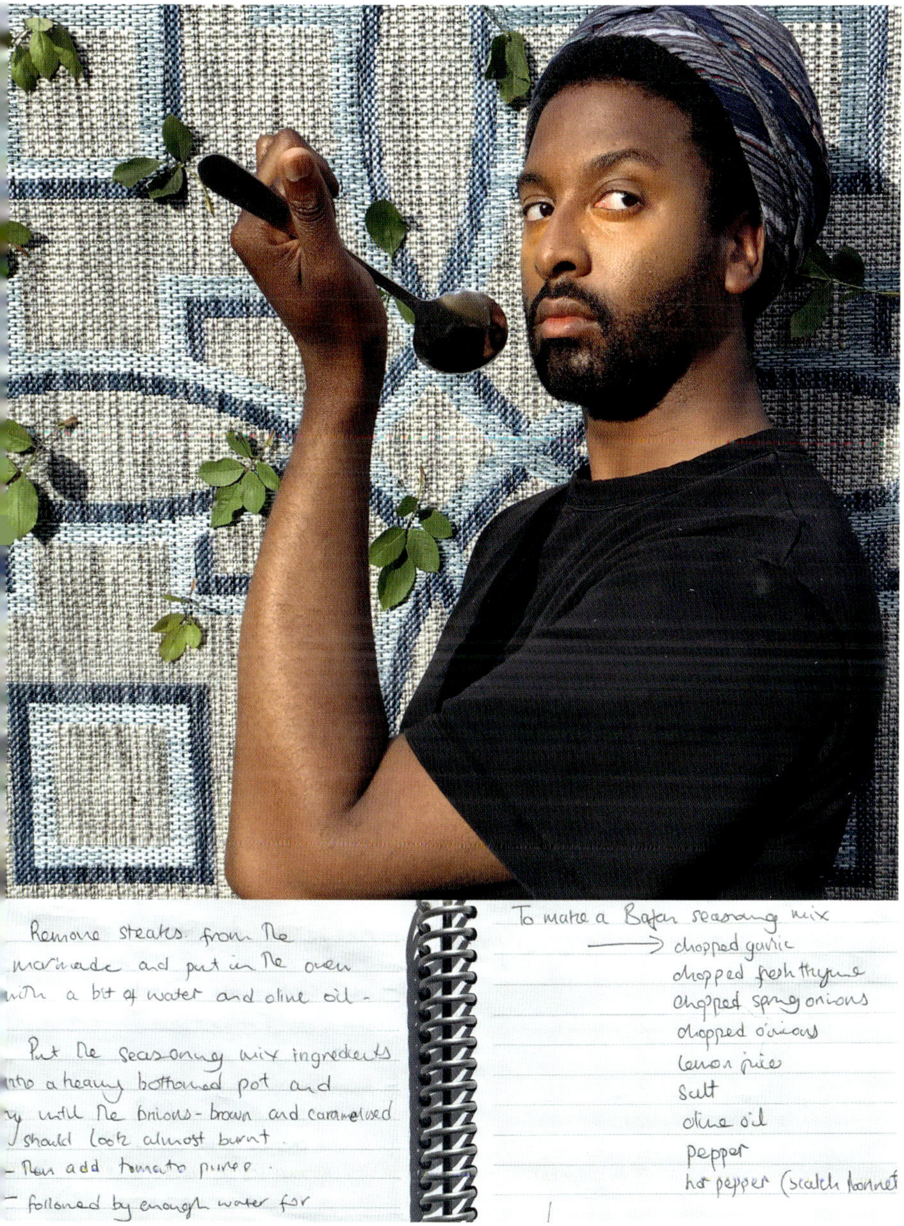

Reworked with a notebook containing my mother's Bajan recipes. In the lower portion of this work, we read a scribbled recollection alongside a list of Afro-Caribbean and British foods, and above the faded scrawl is Boyce herself, positioned in front of what looks like floral-patterned wallpaper. Spoon clutched awkwardly in her raised hand, she looks out to us, lips closed, eyes wide, hair tied. The portrait is striking and complex. Boyce has re-created herself in a stylized way. But there is a defiance in her penetrating gaze, as if challenging the viewer. Boyce is dictating the terms of how we view her, how we judge her, how we know her. In her image, I see all of the anonymous Black figures I have encountered in Western art on this journey of rediscovering Black portraiture—those who were previously silenced, unable to articulate themselves in the face of whiteness. Boyce reclaims the very space of the portrait, making it truly hers, ours, mine.

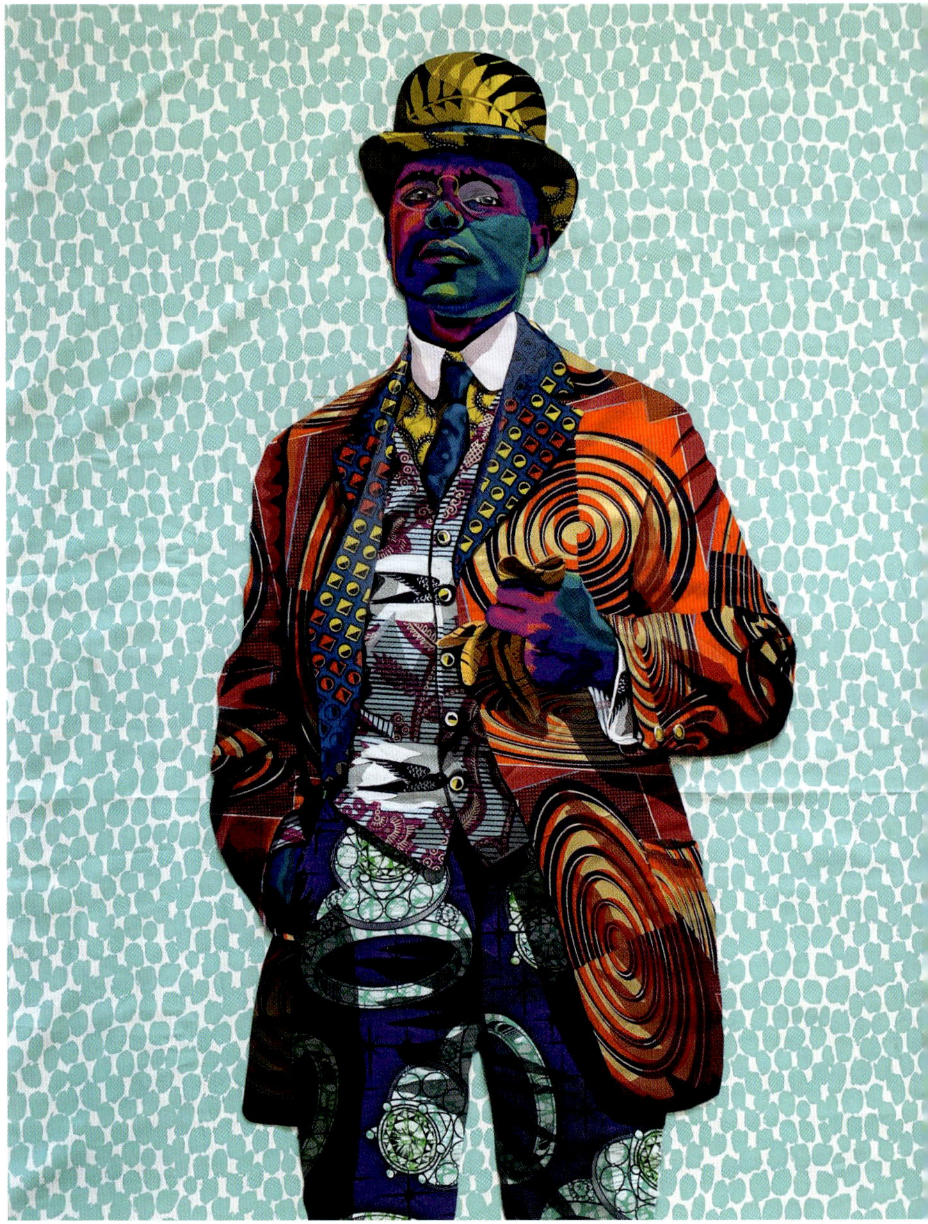

Africa, the Land of Hope and Promise for Negro Peoples of the World

2020

Bisa Butler
American, b. 1973

Cotton, silk, wool, and velvet quilted and appliquéd (detail, early state)
223.5 × 132.1 × 5.1 cm
(88 × 52 × 2 in.)
Private collection

Quilted portrait reworked with face paint and African wax fabric remnants. Butler's art deals with absent or silenced histories. She extends the ancient tradition of quilting in the Black community by fusing portraiture with collage, using vividly patterned African fabrics. Many of her subjects are anonymous, but here she portrays Emmett J. Scott, a Black journalist, educator, author, and government official. Scott was Booker T. Washington's

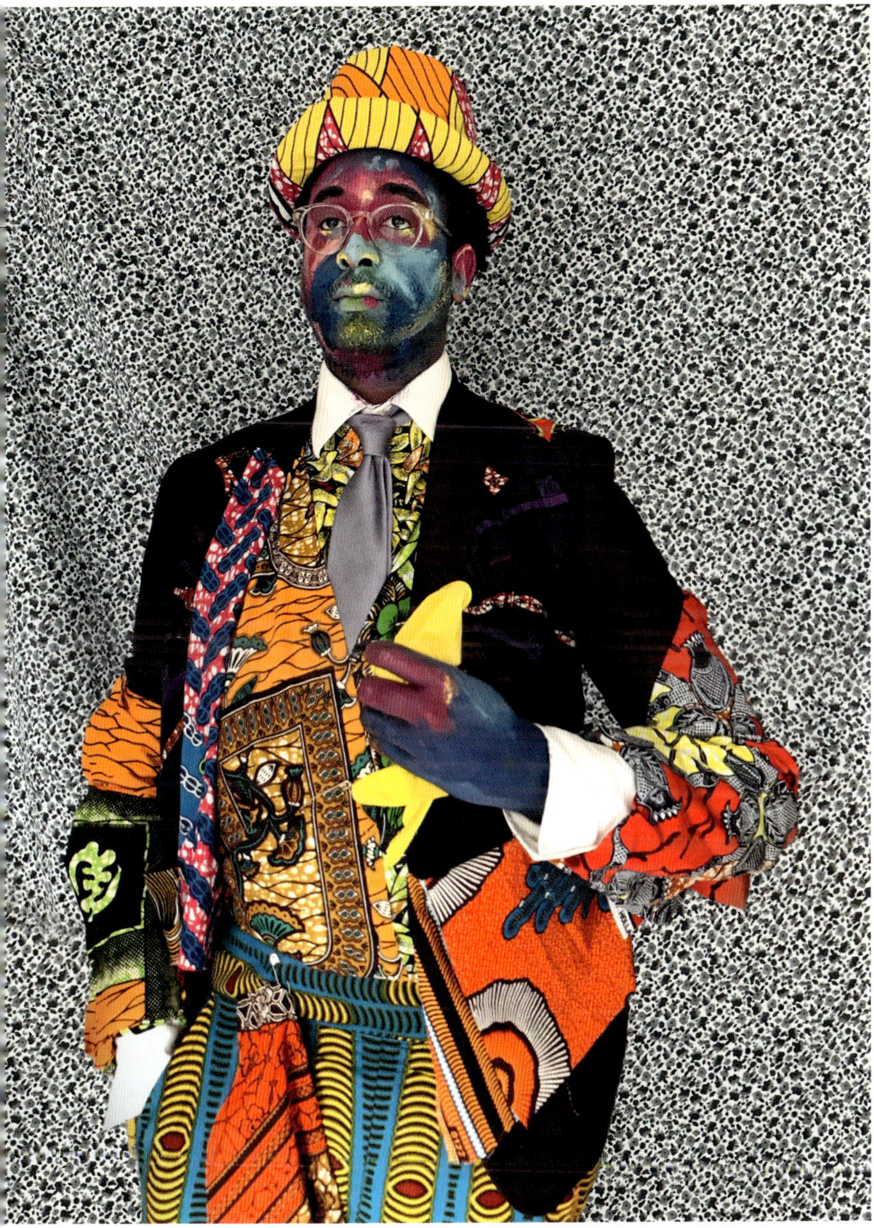

chief aide at the Tuskegee Institute and later became the highest-ranking African American in President Woodrow Wilson's administration. This re-creation underscores how central the patchwork quilt made by my maternal grandmother, Ina Elrita Brathwaite, has been to the Rediscovering Black Portraiture series. Through it, I am connected to her, to hundreds of years of Barbadian history, and even further back to West Africa. The quilt I inherited has become a visible manifestation of the spirits of departed ancestors. Through these disparate scraps of fabric, they enter the room for remembrance, celebration, and blessings.

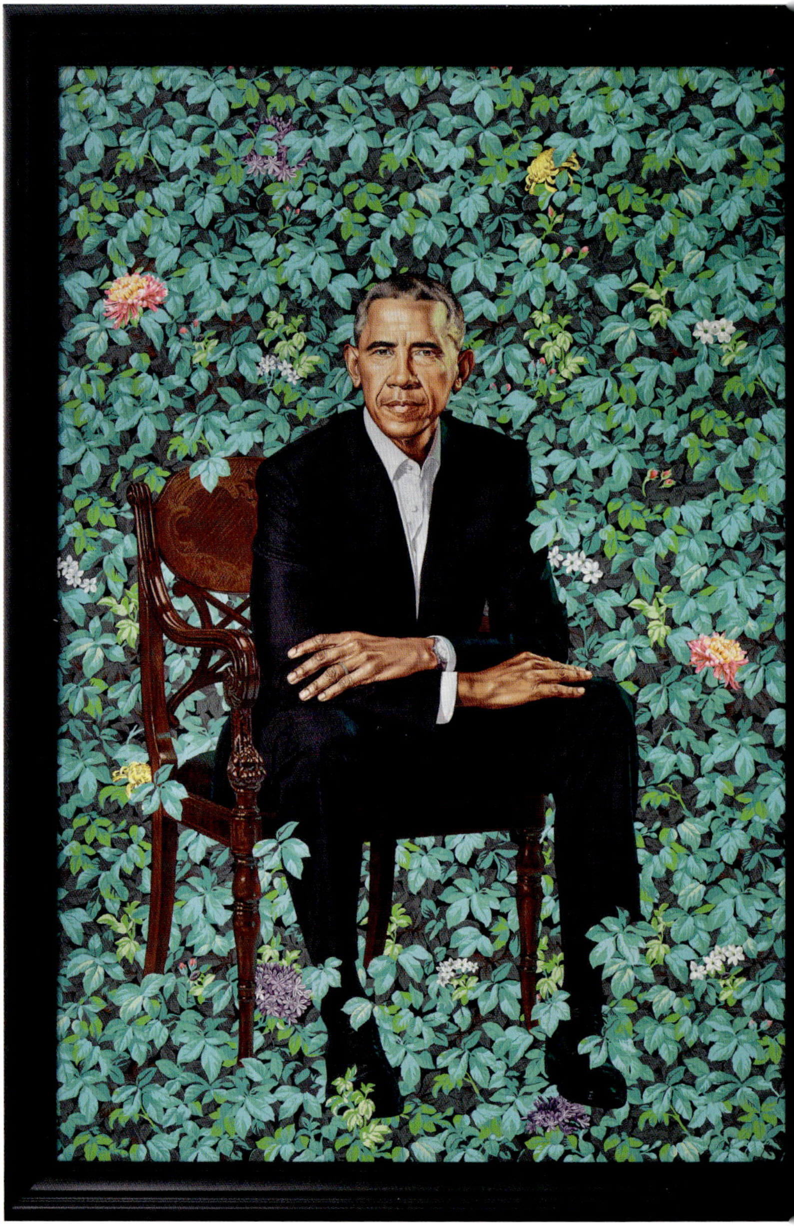

Barack Obama

2018

Kehinde Wiley
American, b. 1977

Oil on canvas
213.4 × 147.3 cm
(84 × 58 in.)
Washington, DC,
National Portrait Gallery,
Smithsonian Institution,
NPG.2018.16

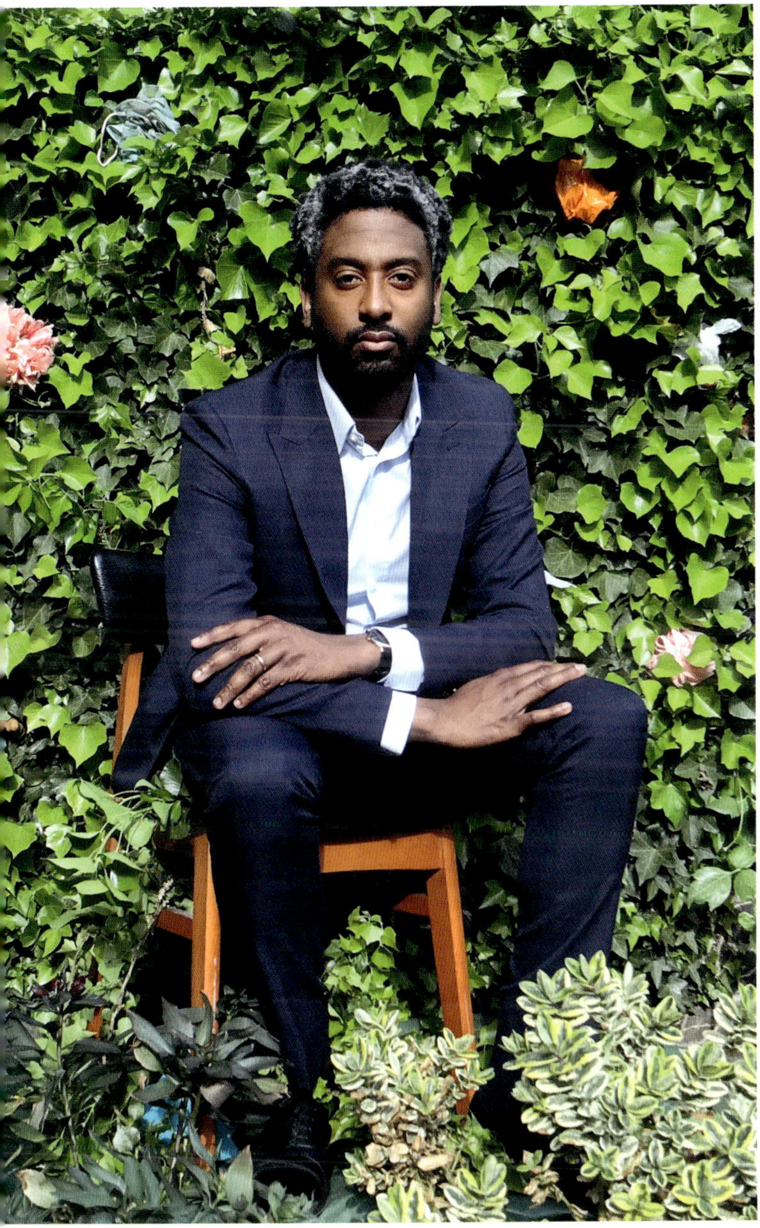

Act 3

Portrait of Barack Obama, forty-fourth president of the United States, reworked in front of my garden wall with exfoliating mesh sponges. Wiley's large-scale works aim to redress the absence of Black individuals, especially Black men, in the canon of Western painting. His sitters' poses are usually modeled after famous figures in historical portraits. Here Obama sits easily and open-collared in front of a lush backdrop of plants and flowers that evoke his biography and background: African blue lilies honor his late Kenyan father; jasmine recalls his childhood in Hawaii; and chrysanthemums are the official flower of the city of Chicago. Wiley's portrait is a meditation on self-ownership and self-representation, which are as essential for the "leader of the free world" as they are for every one of us.

The "gaze" has been and is a site of resistance for colonized black people globally. Subordinates in relations of power learn experientially that there is a critical gaze, one that looks to document, one that is "oppositional." In resistance struggle, the power of the dominated to assert agency by claiming and cultivating "awareness" politicizes "looking" relations—one learns to look a certain way in order to resist.

— bell hooks, "The Oppositional Gaze: Black Female Spectators," in *Black Looks: Race and Representation*, 1992

Encore

Cheryl Finley

Around 1643, a Dutch painter named Jasper Becx painted the portrait of a splendidly dressed man named Don Miguel de Castro, an emissary from Kongo who had traveled with two servants via Brazil in an attempt to negotiate peace with the Netherlands. The painting (p. 40) shows Don Miguel dressed in contemporary Portuguese style, including a wide-brimmed, asymmetrical hat with a red plume and a cross-body belt to carry his sword. In Peter Brathwaite's retooling of Becx's image (p. 41), he replaces the belt with a striped Vivienne Westwood tie and tucks a couple of cream crackers into the band of his hat. Brathwaite also re-creates the companion portraits of Castro's servants, Diego Bemba and Pedro Sunda, wearing matching wax-print fabrics (p. 104). Here he replaces the objects held by the men with a packet of salted cod and a treasured cou-cou stick carved by his grandfather—a prop by now familiar to any reader of this book.

In earlier writings, I have used the concept of "mnemonic aesthetics," a ritualized practice of remembering and recovery, to describe work by contemporary artists whose practices mine the archives to highlight the relationship of the present moment to past histories of slavery and colonialism.[1] Such artists often work in recurring series or repurpose previous motifs, objects, images, or symbols. Brathwaite's strategic reuse of the cou-cou stick, among other repeating props and settings, offers a perfect illustration of the concept. His photographic re-creations reveal hidden histories, invite us to question, and ask us to remember. In doing so, his project aligns with the practices of other artists concerned with history and the archive, identity and memory, portraiture and performance, the gaze and looking back. Representing a generation that harnesses the promise of technology to push back against the teachings of Western (art) history, these artists strive to shed light on figures and narratives of African, African American, and African diasporic history that have been overlooked or hidden from view.

Omar Victor Diop, Yinka Shonibare CBE, Joy Gregory, Samuel Fosso, and Titus Kaphar are just some of the artists productively confronting the historical canon of painting, printmaking, and sculpture from the Renaissance era forward. Their works, often produced in series, take the form of photography, installation, film, performance, and digital interventions like Brathwaite's. And like Brathwaite, they ask: How is art history made, and who makes it? Which figures are privileged within art history, and why? Who is doing the looking, controlling the gaze, returning the gaze, deflecting the gaze? Their works cleverly rebut the idea that the archive is objective. Indeed, they reveal the power of images to command historical narratives—to uplift some, to subjugate others, and to foment change. Filling the weathered and worn gaps created by the legacies of slavery and colonialism as well as ongoing migration crises, this coterie of artists offers a fitting encore to Brathwaite's pioneering project. Each deploys a mnemonic aesthetic to reaffirm and insist upon Black presence in art history.

A close antecedent of Brathwaite is the Senegalese photographer Omar Victor Diop, whose Project Diaspora (2014) explores notable African figures in European painting from the fifteenth to the nineteenth century through metaphorical self-portraits. In these elaborately staged photographs, Diop appears as both subject and object, re-creating the pose in the referent painting while fastidiously dressed in sumptuous period clothing. According to the artist, "I wanted to bring these rich historical characters into the current conversation about the African diaspora and contemporary issues around immigration, integration and acceptance."[2]

Like Brathwaite, Diop incorporates contemporary objects in his re-creations, but he does so to different effect. A fan of the globally popular sport of football (soccer in US parlance), Diop sees the game as a bellwether for race relations. He places a defining element—a ball, gloves, a red flag, a trophy cup—to signify how the sport has uplifted the lives and careers of African and diasporic players even as they are frequently insulted by racist heckling from the stands. The repurposed props add a contemporary dimension to the series' potent commentary on histories of disenfranchisement, global capital, and migration. Notably, Diop produced his own version of Becx's Don Miguel (right), the same painting later performed by Brathwaite.[3] Diop wears the requisite cross-body belt and hat with red plumage, but he makes the portrait his own by adding white gloves of a type used by soccer goalies, suggesting a connection between the diplomatic function of a political emissary and that of a goalie on a sports team. The food-related props chosen by Brathwaite, on the contrary, are meant to invoke traditional culinary staples of the Caribbean. Brathwaite notes that the unhealthful diet of salted fish and other inexpensive foods given to the enslaved population continues to reverberate through the generations, contributing to disproportionate rates of hypertension in the region today.

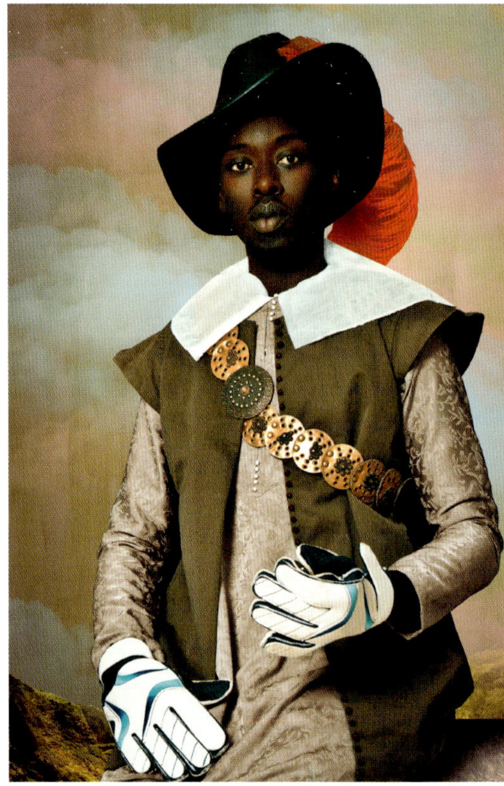

◂ Omar Victor Diop (Senegalese, b. 1980), *Don Miguel de Castro*, 2014. Pigment inkjet print, 120 × 80 cm ($47\frac{1}{4} \times 31\frac{1}{2}$ in.). Courtesy the artist and MAGNIN-A Gallery, France

Both Diop and Brathwaite operate in the wake of a generation of Black British artists who came of age in the 1980s (the era of the Brixton riots, a series of clashes provoked by police brutality and racist treatment of South London's primarily Caribbean- and African-immigrant-descended Black residents) and flourished in the 1990s. Artists such as Joy Gregory and Yinka Shonibare, children of immigrants who both attended preeminent London art schools, adopted photography and print-based media to question and recast their histories and those of their ancestors. They deftly used visual material found in the archive to expose powerful forces of institutional racism and chart a postcolonial narrative to counter the British mythology of empire and the sources of its present-day wealth.

The London-based Gregory's Amberley Queens series (1999), for instance, was inspired by a residency at Pallant House Gallery in Chichester, England, where the artist encountered the sixteenth-century Amberley Castle Panels, commissioned by Robert Sherborne, Bishop of Chichester, in 1526 to dissuade King Henry VIII from his desire for a male heir. The original nine paintings (of which eight survive today) depict notable women in history who were successful empire builders and great leaders. According to the scholar Francesco Nevola, "The inscriptions beneath each panel, possibly composed by the humanist scholar-bishop, may be derived from the ballad of *The Nine Ladies Worthy* attributed to Chaucer in the late fifteenth century."[4] Gregory set about updating the works as large-format color photographs, casting women from diverse backgrounds to portray heroines of antiquity who showed great courage in the face of adversity. In Gregory's portraits, the women assume powerful poses according to the historic roles in their captions: "zenobia well versed in the arts of war seized egypt, asia minor and syria all" (left) or "semiramis, assyrian queen of babylon mighty conqueror of barbary & ethiopia." The same objects—a walking stick, a piece of brocade fabric, jewelry—recur throughout the nine portraits. The repetition of defining props serves to unite the individual queens from various lands and time periods while also, as in Brathwaite's similarly recuperative project, exposing the artifice of the performance.

Performance likewise has been a staple for Shonibare, a British Nigerian artist and a close colleague of Gregory's. Shonibare's breakout series of 1998, Diary of a Victorian Dandy—the title a reference to the eighteenth-century satirist William Hogarth's popular Rake's Progress series of paintings (1734) and prints (1735)—uses elaborate sets and the presence of actors, including the artist himself, to question constructions of identity, British-ness, power, class structure, and sexuality.[5] For Shonibare and Gregory, as for Brathwaite, the role of performance as an element of (Black) portraiture cannot be emphasized enough.

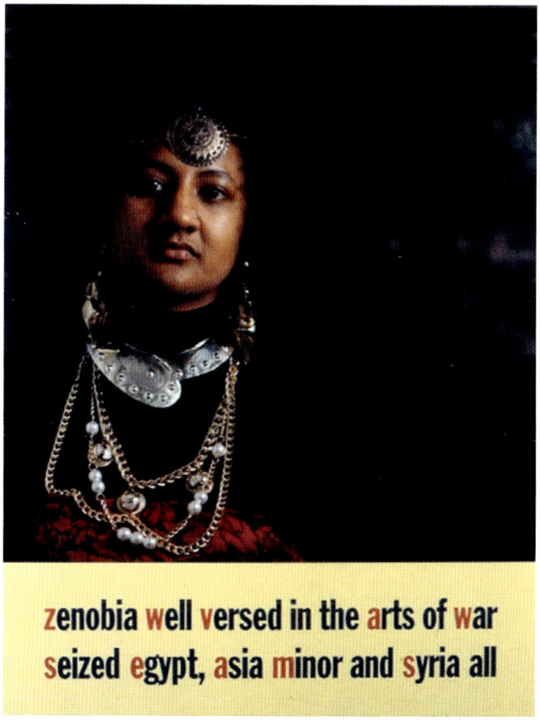

▼ Joy Gregory (British, b. 1959), *Zenobia*, from the series the Amberley Queens, 1999/2000. C-type print on board, 63.3 × 49.3 cm (24 15/16 × 19 7/16 in.). Chichester, England, Pallant House Gallery

Moving beyond Britain, the work of the Cameroonian photographer Samuel Fosso reflects a different tradition of performance portraiture. Fosso, who grew up in Igboland in postcolonial Nigeria until the age of ten, opened his own photography studio at age thirteen in Bangui, Central African Republic, and made a living by creating likenesses of others while simultaneously developing a practice of self-portraiture. Enamored of the simple yet boldly patterned backdrops characteristic of classic mid-twentieth-century African studio portraiture popularized by the Malian photographers Seydou Keïta and Malick Sidibé, Fosso styles elaborate backdrops and costumes to present himself in a variety of guises, often challenging gender and cultural norms and engaging in the consciously and necessarily narcissistic performance of self-portraiture before the camera.[6]

In several of his works, Fosso, like Brathwaite, plays with everyday found objects to convey meaning, character, and time period. In the series Tati (1997), where Fosso's characters satirize the liberated Black American woman of the 1970s, he wears high heels, dresses, makeup, and wigs. In his later series African Spirits (2008), Fosso poses as icons of the African liberation and US civil rights movements, including Patrice Lumumba, Angela Davis (right), and Malcolm X, conveying how their self-styling for the media contributed to their iconic resonance in history and memory. Further probing the performative nature of photographic portraiture, Fosso occasionally exposes the apparatus of the studio, including lighting and the edges of contrasting backdrops. Such choices bring to mind Brathwaite's unabashed ownership of the limitations of his own studio settings during the COVID-19 pandemic, during which he sometimes repurposed the same backgrounds and spaces (the brick wall in his garden, for example) in successive images.

Brathwaite has also innovated technologically within the rubric of the mnemonic aesthetic. Making art during the darkest days of a global pandemic, he engaged digitally with the archive and with his audience, discovering historical sources via digital repositories and disseminating the resulting artworks via social media. In doing so, he succeeded in reaching a broad global audience via performance, much as the US artist Titus Kaphar did in 2017, when he

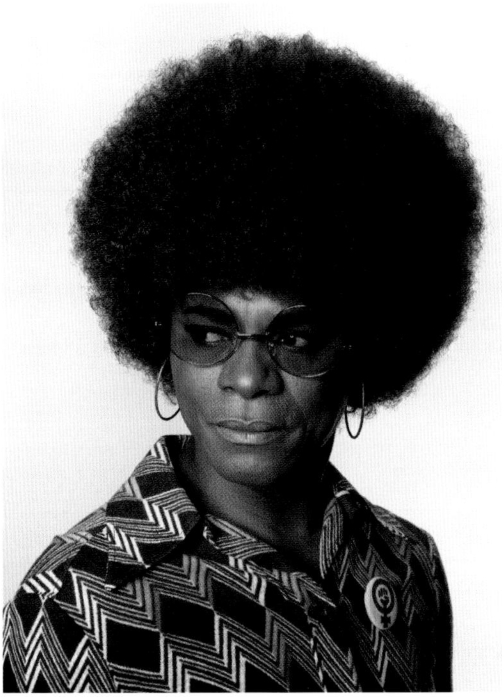

◄
Samuel Fosso (French-Cameroonian, b. 1962), *Angela Davis*, from the series African Spirits, 2008. Gelatin silver print, 162.6 × 122 cm (64 × 48 in.). Courtesy the artist and Jean Marc Patras, Paris

used the popular platform of the TED Talk to ask a crucial question: Can art amend history? Showing a reproduction of a seventeenth-century Frans Hals painting of Dutch royalty, he explains how his young son influenced his painting practice by encouraging him to shift his gaze. The Hals painting in question shows an elite Dutch family with a young Black boy whose status as property of the family is indicated by a metal collar around the neck. During the TED Talk, Kaphar brushes white paint over the faces and figures of the family, leaving only the young boy in view. Then, slowly, he uses linseed oil to reverse the process ever so slightly, allowing some of the white faces to reemerge as ghostly reminders of slavery's past in the present. "We can't erase this history," says Kaphar. "It's real. We have to know it."[7]

Who is seen? Who is hidden from view, pushed to the background, the sidelines? Whose history is documented, relevant, worth preserving? Brathwaite seeks images to which he can pose these difficult questions. His re-creations likewise reposition the gaze, compelling us to discover how historical images not only relate the past to the present but also have the power to manifest resistance and possibility into the future.

1 Cheryl Finley, *Committed to Memory: The Art of the Slave Ship Icon* (Princeton, NJ: Princeton University Press, 2018), 11.

2 Sean O'Hagen, "Omar Victor Diop: I Want to Reinvent the Heritage of African Studio Photography," *The Guardian*, July 11, 2015, https://www.theguardian.com/artanddesign/2015/jul/11/mar-ictor-ioi-want-to-reinvent-great-heritage-of-african-studio photography. For a gallery of images, see Sean O'Hagen, "Omar Victor Diop's Project Diaspora—in Pictures," *The Guardian*, July 11, 2015, https://www.theguardian.com/artanddesign/gallery/2015/jul/11/omar-victor-diops-project-diaspora-in-pictures.

3 Both Diop and Brathwaite also have re-created portraits of Olaudah Equiano and Adolf Ludvig Gustav Albert Couschi, known as Badin; see Brathwaite's Couschi on p. 81.

4 Francesco Nevola, "The Amberley Castle Panels of the Nine Heroines of Antiquity: Queen Xenobia of the Palmyrenes," https://www.vads.ac.uk/digital/collection/NIRP/id/29469/.

5 Diary of a Victorian Dandy, commissioned by the Institute of International Visual Arts in London, consists of five large-format color prints in which the artist plays the role of a dandy in scenes of increasing debauchery that allude to Hogarth's masterful Rake's Progress cycle of eight paintings and related engravings critiquing British society.

6 See Okwui Enwezor, *The Short Century: Independence and Liberation Movements in Africa, 1945–1994* (Munich: Prestel, 2001); André Magnin, *Seydou Keïta* (New York: Scalo, 1997); and Manthia Diawara, Gunilla Knape, and André Magnin, *Malick Sidibé Photographs* (Göttingen, Germany: Steidl; Gothenburg, Sweden: Hasselblad Center, 2004).

7 Titus Kaphar, "Can Art Amend History?," TED2017, https://www.ted.com/talks/titus_kaphar_can_art_amend_history?language=en.

Backstage

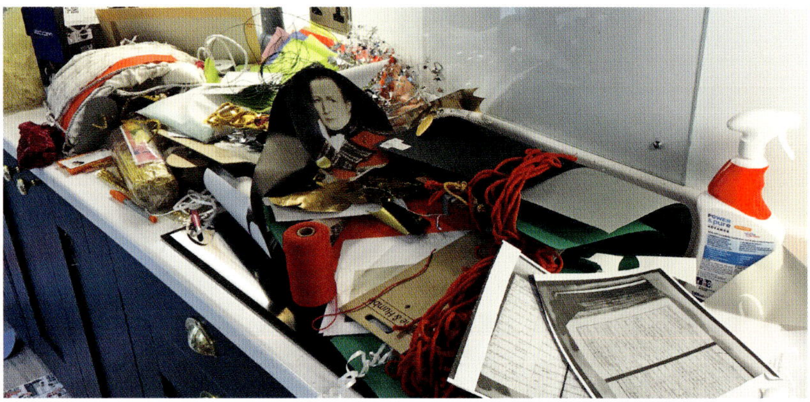

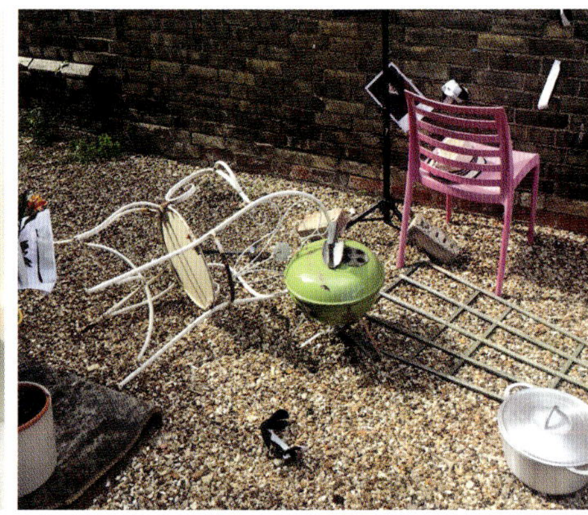

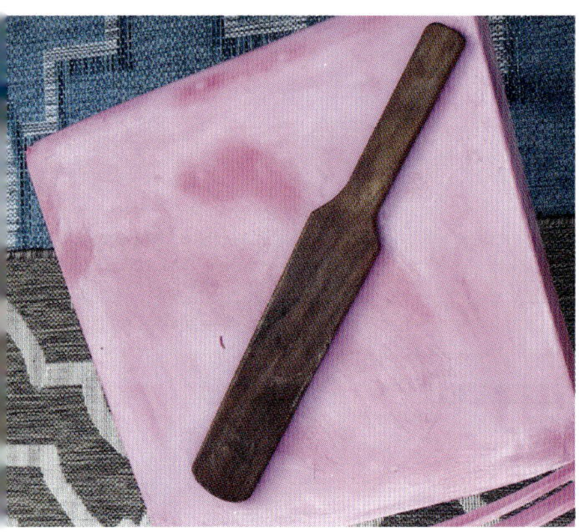

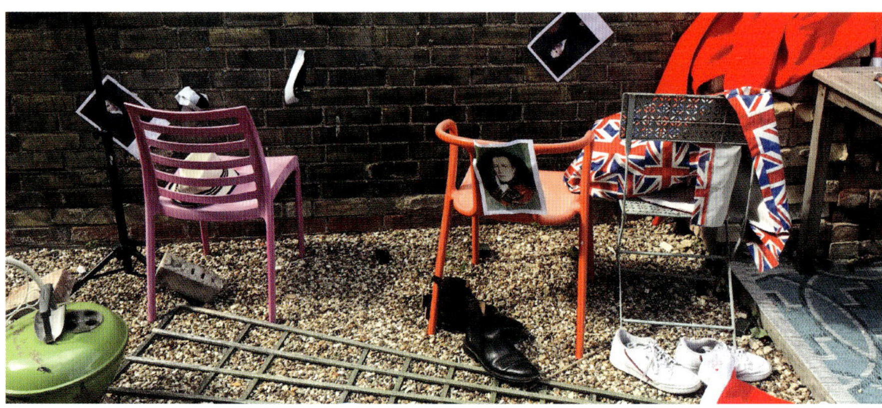

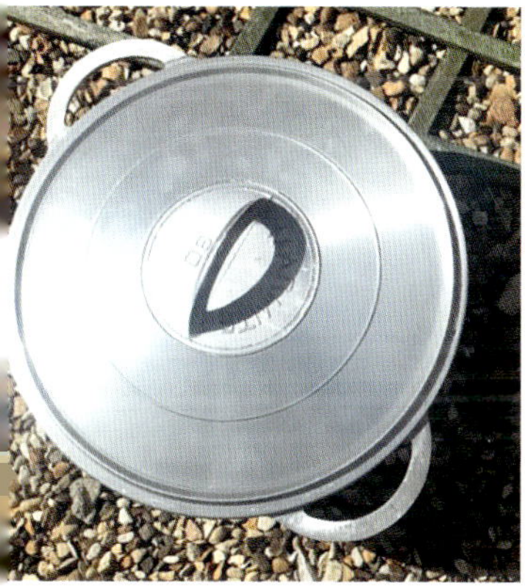

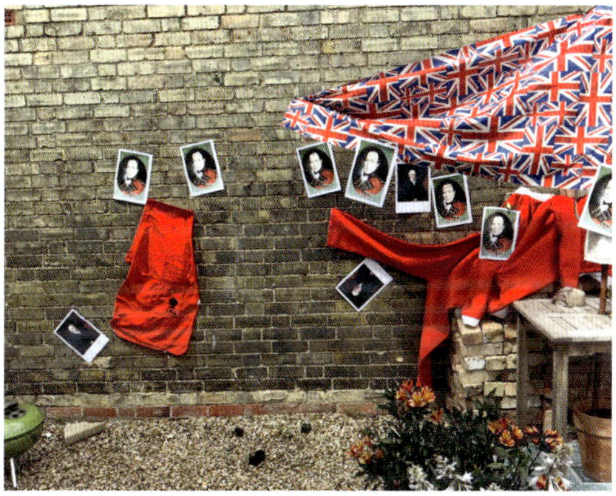

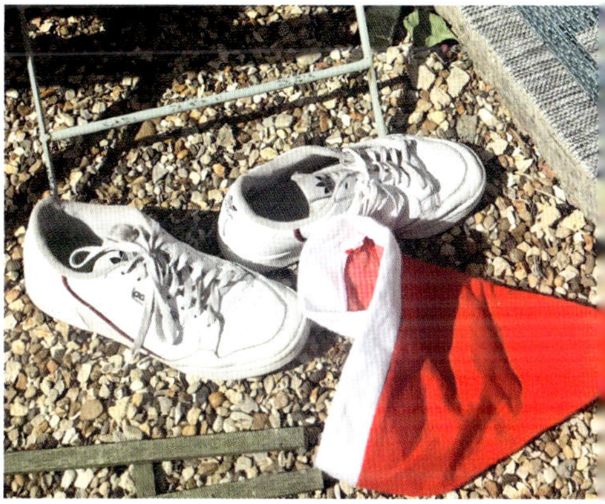

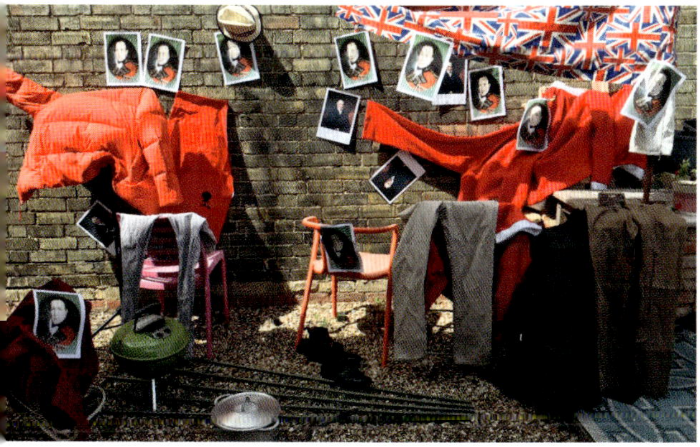

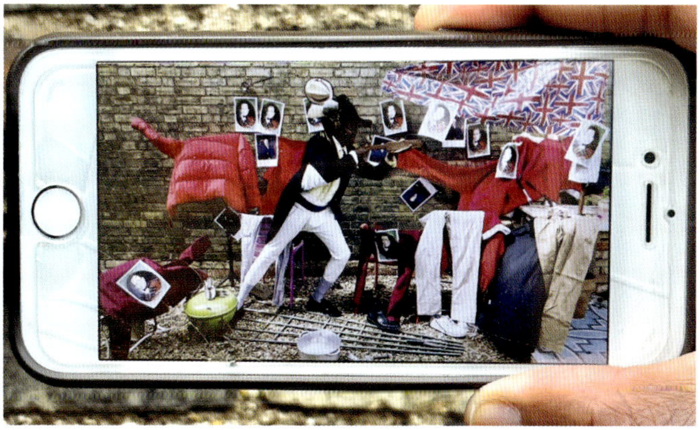

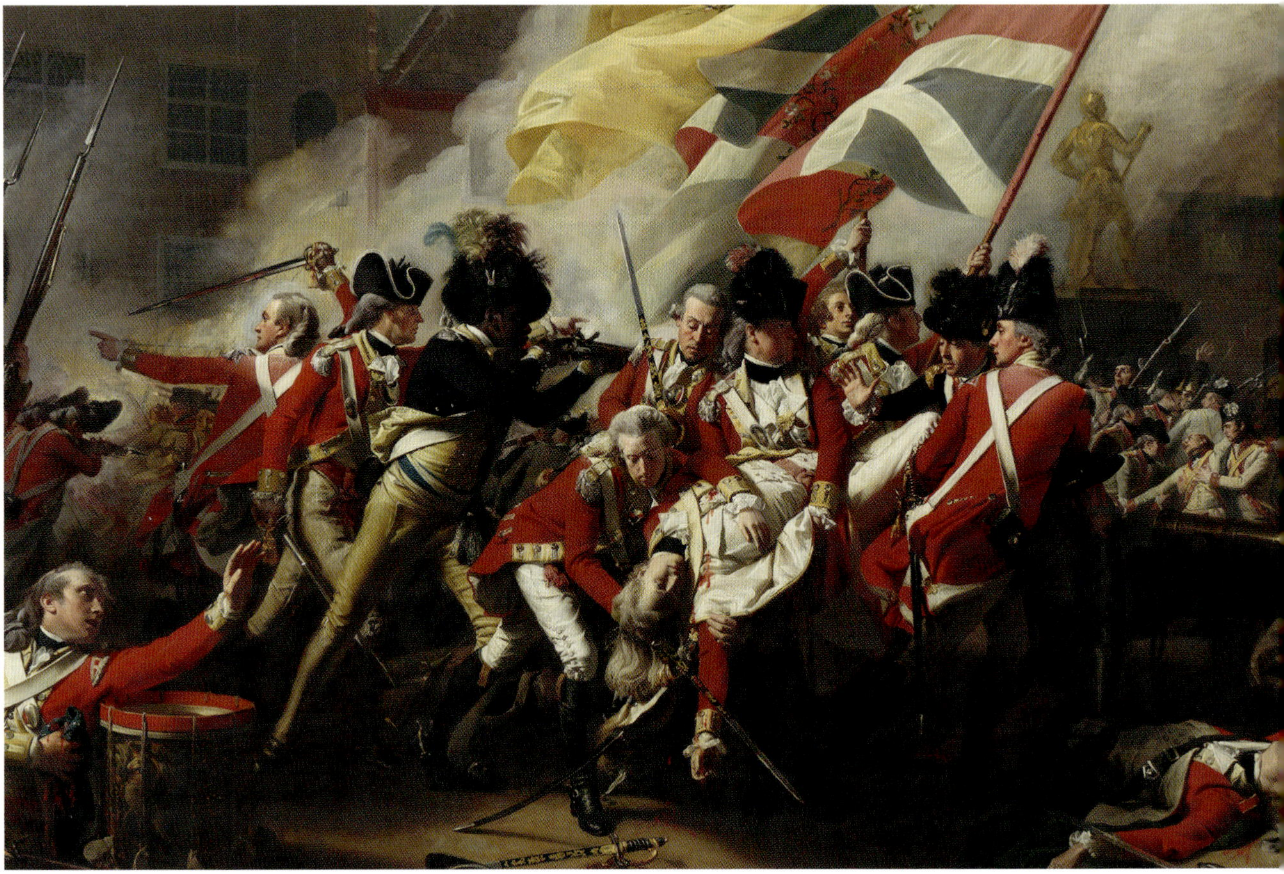

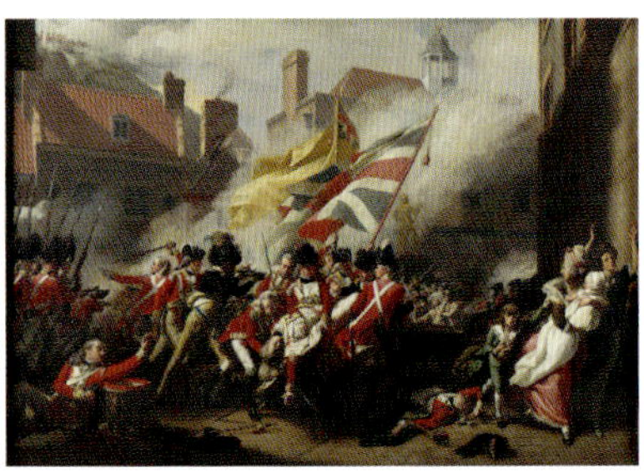

The Death of Major Peirson, 6 January 1781

1783

John Singleton Copley
American, 1738–1815

Oil on canvas
251.5 × 365.8 cm
(99 × 144 in.)
London, Tate, N00733

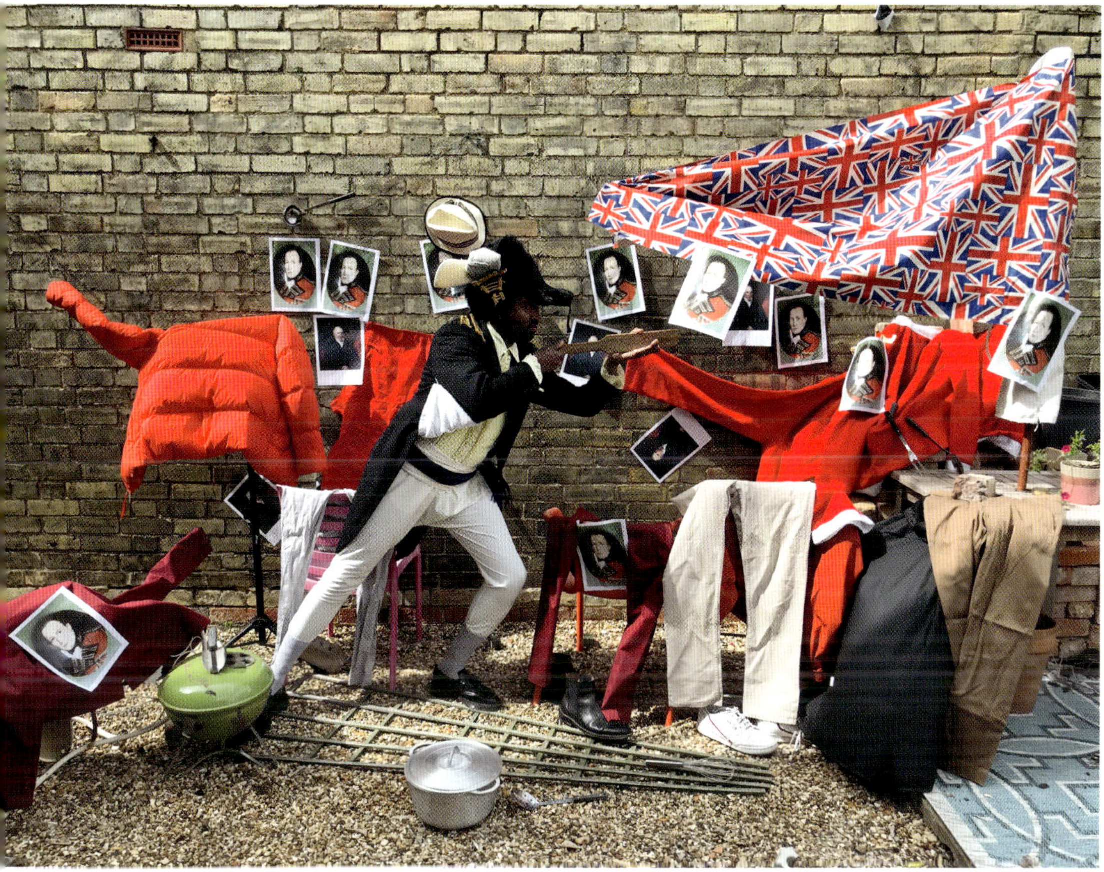

Backstage

This painting commemorates a battle between the British and the French for possession of Jersey, an island in the English Channel then loyal to the British monarchy. Copley painted the work in tribute to the bravery of Major Francis Peirson, who was killed in the skirmish by a French sniper. But at the center of the chaotic scene, we discover an equally heroic Black man: Peirson's servant, Pompey, who avenged Peirson's death by shooting the sniper. Copley's model for the figure of Pompey was the Black servant of James Christie, founder of the renowned Christie's auction house. I was moved to re-create this depiction of a loyal Black subject who exhibits just as much courage in the face of danger as his so-called superior. Reworked in my garden with printouts of a portrait of my five-times-great-grandfather Miles Brathwaite II and Grandpap's cou-cou stick.

Acknowledgments

First, my deepest love and thanks to my mother, Sheila, who taught me the power of speaking with authority in my own voice, and whose intriguing stories sparked the research that underpins this series. Also to my sisters, Sophia, Melanie, and Maureen, for everything they have given. How wonderful it was to grow up imagining and creating with them.

Thank you to Karen Levine at Getty Publications for her unfailing duty of care toward platforming both the works and the many previously silenced voices featured here. Thanks also to the rest of the Getty team, especially Jeffrey Cohen, Tori Gallina, Dina Murokh, and Nancy Rivera. We are inspired and grateful to have contributions by Cheryl Finley, Temi Odumosu, and Mark Sealy in these pages.

I'm indebted to the members of the Black Presence in British Portraiture Network, formed during the first COVID-19 lockdown of 2020, for their friendship, support, and diverse expertise. Many thanks also to Victoria Robey, Brian Allen, Candace Allen, Edward Town, and Miranda Kaufmann for the early conversations that spurred me on.

A great many thanks to Sam for a great many things, not least of which has been the nurturing and diligent partnership on the photography. It is Sam who helped me, in each and every case, to find just the right image to capture these mini-performances.

Last but certainly not least, my re-creations could not have had a life without those of you who engaged so dynamically with them on social media. Your insights, curiosity, provocations, and joy have made this work all the richer.

Suggested Further Reading

There is an expanding body of literature addressing representations of Black subjects and the Black diasporic experience. The following list is admittedly selective, but readers keen to learn more about these topics, or about authors and books that have informed my work, may be interested in seeking out these sources.

Adi, Hakim. *African and Caribbean People in Britain: A History.* London: Allen Lane, 2022.

Akala. *Natives: Race and Class in the Ruins of Empire.* London: Two Roads, 2018.

Bailey, David A., and Allison Thompson, eds. *Liberation Begins in the Imagination: Writings on Caribbean-British Art.* London: Tate, 2021.

Barringer, Tim, Gillian Forrester, and Bárbaro Martínez Ruiz. *Art and Emancipation in Jamaica: Isaac Mendes Belisario and His Worlds.* New Haven, CT: Yale Center for British Art / Yale University Press, 2007.

Bindman, Daniel, and Henry Louis Gates Jr., eds. *The Image of the Black in Western Art.* 5 vols. 2nd ed. Cambridge, MA: Belknap Press of Harvard University Press, 2010–14.

Brathwaite, Edward. *The Arrivants: A New World Trilogy.* Oxford: Oxford University Press, 1973.

Brathwaite, Peter. "Discovering Black Portraiture." Five episodes on *The Essay*, BBC Radio, 2020. https://www.bbc.co.uk/programmes/m000nbdw/episodes/player.

Caragol, Taína, Dorothy Moss, Richard J. Powell, and Kim Sajet. *The Obama Portraits.* Washington, DC: National Portrait Gallery; Princeton, NJ: Princeton University Press, 2020.

Chambers, Eddie. *Black Artists in British Art: A History since the 1950s.* London: I. B. Tauris, 2014.

Collins, Kristen, and Bryan C. Keene, eds. *Balthazar: A Black African King in Medieval and Renaissance Art.* Los Angeles: J. Paul Getty Museum, 2023.

Dabydeen, David. *Hogarth's Blacks: Images of Blacks in Eighteenth Century English Art.* Manchester: Manchester University Press, 1987.

Earle, T. F., and Kate Lowe, eds. *Black Africans in Renaissance Europe.* Cambridge: Cambridge University Press, 2005.

Eddo-Lodge, Reni. *Why I'm No Longer Talking to White People about Race.* London: Bloomsbury, 2017.

Eshun, Ekow. *In the Black Fantastic: The Art of Afrofuturism.* London: Thames & Hudson; Cambridge, MA: MIT Press, 2022.

Finley, Cheryl. *Committed to Memory: The Art of the Slave Ship Icon.* Princeton, NJ: Princeton University Press, 2018.

Galembo, Phyllis, with an introduction by Chika Okeke-Ogulu. *Maske.* New York: Aperture Foundation, 2016.

Gerzina, Gretchen H. *Britain's Black Past.* Liverpool: Liverpool University Press, 2020.

Godfrey, Mark, and Zoé Whitley, eds. *Soul of a Nation: Art in the Age of Black Power.* London: Tate, 2017.

Hochschild, Adam. *Bury the Chains: Prophets and Rebels in the Fight to Free an Empire's Slaves.* Boston: Houghton Mifflin, 2006.

Jackson, Sharna, and Zoé Whitley. *Black Artists Shaping the World.* London: Thames & Hudson, 2021.

Kaufmann, Miranda. *Black Tudors: The Untold Story.* London: Oneworld Publications, 2017.

Kolfin, Elmer, and Epco Runia, eds. *Black in Rembrandt's Time.* Zwolle, Netherlands: W Books, 2020.

Lamming, George. *In the Castle of My Skin.* London: Michael Joseph, 1953.

Lewis, Robin Coste. *Voyage of the Sable Venus: And Other Poems.* New York: Alfred A. Knopf, 2020.

Lugo-Ortiz, Agnes, and Angela Rosenthal, eds. *Slave Portraiture in the Atlantic World.* Cambridge: Cambridge University Press, 2013.

Marin, Natasha. *Black Imagination: Black Voices on Black Futures.* San Francisco: McSweeney's, 2020.

Moore, Andrew, Nathan Flis, and Francesca Vanke, eds. *The Paston Treasure: Microcosm of the Known World.* New Haven, CT: Yale Center for British Art, 2018.

Murrell, Denise. *Posing Modernity: The Black Model from Manet and Matisse to Today.* New Haven, CT: Yale University Press, 2018.

Odumosu, Temi. *Africans in English Caricature 1769–1819: Black Jokes, White Humour.* London: Harvey Miller, 2017.

Off the Walls: Inspired Re-Creations of Iconic Artworks. Los Angeles: Getty Publications, 2020.

Olusoga, David. *Black and British: A Forgotten History.* Rev. ed. London: Picador, 2021.

Otele, Olivette. *African Europeans: An Untold History.* New York: Basic Books, 2021.

Parker, Matthew. *The Sugar Barons: Family, Corruption, Empire and War in the West Indies.* London: Windmill Books; New York: Walker, 2011.

Powell, Richard J. *Cutting a Figure: Fashioning Black Portraiture.* Chicago: University of Chicago Press, 2008.

Sealy, Mark. *Decolonising the Camera: Photography in Racial Time.* London: Lawrence Wishart, 2019.

———. *Photography: Race, Rights and Representation.* London: Lawrence Wishart, 2022.

Spicer, Joaneath, ed. *Revealing the African Presence in Renaissance Europe.* Baltimore: Walters Art Museum, 2012.

Stuart, Andrea. *Sugar in the Blood: A Family's Story of Slavery and Empire.* New York: Vintage, 2013.

Illustration Credits

Front cover (left), pp. 2 (right), 4 (left), 15, 17, 19, 21, 23, 25, 27, 29, 31, 33, 35, 37, 39, 41, 43, 45, 47, 49, 61, 63, 65, 67, 69, 71, 73, 75, 77, 79, 81, 83, 85, 87, 89, 91, 93, 95, 97, 99, 102 (right), 104 (top right, bottom left), 109 (right), 110 (right), 114 (right), 119, 121, 123, 125, 127, 129, 131, 133, 135, 137, 139, 141, 143, 145, 147, 156, 157, 159: Peter Brathwaite (with photographic partner Sam Baldock) © Peter Brathwaite; **front cover (right), back cover, p. 28:** Rijksmuseum; **pp. 2 (left), 84:** © The Trustees of the British Museum; **pp. 4 (right), 40, 104 (top left, bottom right):** Statens Museum for Kunst (SMK), Copenhagen; **p. 14:** BnF; **p. 16:** © Niedersächsische Staats- und Universitätsbibliothek Göttingen; **p. 18 (left):** © Alinari Archives / George Tatge, 1989 / Art Resource, NY; **p. 18 (right):** Scala / Art Resource, NY; **pp. 20, 22, 118:** digital image courtesy of Getty's Open Content Program; **p. 24:** College of Arms MS Westminster, Tournament Roll, 1511, membrane 28. Reproduced by permission of the Kings, Heralds and Pursuivants of Arms; **p. 26:** image courtesy of The Image of the Black Archive & Library, The Hutchins Center for African and African American Research, Harvard University; **p. 30:** Germanisches Nationalmuseum, Nuremburg; **p. 32:** Widener Collection; **p. 34:** photo © National Gallery of Ireland; **p. 36:** Kunstpalast / Wikimedia Commons; **p. 38:** image courtesy of Dorotheum; **p. 42:** The Menil Collection, Houston; **p. 44:** The Picture Art Collection / Alamy Stock Photo; **p. 46:** Museum van de Stad Brussel, Brussels; **p. 48:** Norfolk Museums Service (Norwich Castle Museum & Art Gallery); **p. 53 (top):** © National Portrait Gallery, London; **p. 53 (bottom):** Davis Museum at Wellesley College, Wellesley, Massachusetts, Museum purchase, The Nancy Gray Sherrill, Class of 1954, Collection Acquisition Fund; **p. 54:** Victoria Art Gallery, Bath, and North East Somerset Council / © Victoria Art Gallery, Bath / Bridgeman Images; **p. 60:** bpk Bildagentur / Gemäldegalerie / Staatliche Museen / Jörg P. Anders / Art Resource, NY; **p. 62:** Victoria and Albert Museum, London, Gift of Viscount Bearsted M.C. and Spink and Son Ltd. through the National Art Collections Fund, 1928; **p. 64:** Barbados Museum and Historical Society; **p. 66:** image from Wikimedia Commons (CC BY 4.0); **p. 68:** agefotostock / Alamy Stock Photo; **p. 70:** North Carolina Museum of Art / Bridgeman Images; **p. 72:** Carlton Hobbs LLC; **p. 74:** photo © Philip Mould Ltd, London / Bridgeman Images; **p. 76:** Cameraphoto Arte, Venice / Art Resource, NY; **p. 78:** courtesy of Earls of Mansfield collection; **p. 80:** photo: © Nationalmuseum, Stockholm; **p. 82:** Cummer Museum of Art & Gardens; **p. 86:** © Musée McCord – McCord Museum, Montreal / Art Resource, NY; **p. 88:** History and Art Collection / Alamy Stock Photo; **p. 90:** The Metropolitan Museum of Art, New York, Gift of William H. Huntington, 1883; **p. 92:** Schomburg Center for Research in Black Culture, New York Public Library; **pp. 94, 122:** © Victoria and Albert Museum, London; **p. 96:** Tasmanian Museum and Art Gallery, Presented by Mr. C. E. Docker, 1956; **p. 98:** Yale Center for British Art; **p. 102 (left):** The National Archives, Kew; **pp. 106, 126:** Library of Congress; **p. 107:** © Yinka Shonibare CBE, All Rights Reserved, DACS / Artimage 2022; **p. 109 (left):** North Wind Picture Archives via Bridgeman/ Alamy; **p. 110 (left):** © 2020 Kehinde Wiley, courtesy of Sean Kelly, New York; **pp. 111, 128:** © RMN-Grand Palais / Art Resource, NY; **p. 114 (left):** Art Institute of Chicago, Henry Tiefenbronner Endowment; **p. 120 (top):** National Portrait Gallery, Smithsonian Institution; **p. 120 (bottom):** © Manchester Art Gallery / Bridgeman Images; **p. 124:** Courtesy of The Hispanic Society of America, New York; **p. 130:** National Gallery of Art, Washington, DC, Collection of Mr. and Mrs. Paul Mellon; **p. 132:** Garden Museum, London; **p. 134:** Album / Alamy Stock Photo; **pp. 136, 138:** © The Estate of Alice Neel, courtesy The Estate of Alice Neel and David Zwirner; **p. 140:** © Kerry James Marshall / courtesy the artist and David Zwirner, London / photo © Museum Associates / LACMA; **p. 142:** © Sonia Boyce / Artists Rights Society (ARS), New York / DACS, London / courtesy of Simon Lee Gallery / photo: Denise Swanson; **p. 144:** © Bisa Butler; **p. 146:** © Kehinde Wiley, courtesy of the National Portrait Gallery, Smithsonian Institution; **p. 150:** © Omar Victor Diop / courtesy MAGNIN-A Gallery, France; **p. 151:** © Joy Gregory /Artists Rights Society (ARS), New York / DACS, London / image courtesy Pallant House Gallery; **p. 152:** courtesy the artist and Jean Marc Patras, Paris; **p. 158:** TATE

Index

Page numbers in *italics* refer to illustrations.

A

Abbreviatio of Domesday, 101, *102*
Adolf Ludvig Gustav Albert Couschi, Called Badin (Lundberg), 80–81, *80*, *81*
Adoration of the Magi, The (Trubert), 20, 21, *21*
Africa, the Land of Hope and Promise for Negro Peoples of the World (Butler), 144–45, *144*, *145*
African King Caspar, The (Heerschop), 60–61, *60*, *61*
African Spirits series (Fosso), 152, *152*
Aïcha (Vallotton), *134*, 135, *135*
Aksum, 23
Algorithms of Oppression (Noble), 51–52
Allegory of the Sense of Smell (follower of Bartolomeo Passarotti), 42, 43, *43*, 105
Amberley Queens series (Gregory), 151, *151*
Angela Davis (Fosso), 152, *152*
Arrieta, Agustín, *The Young Man from the Coast*, *124*, 125, *125*
Artist Completing a Portrait of Maria Anna of Austria (unknown), 72, 73, *73*
Atlas of Maritime Charts (*The Catalan Atlas*) (Cresques), *14*, 15, *15*

B

Bach, Johann Sebastian, 35, 77, 103
Badin (Couschi, Adolf Ludvig Gustav Albert), 80–81, *80*, 153n3
Barack Obama (Wiley), *146*, 147, *147*
Bazille, Frédéric, *Young Woman with Peonies*, 130–31, *130*, *131*
Beaucourt, François, *Portrait of a Haitian Woman*, *86*, 87, *87*
Becx, Jasper, *Don Miguel de Castro: Emissary of Kongo*, *40*, 41, *41*, 103–5, 149, 150, *150*
Becx, Jasper, or Albert Eckhout (attr.), *Diego Bemba, a Servant of Don Miguel de Castro*, 103, *104*, 149
Becx, Jasper, or Albert Eckhout (attr.), *Pedro Sunda, a Servant of Don Miguel de Castro*, 103, *104*, 149
Belisario, Isaac Mendes, *Lovey*, *98*, 99, *99*
Bell, Maria, 79
Belle, Dido Elizabeth, *78*, 79
Bellifortis (Kyeser), *16*, 17, *17*
Bemba, Diego, 41, 103, *104*, 149
Black Boy, A (Hollar), 52–53, *53*
Black Boy, The (Jones), *54*, 55
Black Boy (Wright), 55
Black Charley, Norwich (Dempsey), *96*, 97, *97*
Black Draftee (*James Hunter*) (Neel), *138*, 139, *139*
Black Madonnas, *66*, 67
Black Man (Neel), 110, 111, *136*, 137, *137*
Blanke, John, *24*, 25
Blue Black Boy (Weems), 55
Bologne, Joseph (Chevalier de Saint-Georges), 10, *84*, 85, *85*
Boyce, Sonia, *Rice n Peas*, 110–11, *142*, 143, *143*
Brathwaite, Addo, 77, 108–10
Brathwaite, Charles Richard, 113
Brathwaite, Edward Kamau, 10
Brathwaite, Ina Elrita, 145
Brathwaite, John, 12n, 106
Brathwaite, Miles, II, 33, 127, 159
Briggs, Henry Perronet, *Ira Aldridge as Othello*, *120*, 121, *121*
Brixton riots, 150
Brown, Mather, *Monsieur de Saint-Georges*, 10, *84*, 85, *85*
Brown Study, A [Portrait of a Boy with a Slate] (Hunt), *122*, 123, *123*
Brunias, Agostino, *Women in Barbados*, 92–93, *92*, *93*
Burbank, Elbridge Ayer, *Portrait of a Young Black Boy*, 53, *53*, 55
Butler, Bisa, *Africa, the Land of Hope and Promise for Negro Peoples of the World*, 144–45, *144*, *145*

C

Captain Lord George Graham, in His Cabin (Hogarth), *68*, 69, *69*
Carpaccio, Vittore, Gondolier (det., *Miracle of the Relic of the Cross at the Rialto Bridge*), *18*, 19, *19*
Catherine of Aragon (queen of England), 31
Césaire, Aimé, 52
Charles I at the Hunt (Van Dyck), 111, *111*
Charles V (Holy Roman emperor), 29, 31
Christie, James, 159
Christopher the Moor, 29
Coleridge-Taylor, Samuel, 9
Copley, John Singleton, *Death of Major Peirson, 6 January, 1781*, *158*, 159, *159*
Costume Book (Weiditz), *30*, 31, *31*
"Cotton," Norwich (Dempsey), *96*, 97, *97*
Couschi, Adolf Ludvig Gustav Albert (Badin), 80–81, *80*, 153n3
Cresques, Abraham, Mansa Musa (det., *Atlas of Maritime Charts* [*The Catalan Atlas*]), *14*, 15, *15*

D

Davis, Angela, 152
Death of Major Peirson, 6 January, 1781 (Copley), *158*, 159, *159*
de Heem, Jan Davidsz, *Still Life with Servant and Parrot*, *46*, 47, *47*, 105–6
Dempsey, John
Black Charley, Norwich, *96*, 97, *97*
"Cotton," Norwich, *96*, 97, *97*
Diary of a Victorian Dandy (Shonibare), 151, 153n5
Dido Elizabeth Belle and Lady Elizabeth Murray (Martin), *78*, 79, *79*

Diego Bemba, a Servant of Don Miguel de Castro (Becx or Eckhout [attr.]), 103, *104*, 149
Diop, Omar Victor, 108, 149–50
Domesday Book, 101, *102*
Donizetti, Gaetano, 9
Don Miguel de Castro: Emissary of Kongo (Becx), 40, 41, *41*, 103–5, 149, 150, *150*
Drax, James, 106
Drummer (det., *Costume Book*) (Weiditz), 30, 31, *31*
Du Bois, W. E. B., 112
  Types of American Negroes, 106, 107

E

Eckhout, Albert, circle of, *Portrait of a Man Crowned with Laurel*, 38, 39, *39*
Eckhout, Albert, or Jasper Becx (attr.), *Diego Bemba, a Servant of Don Miguel de Castro*, 103, *104*, 149
Eckhout, Albert, or Jasper Becx (attr.), *Pedro Sunda, a Servant of Don Miguel de Castro*, 103, *104*, 149
Ellison, Ralph, 113, 140–41
Equiano, Olaudah, 153n3

F

Floyd, George, 113
Folio of British Street Portraits, A (Dempsey), 96, 97, *97*
Fosso, Samuel, 149
  African Spirits series, 152, *152*
  Angela Davis, 152, *152*
  Tati series, 152
France, 119, 128–29, 131, 135
  See also Caribbean
Francis Williams, the Scholar of Jamaica (unknown), 62–63, *62*, *63*
Franklin, Aretha, 103
Freeman, Thomas Birch, 133
Furioso all'isola di San Domingo, Il (Donizetti), 9

G

Genoa, 33
Géricault, Théodore
  Raft of the Medusa, The, 119
  Study of the Model Joseph, 118, 119, *119*
Germany, 27
Gilman, Harold, *Portrait of a Gardener*, 132, 133, *133*
Goblet, Aïcha, *134*, 135
Gondolier (det., *Miracle of the Relic of the Cross at the Rialto Bridge*) (Carpaccio), 18, 19, *19*
Gordon, Avery, 56
Grasset, Henry W., 73
Gregory, Joy, 149, 150–51
  Amberley Queens series, 151, *151*
  Zenobia, *151*
Guardi, Francesco, *Votive Portrait of Lazzaro Zen*, 76, 77, *77*

H

Haiti, 87, 90, 91, 108, 109, 119
Hall, Stuart, 107
Hals, Frans, 153
Heerschop, Hendrick, *The African King Caspar*, 60–61, *60*, *61*
Henry VIII (king of England), 25
Historical Account of the Black Empire of Hayti, An (Rainsford), *109*
Hogarth, William, 103
  Musician (det., *Captain Lord George Graham, in His Cabin*), 68, 69, *69*
  Rake's Progress series, 151, 153n5
Hollar, Wenceslaus ("Wenzel"), *A Black Boy*, 52–53, *53*
Hunt, William Henry, *A Brown Study* [Portrait of a Boy with a Slate], *122*, 123, *123*
Hunter, James, *138*, 139

I

Image of the Black in Western Art, The (Bindman and Gates), 62
Instructions for the Management of a Plantation in Barbadoes, and for the Treatment of Negroes (Brathwaite), 12n
In the Castle of My Skin (Lamming), 27
Invisible Man (Ellison), 113, 140–41
Ira Aldridge (Northcote), *120*, 121, *121*
Ira Aldridge as Othello (Briggs), *120*, 121, *121*
Italy, 19, 33, 77

J

Jamaica, 62–63, 99
John Blanke (det., Westminster Tournament Roll), *24*, 25, *25*
Johnson, Joseph, 94–95, *94*, 112
Jones, William, *The Black Boy*, *54*, 55
Joseph Johnson (Smith), 94–95, *94*, *95*, 112

K

Kaphar, Titus, 149, 152–53
Keïta, Seydou, 152
King, Martin Luther, Jr., 137
Kitchen Maid with the Supper at Emmaus (Velázquez), *34*, 35, *35*, 102–3
Kneller, Godfrey (or follower), *Portrait of a Man in Livery*, *64*, 65
Kongo, *40*, 41, 103–4
Kyeser, Konrad, Queen of Sheba (det., *Bellifortis*), *16*, 17, *17*

L

Lamming, George, 27
Laure (det., *Olympia*) (Manet), 128–29, *128*, *129*, 130
Lemoine, Marie Victoire, *Portrait of a Youth in an Embroidered Vest*, 82, 83, *83*
Levinas, Emmanuel, 103
Ligon, Richard, 47, 106
Lincoln, Abraham, 126
Lindsay, John, 79

Louisa Ulrika of Prussia (queen of Sweden), 80
Louverture, Toussaint, *90*, 91, 108, *109*
Lovey (Belisario), *98*, 99, *99*
Lumumba, Patrice, 152
Lundberg, Gustaf, *Adolf Ludvig Gustav Albert Couschi, Called Badin*, 80–81, *80*, *81*

M

Mali, 15
Manet, Edouard, 130, 131
  Laure (det., *Olympia*), 128–29, *128*, *129*, 130
Mansa Musa (det., *Atlas of Maritime Charts* [*The Catalan Atlas*]) (Cresques), *14*, 15, *15*
Man Scraping Chocolate, A (unknown), *70*, 71, *71*
Marchesa Elena Grimaldi Cattaneo (Van Dyck), *32*, 33, *33*
Marie-Thérèse-Zémire, *86*, 87
Marshall, Kerry James, *A Portrait of the Artist as a Shadow of His Former Self*, 112–13, 140–41, *140*, *141*
Martin, David, *Dido Elizabeth Belle and Lady Elizabeth Murray*, *78*, 79, *79*
Mexico, 67, 125
Miracle of the Relic of the Cross at the Rialto Bridge (Carpaccio), *18*, 19, *19*
Modigliani, Amedeo, 135
Moi Libre (unknown), *88*, 89, *89*
Monsieur de Saint-Georges (Brown), 10, *84*, 85, *85*
Mostaert, Jan, *Portrait of an Unknown Man*, *28*, 29, *29*
Murray, William (Earl of Mansfield), 79
Musician (det., *Captain Lord George Graham, in His Cabin*) (Hogarth), *68*, 69, *69*

N

Neel, Alice
  Black Draftee (James Hunter), *138*, 139, *139*
  Black Man, 110, 111, *136*, 137, *137*
Netherlands, 37, 41, 45, 53, 60, 61
Nevola, Francesco, 151
Nine Ladies Worthy, The, 151
Noble, Safiya, 51–52
Northcote, James, *Ira Aldridge*, *120*, 121, *121*

O

Obama, Barack, *146*, 147
Olympia (Manet), 128–29, *128*, *129*, 130

P

Passarotti, Bartolomeo, follower of, *Allegory of the Sense of Smell*, *42*, 43, *43*, 105
Paston, William, 49
Paston Treasure, The (unknown), *48*, 49, *49*, 112, 113
Pedro Sunda, a Servant of Don Miguel de Castro (Becx or Eckhout [attr.]), 103, *104*, 149
Peirson, Francis, *158*, 159
Peters, Erskine A., 55, 58n7
Portrait of a Gardener (Gilman), *132*, 133, *133*
Portrait of a Haitian Woman (Beaucourt), *86*, 87, *87*
Portrait of a Man Crowned with Laurel (circle of Albert Eckhout), *38*, 39, *39*
Portrait of a Man in Livery (Kneller or follower), *64*, 65
Portrait of an Unknown Man (Mostaert), *28*, 29, *29*
Portrait of a Young Black Boy (Burbank), 53, *53*, 55
Portrait of a Youth in an Embroidered Vest (Lemoine), *82*, 83, *83*
Portrait of Emmanuel Rio (Schindler), 113, *114*
Portrait of the Artist as a Shadow of His Former Self, A (Marshall), 112–13, 140–41, *140*, *141*
Price, Leontyne, 9

Q

Queen of Sheba (det., *Bellifortis*) (Kyeser), *16*, 17, *17*

R

Raft of the Medusa, The (Géricault), 119
Rainsford, Marcus, *109*
Rake's Progress series (Hogarth), 151, 153n5
Ray, Man, 135
Rice n Peas (Boyce), 110–11, *142*, 143, *143*
Rio, Emmanuel, 113, 114, *114*
Roi a la Chasse, Le (Wiley), *110*, 111–12

S

Saint-Domingue. *See* Haiti
Saint John (Ethiopian gospel book), *22*, 23, *23*
Saint John Passion (Bach), 35, 103
Saint Maurice (unknown), *26*, 27, *27*
Schindler, Albert, *Portrait of Emmanuel Rio*, 113, *114*
Scott, Emmett J., 144–45, *144*
Servant, A (unknown), *74*, 75
Sherborne, Robert, 151
Shonibare, Yinka, 107–8, 149, 150–51
  Diary of a Victorian Dandy, 151, 153n5
  Untitled (*Effnik*), *107*
Sibyl Agrippina, The (Van den Hoecke [attr.]), *36*, 37, *37*
Sidibé, Malick, 152
Sketches of Character in Illustration of the Habits, Occupation, and Costume of the Negro Population in the Island of Jamaica (Belisario), *98*, 99

Smith, John Thomas, *Joseph Johnson*, 94–95, *94*, *95*, 112
Stephens, Henry Louis, *Untitled* [Man Reading a Newspaper by Candlelight], 126–27, *126*, *127*
Still Life with Peaches and a Lemon (Van Streeck), 44, 45, *45*
Still Life with Servant and Parrot (de Heem), 46, 47, *47*, 105–6
Study of the Model Joseph (Géricault), 118, 119, *119*
Sunda, Pedro, 41, 103, *104*, 149
Sweden, 80–81

T

Tati series (Fosso), 152
Titian, 33
Toussaint Louverture on Horseback (unknown), 90, 91, *91*, 108
Trubert, Georges, *The Adoration of the Magi*, 20, 21, *21*
True and Exact History of the Island of Barbadoes, A (Ligon), 47, 106
Types of American Negroes (Du Bois), 106, 107

U

Untitled (*Effnik*) (Shonibare), *107*
Untitled [Man Reading a Newspaper by Candlelight] (Stephens), 126–27, *126*, *127*

V

Vallotton, Félix, *Aïcha*, 134, 135, *135*
Van den Hoecke, Jan (attr.), *The Sibyl Agrippina*, 36, 37, *37*
Van Dyck, Anthony
  Charles I at the Hunt, 111, *111*
  Marchesa Elena Grimaldi Cattaneo, 32, 33, *33*
Van Streeck, Juriaen, *Still Life with Peaches and a Lemon*, 44, 45, *45*
Velázquez, Diego, *Kitchen Maid with the Supper at Emmaus*, 34, 35, *35*, 102–3
Venice, 19, 77
Virgin of Guadalupe, The (unknown), 66, 67, *67*
Votive Portrait of Lazzaro Zen (Guardi), 76, 77, *77*

W

Walcott, Derek, 8, 10, 57
Ward, William, 10, 84
Washington, Booker T., 144–45
Weems, Carrie Mae, *Blue Black Boy*, 55
Weiditz, Christoph, I, Drummer (det., *Costume Book*), 30, 31, *31*
Westminster Tournament Roll, 24, 25, *25*
Wiley, Kehinde
  Barack Obama, 146, 147, *147*
  Roi a la Chasse, Le, *110*, 111–12
Williams, Francis, 62–63, *62*
Wilson, Woodrow, 145
Women in Barbados (Brunias), 92–93, *92*, *93*
Wright, Richard, 55

X

X, Malcolm, 137, 152

Y

Yearly, Charles Willis, 97
Young Man from the Coast, The (Arrieta), 124, 125, *125*
Young Woman with Peonies (Bazille), 130–31, *130*, *131*

Z

Zen, Lazzaro, *76*, 77
Zenobia (Gregory), 151

About the Authors

British opera singer **Peter Brathwaite** works across different art forms to excavate and platform suppressed stories and voices. In addition to performing on major international opera stages, he devises his own theater productions. He has been shortlisted for a Royal Philharmonic Society Award, and his collaborative work has won a Laurence Olivier Award. Brathwaite's photographic series has been exhibited by King's College London / Wellcome Trust and the Bristol Museum and Art Gallery. As a broadcaster for BBC Radio 3, he has authored and presented programs on Black portraiture and the cultural legacy of enslavement in Barbados. He has written for *The Guardian* and *The Independent* and is a prominent speaker on performance, identity, and restorative justice in the arts.

Cheryl Finley is the inaugural distinguished visiting director of the Atlanta University Center Art History and Curatorial Studies Collective, distinguished visiting professor of art and visual culture at Spelman College, and associate professor of art history at Cornell University. A member of the advisory committee of the Getty Research Institute's African American Art History Initiative, Finley is the award-winning author of *Committed to Memory: The Art of the Slave Ship Icon* (2018), and her writings have appeared in numerous catalogues and periodicals, including *Aperture*, *Nka: Journal of Contemporary African Art*, *American Quarterly*, *Artforum*, and *Small Axe*.

Temi Odumosu is an art historian, curator, and assistant professor at University of Washington Information School. She is the author of the book *Africans in English Caricature 1769–1819: Black Jokes, White Humour* (2017). Her research and curatorial interests include colonial visual cultures, archives and archival praxis, postmemorial art and performance, digitization of cultural heritage, and ethics of care in representation. Overall she is focused on the ways art can mediate social transformation and healing.

Mark Sealy is interested in the relationship between photography and social change, identity politics, race, and human rights. He has been director of Autograph, London, since 1991 and is presently professor of photography, race, and human rights at University of the Arts London. In 2022, he was awarded an OBE for services to art. He has written for many international photography publications, including *Foam Magazine*, *Aperture*, and *Vogue*. His numerous publications include *Different* (2001), coauthored with Stuart Hall; *Decolonising the Camera: Photography in Racial Time* (2019); and *Photography: Race, Rights and Representation* (2022).

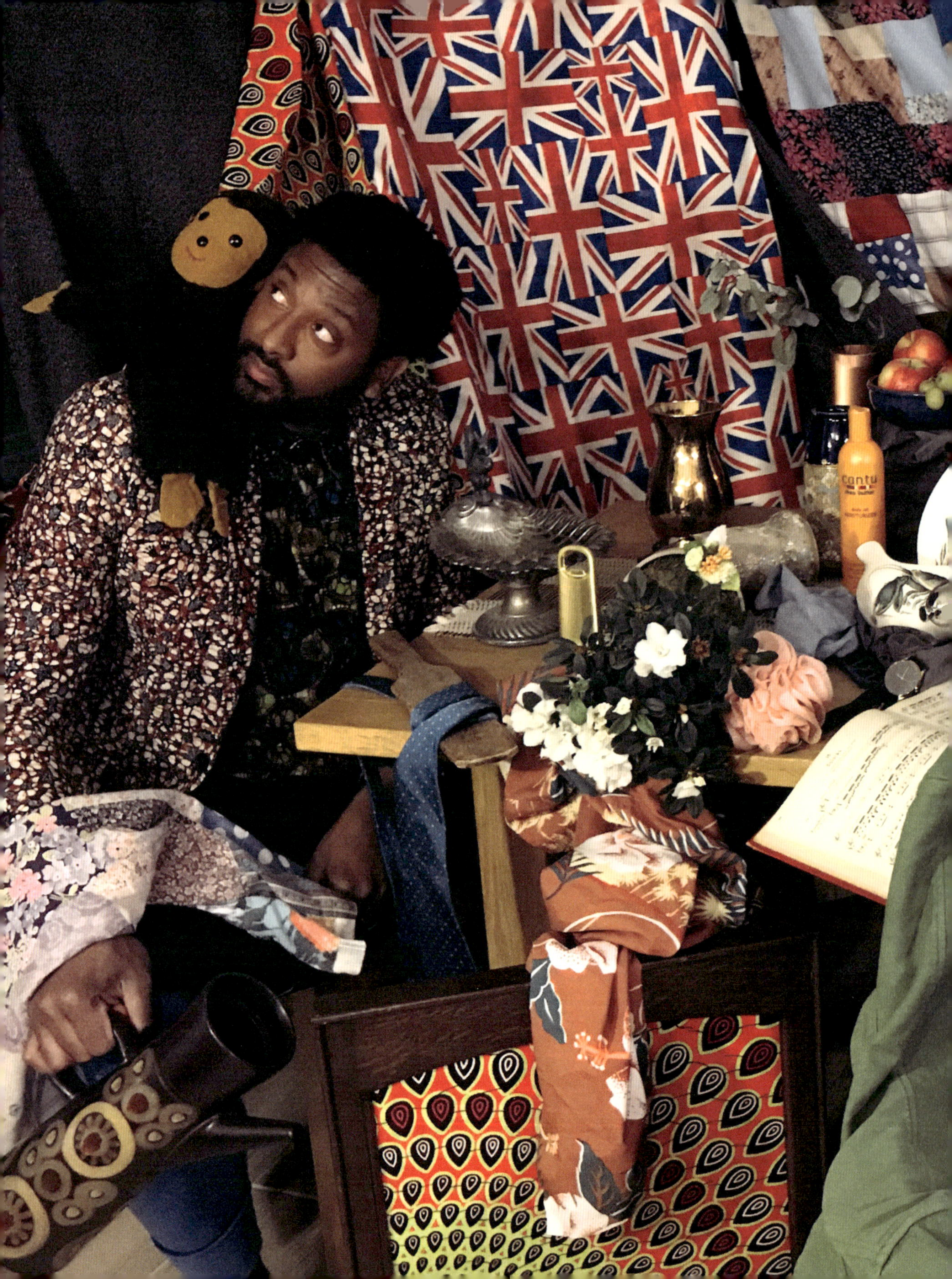
cantu